IMAGES
of America

MUCKENTHALER CULTURAL CENTER

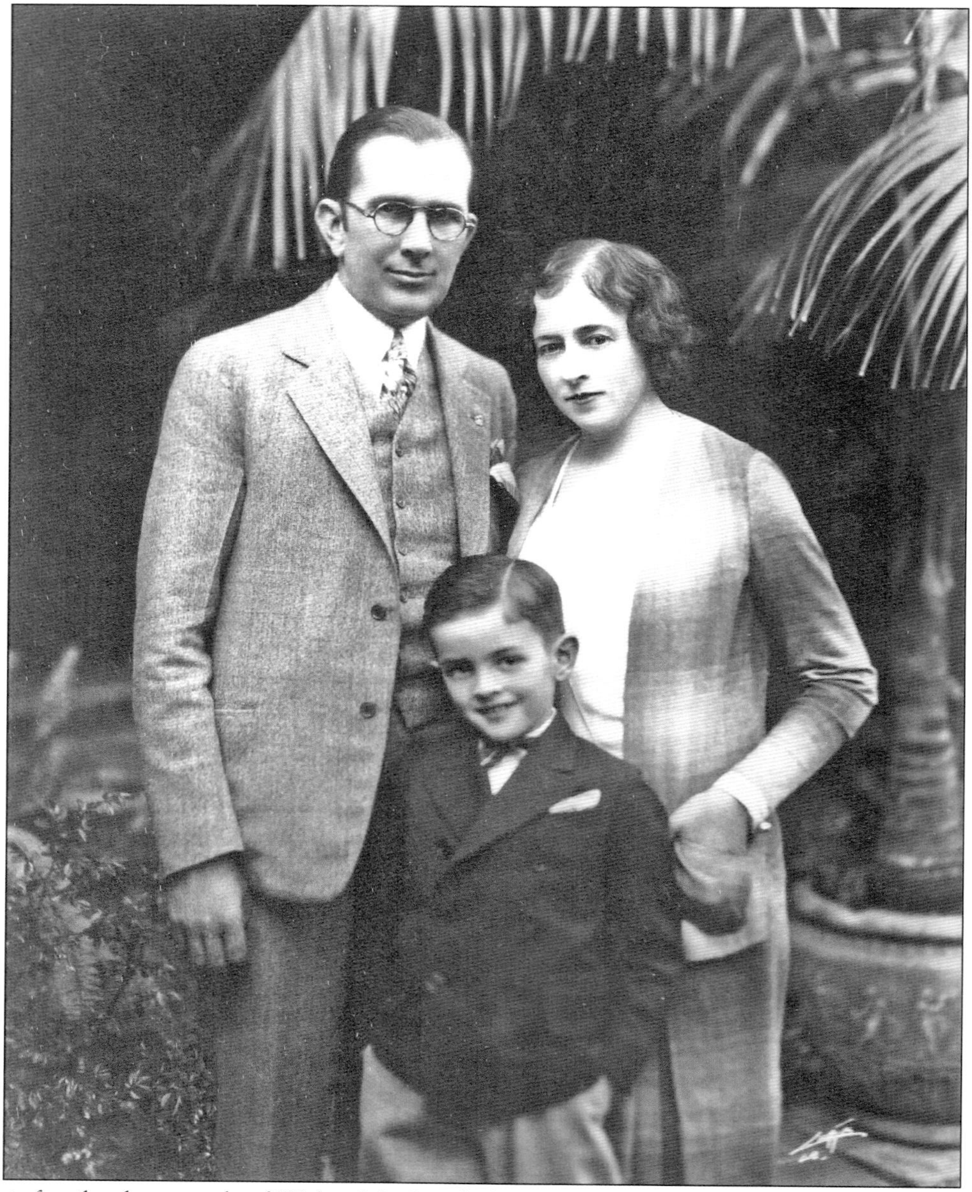

This family photograph of Walter Muckenthaler, Adella Kraemer Muckenthaler, and their nine-year-old son, Harold Muckenthaler, was taken in the courtyard of their villa in 1930. This photograph welcomes you into the cultural center. Through their generosity—Walter as a city councilman and Adella and Harold by their gift of the estate—the Muckenthalers influenced the city of Fullerton for generations to come. (Courtesy of the Muckenthaler Family Archives.)

ON THE COVER: Taken in 1929, this photograph of the east side of the Muckenthaler villa shows off Walter Muckenthaler's new Cadillac with the solarium in the background. The solarium has become an icon of the Muckenthaler, used in logos, trademarks, drawings, paintings, and photographs over its 45-year history and represents the grandeur of the estate. (Courtesy of the Muckenthaler Family Archives.)

IMAGES
of America

MUCKENTHALER CULTURAL CENTER

Muckenthaler Cultural Center Foundation

ARCADIA PUBLISHING

ISBN 978-0-7385-7551-3

Published by Arcadia Publishing
Charleston, South Carolina

Printed in the United States of America

Library of Congress Control Number: 2011920909

For all general information, please contact Arcadia Publishing:
Telephone 843-853-2070
Fax 843-853-0044
E-mail sales@arcadiapublishing.com
For customer service and orders:
Toll-Free 1-888-313-2665

Visit us on the Internet at www.arcadiapublishing.com

To Walter, Adella, Harold, and Shirley Muckenthaler, for their family contributions to North Orange County and their gift of culture to our region

Contents

Acknowledgments

Neither the Muckenthaler Cultural Center nor this book chronicling the history of its site would be possible without the cooperation and support of the Muckenthaler family. Harold Muckenthaler has been a generous supporter of the center for many years. His late wife, Shirley, who founded our women's auxiliary—the Center Circle—is greatly missed. Their daughter, Peggy Muckenthaler Albert, has given of her time as a board member, a volunteer, a docent, and a contributor of her family's history in photographs and her own personal memories.

Our great thanks go also to cousins of the family: Ronald Muckenthaler, Marilyn Muckenthaler Bolcer, and Mary Adair for sharing their personal collections of photographs and their stories.

All photographs were assembled and captions were written by Zoot Velasco, executive director; Matthew Leslie, director of exhibitions; and Kevin Staniec, marketing director. Karen Lucas culled information from several sources, including *Walter M. Muckenthaler* by Keith Terry, a history commissioned by Walter's son, Harold, in 1974; and *The Martin Muckenthaler Family*, a genealogical history supplied by Joan Muckenthaler. Initial editing was done by Monette Velasco. We thank Fred Ouweleen, Muckenthaler Cultural Center board president, Jane Parker, Muckenthaler Cultural Center Foundation president emerita, and our board of directors for their unwavering support.

We also thank our curatorial interns Marissa Massie and Alexandra Tiedeman, who procured and prepared images and other materials; Daniel Hilger, who prepared the original proposal; and our editorial team: Kristina Buckett, Joe Devera, Timothy Daniel Flynn, Katrina Heinzelmann, Janet Kim, Skye Lyon, and Allison Town.

Cathy Thomas and her successor, Cheri Pape, of the Fullerton Public Library's Launer Local History Room, and Warren Bowen of Fullerton Heritage were crucial in the search for photographs of Walter Muckenthaler in his role as a city councilman as well as several fine images of the Muckenthaler estate. Jane Newell of the Anaheim Public Library's Heritage Center provided images of the Kraemer family.

Arcadia editor Debbie Seracini provided much-needed advice and guidance throughout the process of writing this book.

Unless otherwise noted, all images appear courtesy of the Muckenthaler Family Archives. Other images in this volume appear courtesy of the Anaheim Public Library Heritage Center (APLHC) and the Fullerton Public Library Launer Local History Room (Launer).

INTRODUCTION

Once upon a time, a young couple built their dream house on a hill overlooking orchards in sunny Southern California. It was a vision of murmuring fountains and swaying palm trees, of verdant grounds through which to stroll in the sunlight or under the stars of a clear sky. It was the 1920s, a time of growing prosperity for the region. Though they were practical people, they indulged their love of Mediterranean architecture, landscape gardening, and fine furniture for their beautiful new home. They created not only a residence admired for its elegant style but also a welcoming home for the surrounding community through the decades to follow.

The Renaissance Revival–style villa featured a red tile roofline, wrought iron gates, an imported antique Italian banister, arched glass-panel doorways, Batchelder tile fireplaces, mahogany windows, hand-combed plaster moldings, and a double-story solarium. The house was surrounded by gardens, a small reservoir for irrigating orchards, a rustic stone gazebo, and even an aviary for raising rare birds.

For Walter and Adella Kraemer Muckenthaler, it was a house to last a lifetime. For their only son, Harold, it was a boyhood paradise. For Harold's grandparents, aunts, uncles, cousins, and finally, grandchildren, it was a place to celebrate birthdays, anniversaries, and holidays, as well as a wonderful place to visit. For the people of North Orange County, it would eventually become a center for arts and culture.

As in any story, there were ancestors who paved the way for what was to come. Both Walter and Adella came from industrious families who helped to define the direction of early Orange County. Walter was the grandson of immigrants who originally settled in the Midwest. Like many Americans of German descent, however, his parents eventually moved to Anaheim, where they prospered in ranching and other businesses. The family's pioneering spirit led to the many successes that helped to prepare Walter for his adult life.

Adella Kraemer's father was a founder of Fullerton's neighboring city of Placentia. Like the Muckenthalers, he had roots in Germany, but her mother, Angelina, descended from José Antonio Yorba—a Spanish volunteer soldier who escorted Fr. Junipero Serra and won a land grant along the Santa Ana River. His son Bernardo Antonio built a rancho that would become Yorba Linda. Bernardo was Angelina's grandfather. The marriage of Walter and Adella in 1919 brought together two remarkable families during a time of great promise and difficult challenges in Southern California.

Like many farmers and ranchers of their era, Adella's father, Samuel Kraemer, leased land to the burgeoning oil industry. He passed the lease for an oil well on his property to his daughter and son-in-law soon after their wedding, providing them with an unexpected source of financial security.

Walter was employed by the Santa Fe Railroad as a land surveyor for the city of Fullerton. The gift from his father-in-law gave his young family the means to a spectacular home and a wealthier life. But he had been a hard worker from an early age, and though the family could now afford travel and other luxuries of the time, Walter's life was not idyllic.

Walter involved himself intimately with the design of the grounds and the management of the estate. He was also deeply involved in his city, serving on both Fullerton's city council and its planning commission. In financially difficult times, he oversaw the construction of both a flood control project and a new city hall for the growing town.

Harold served in the US Navy in World War II. He married Shirley Zoeter, also of Fullerton, and raised three beautiful daughters in their hometown. The family visited their grandparents often. Peggy, the oldest child, sometimes stayed overnight with them as a special treat. She has fond memories of Christmases spent in the villa's newly enclosed atrium, as well as traveling to Palm Springs with her sisters, parents, and grandparents for Easter.

Fullerton has many structures of historical significance, and the Muckenthaler home has taken its place as one of Fullerton's treasures from the past—but its story does not end with the departure of its first family. Several years after Walter's passing, Adella and Harold arranged to have their family home preserved for all time. In 1965, in an extraordinary gesture to the town they loved, they donated the villa and the eight acres that surrounded it to the city of Fullerton as a cultural center for the visual and performing arts. Five years later, a full schedule of art exhibitions began.

Although some changes were made to the property, the historic home is largely unchanged from the time the Muckenthaler family lived in it. The grounds now serve as a city park. Gone are the aviaries and free-roaming peacocks. The dumbwaiter to the basement has been decommissioned, and the reservoir has been filled in. An amphitheater was built just south of the house in 1995 to host performing arts programs; two studios were added for art classes, one in a former garage. A grand entrance was constructed to welcome visitors to the cultural center from the main parking lot. But Walter's barbecue is still there in the rear patio. The solarium can still be seen at night, its tall windows warmly lit by the original hanging lamp.

In 1999, the Muckenthaler villa received designation in the National Register of Historic Places. Each year, more than 100,000 visitors for cultural events and weddings enjoy the distinctive architecture, gardens, and grounds of the Muckenthaler Cultural Center, where they can experience community celebrations, art exhibitions, theater, music, dance, storytelling, classes, and seasonal festivals. This book is the story of an extraordinary family, their wonderful estate, and the gift of culture born from their love of Fullerton.

One

THE MUCKENTHALERS OF KANSAS

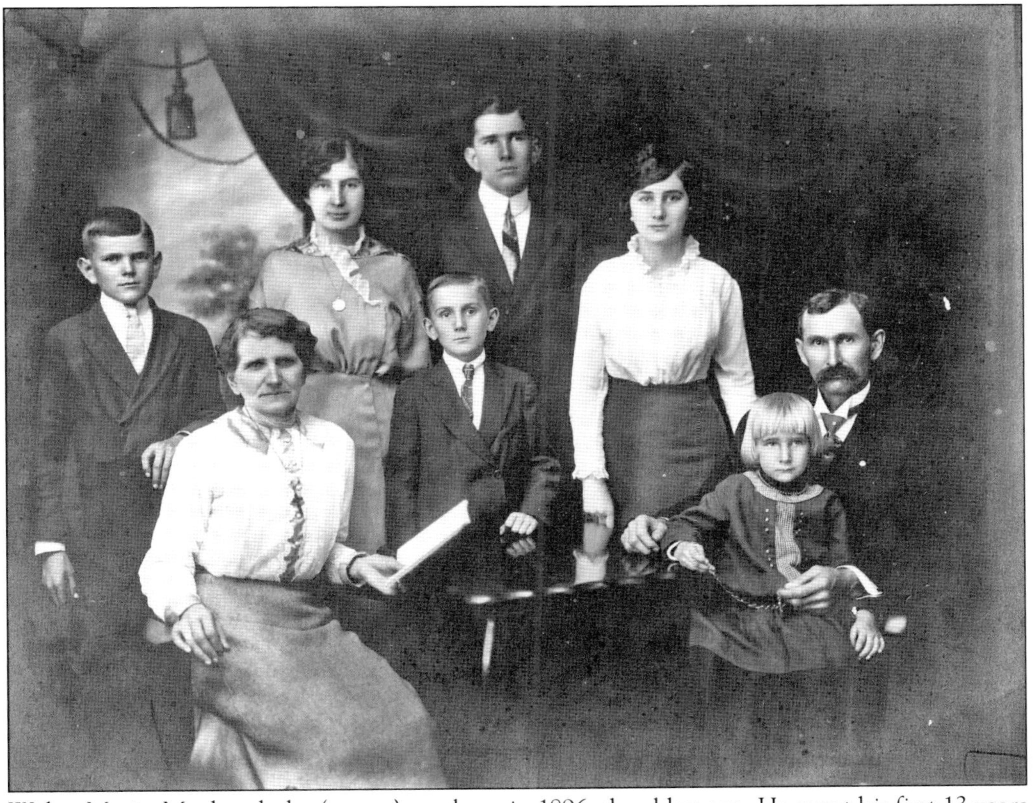

Walter Moritz Muckenthaler (center) was born in 1896, the eldest son. He spent his first 13 years in Paxico, Kansas (located approximately 30 miles from Topeka), with his siblings, Viola, Abbie (Apollonia Agnes), Martin, Lawrence, and Augusta (Gussie). Another son, Clarence, died at only nine months of age. Walter was born with the help of a midwife in his parents' upstairs bedroom. Walter's grandparents Martin and Elizabeth had immigrated to the United States in 1854, originally settling in Minnesota before moving south to Kansas. The family surname had been Muggenthaler in Germany, but, like so many immigrants' names at the time, it was changed to Muckenthaler when his grandparents traveled through Ellis Island.

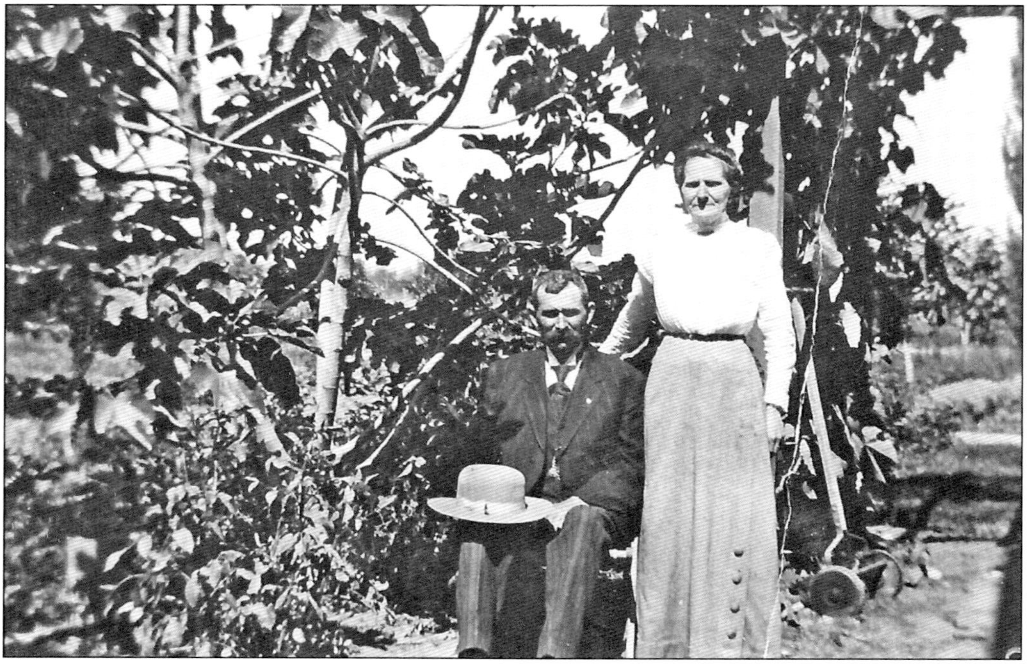

Martin and Elizabeth Muckenthaler (above) were photographed outside their home. Growing up as one of nine children, their son Albert visited Anaheim as a young man of 20 but moved back to Kansas, where he married Augusta Ebert in 1889. Albert and Augusta had a successful farm and dairy in the nearby town of Paxico. Although the family had a farm in Kansas, Albert never forgot the seasons spent working in Anaheim as a young man, and he would dream one day of moving to California with his family. Martin Muckenthaler helped lay out the town of Newbury, Kansas, where the family's two-story gabled home (below) was open to local Jesuit priests for services while the town's church was under construction.

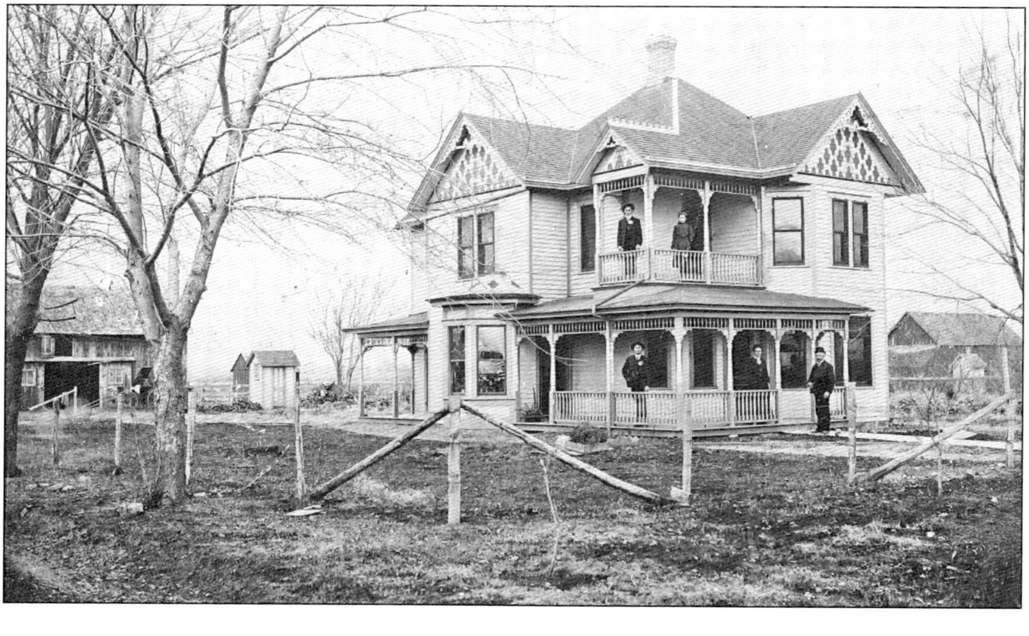

Walter's life in Kansas was typical of a farm boy of the time. He loved to fish in nearby Mill Creek, trap animals in the woods, and wander the open spaces of the plains. He also had serious responsibilities on the family farm, and this shaped his character. As an adult, he expected workers to pull their weight and rewarded those who did. Many workers stayed with the family for more than 30 years.

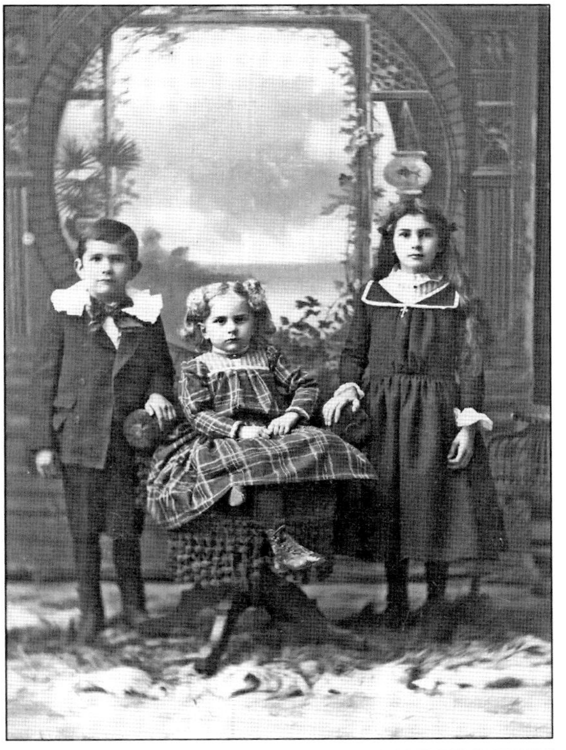

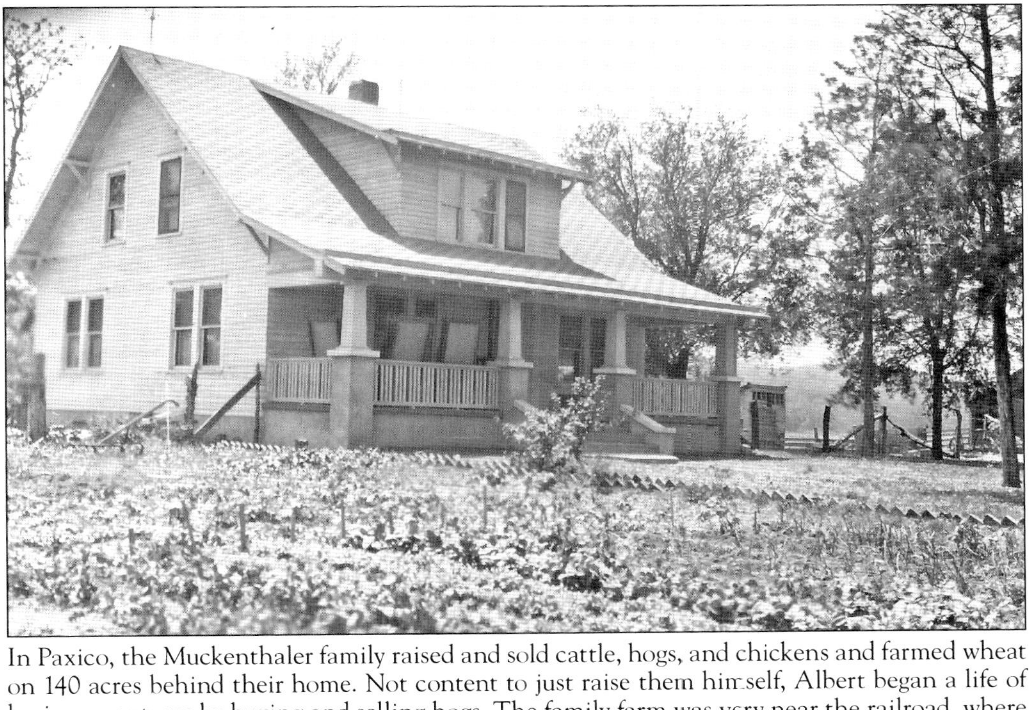

In Paxico, the Muckenthaler family raised and sold cattle, hogs, and chickens and farmed wheat on 140 acres behind their home. Not content to just raise them himself, Albert began a life of business ventures by buying and selling hogs. The family farm was very near the railroad, where Albert would see the *Golden State Limited* heading for California.

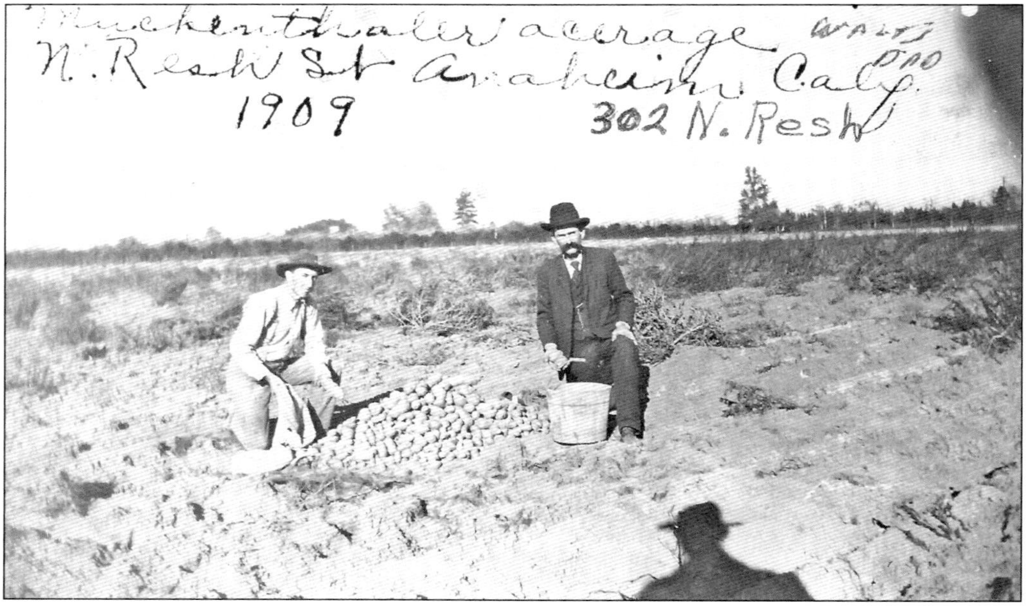

In 1909, Albert realized his dream of moving permanently to Anaheim with his family. Settling there, they first rented a cottage on North Olive Street. At Augusta's insistence, Albert purchased an L-shaped lot of their own from St. Catherine's Orphanage (later St. Catherine's Military Academy). They began by planting potatoes and continued with orange trees. Two local German carpenters, Bender and Silbernagle, constructed a two-story Craftsman house on North Resh and West Cypress Streets in what is now known as the Anaheim Colony District.

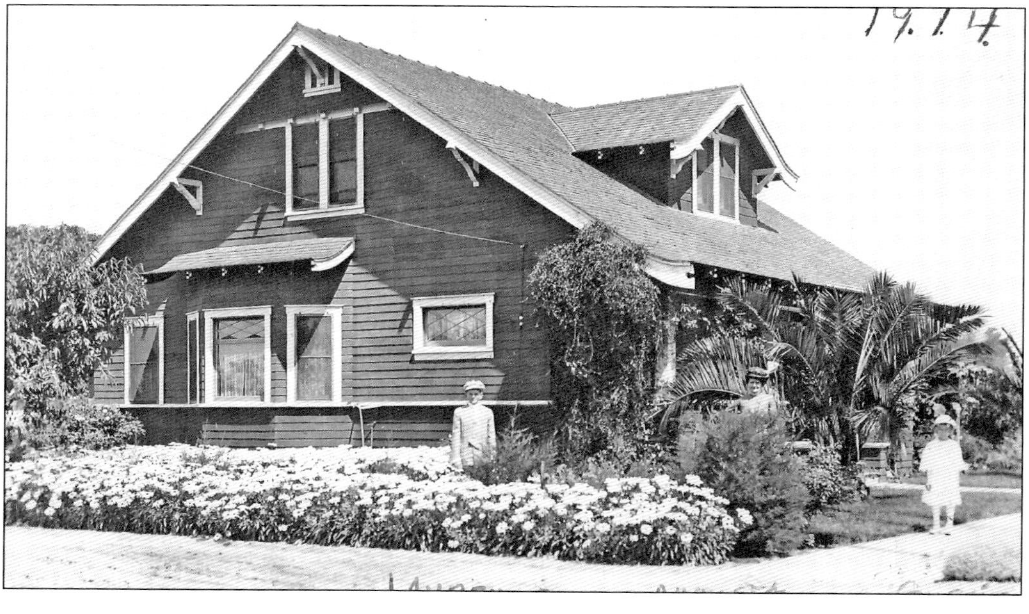

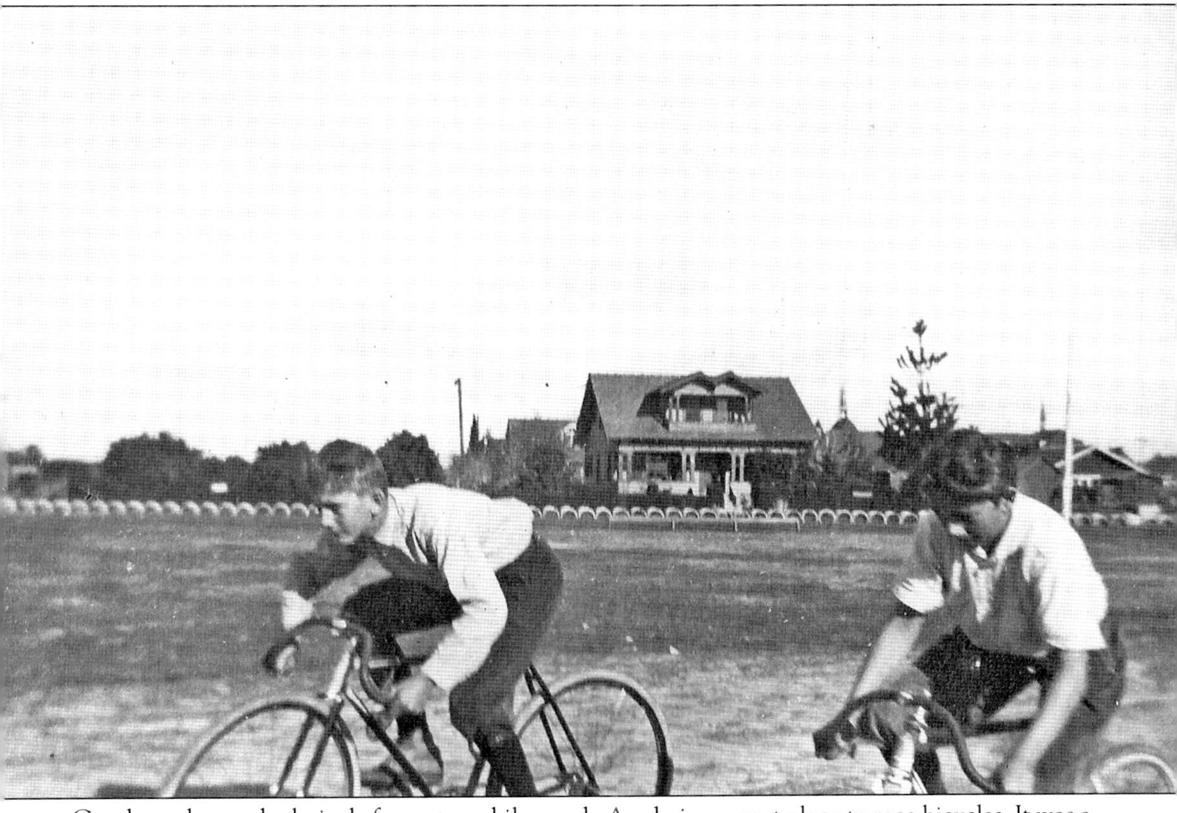

Good weather and relatively few automobiles made Anaheim a great place to race bicycles. It was a German Catholic colony founded in 1850. The families bought land from the Yorbas and depended on each other. These farmers grew up with a strong sense of community and interdependence. They became very close knit in this country of unsurpassed beauty. They had a sense of the American dream of the Old West—that with grit and determination, anything was possible.

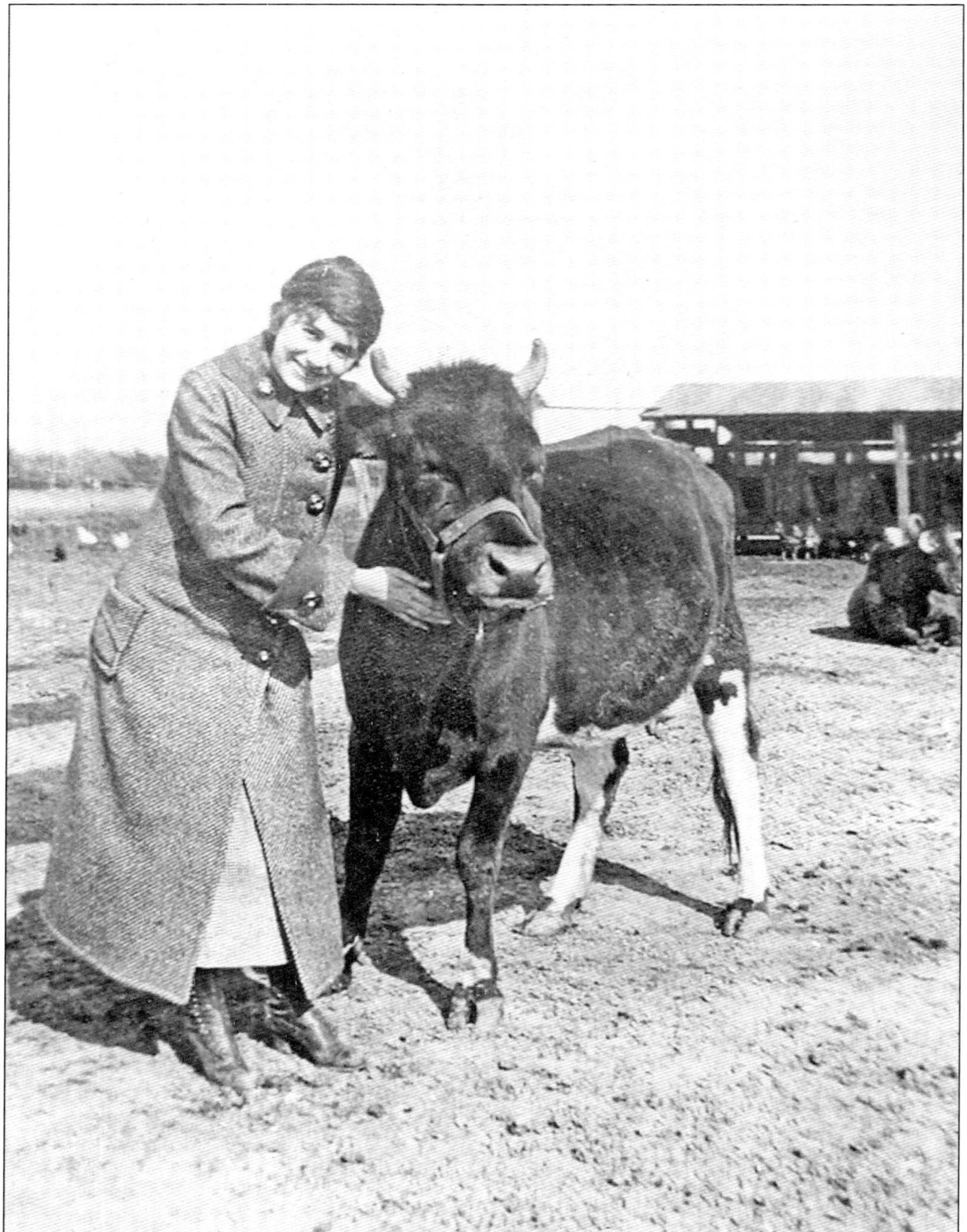

What worked for the Muckenthalers in Kansas also worked in California. The family soon opened a professional dairy, selling butter and milk, which was packaged in standard bottles with paper caps. They started with one cow, and as demand grew, their stock increased until they owned at least a dozen cows. As the Muckenthalers prospered, so did their neighbors, and Anaheim became an important colony in the county. The growers of Anaheim would often take their crops a few miles up the road to Fullerton and send them by train around the country.

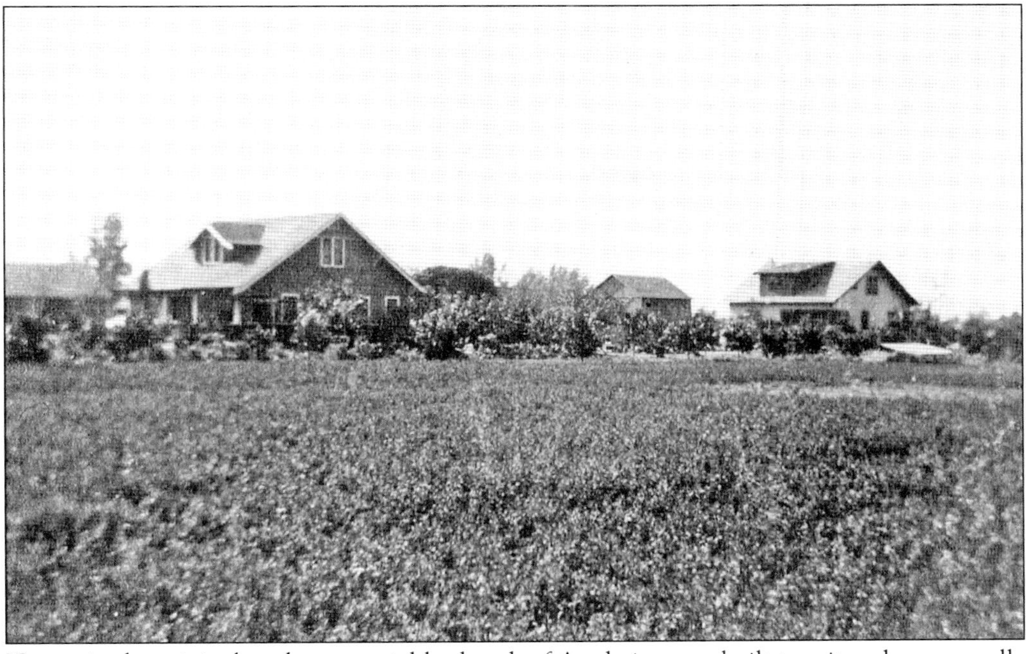

Homes in the original settlement neighborhoods of Anaheim were built to suit and were usually surrounded by fields for farming. The Muckenthaler land had to be cleared of brush and grass from its days as a vineyard before it could be planted with other crops. Houses like this still exist in the Colony District, though they are now surrounded by later homes built in between the older ones. The home on Resh Street began to seem small for the family of six children and their parents. Albert contracted with the same two German carpenters who built it to construct a larger house nearby (below). Although this house had a small third story, the family eventually realized that they preferred the original home on Resh Street. They moved back in and leased the newer home to another family.

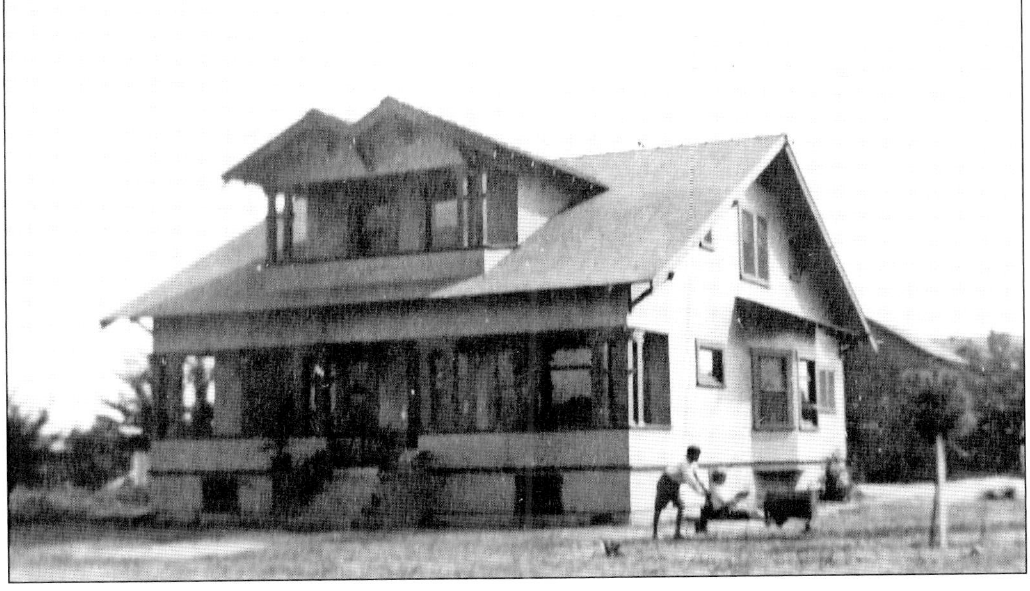

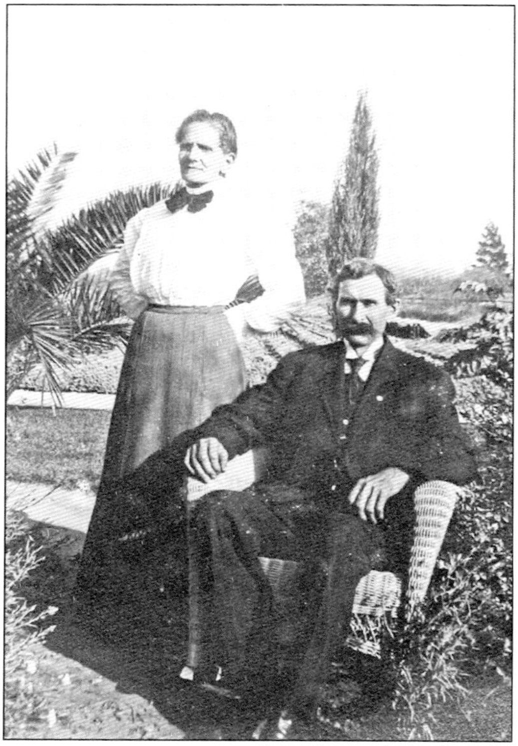

Albert and Augusta Muckenthaler pose for a photographer. Augusta was a strong, resolute woman with fine business sense. She supported her husband's desire to move to California and helped relocate the entire family halfway across the country by railcar, leaving behind a successful life in Paxico. In the library of the Muckenthaler villa, the Batchelder tile fireplace sports a frieze of the Chisholm Trail from Kansas to the west, reminding them of their journey. (Batchelder only sold this relief to families that had migrated west from Kansas.)

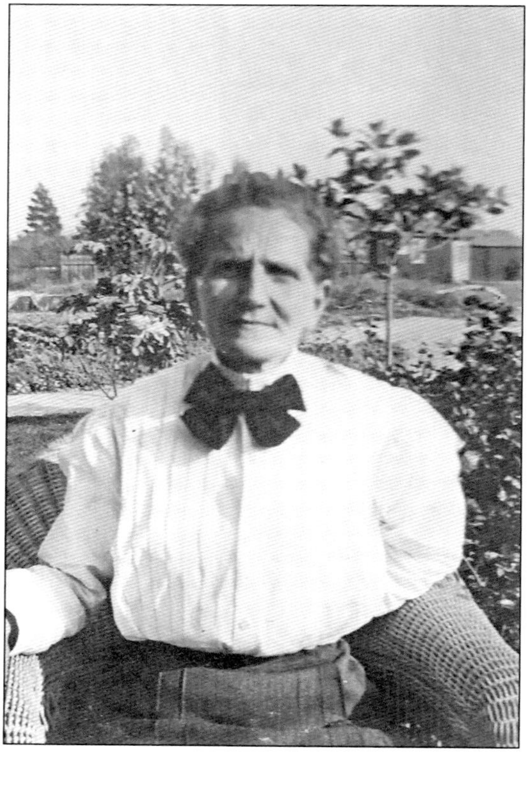

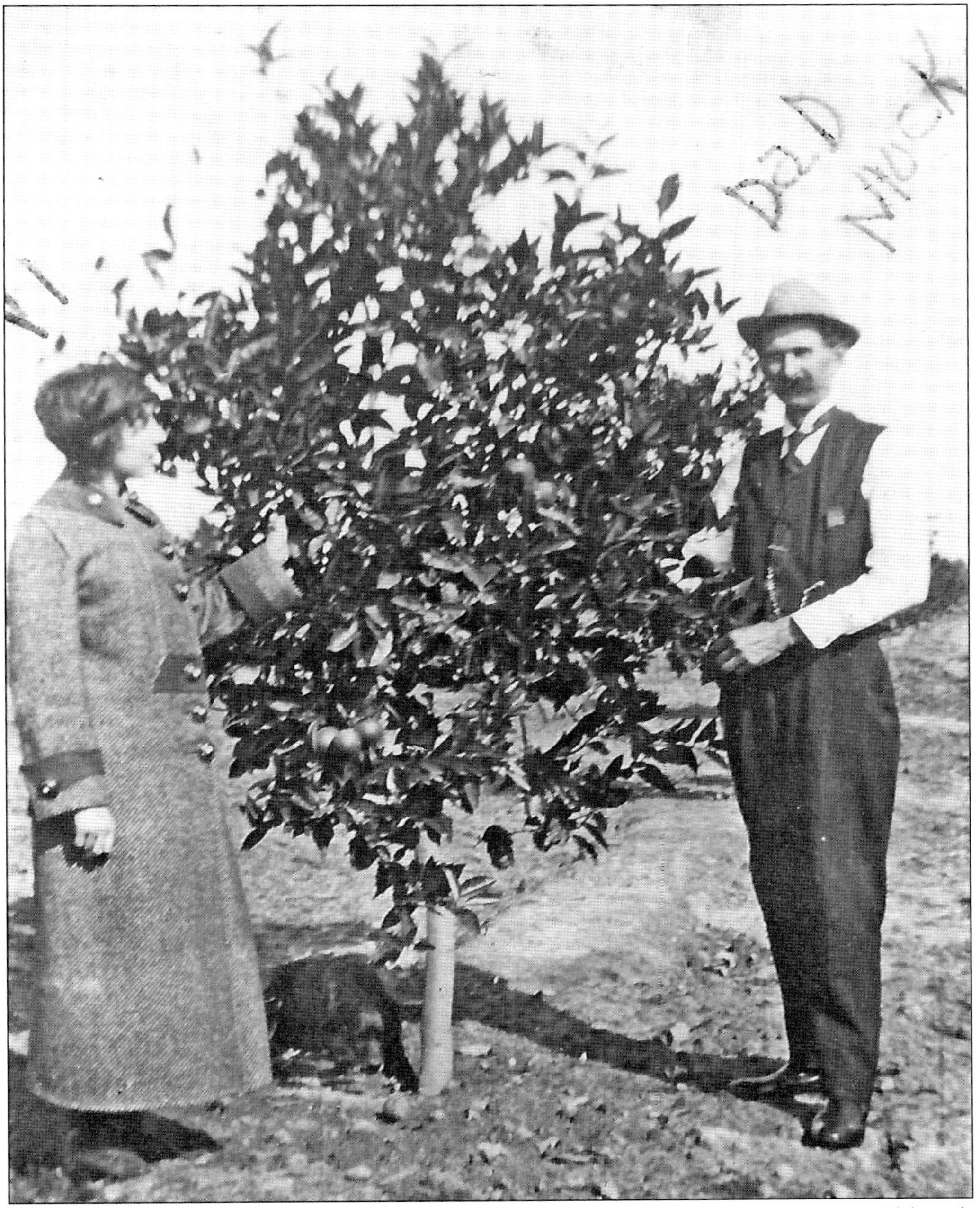

Martin and his daughter Viola "Vi" Muckenthaler pose beside one of their orange trees. Although many of Anaheim's original settlers had tried growing grapes, disease decimated the crop. The introduction of citrus and walnuts proved much more successful, ultimately defining an era of agriculture in Southern California. The picture is labeled "Dad Muck," showing that even within the family Muck became shorthand for Muckenthaler. Today, the cultural center is often affectionately referred to as the Muck, which has even become the web address (TheMuck.org). When the cultural center decided to brand the name, the family was consulted first. Always supportive, they said, "That's what we call it. If it brings people inside, go ahead!"

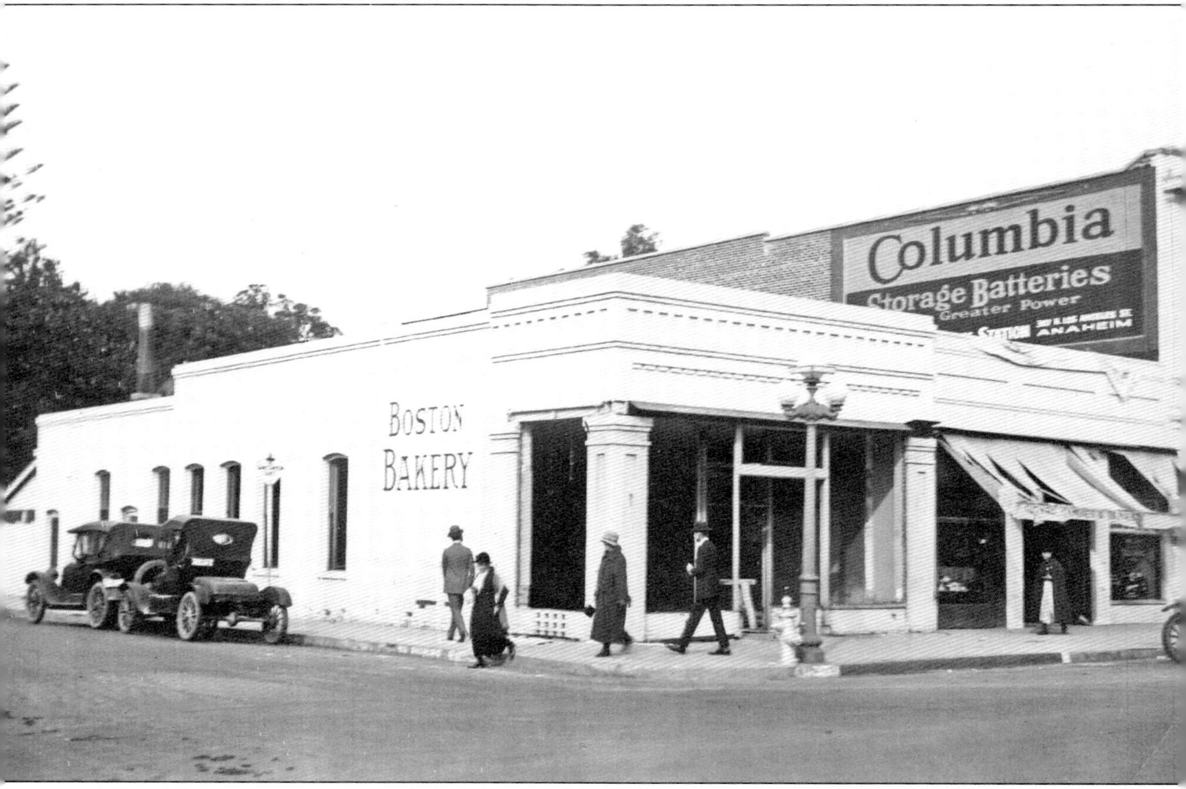

Albert's business interests included the purchase of the Boston Bakery in downtown Anaheim. Walter graduated from Anaheim Union High School in 1914 and worked for a year at the bakery's soda fountain, managing the shop while saving money for college. At the time this photograph was taken, Anaheim was a burgeoning settlement for German immigrant farmers, and Fullerton was established because of the railroad. Other North Orange County towns had yet to be created, making Anaheim and Fullerton hubs for downtown business. During this time, the Muckenthalers attended St. Boniface Church. It was there that Walter first met the Kraemer family's eldest daughter, Adella. (APLHC.)

Two

The Kraemers in California

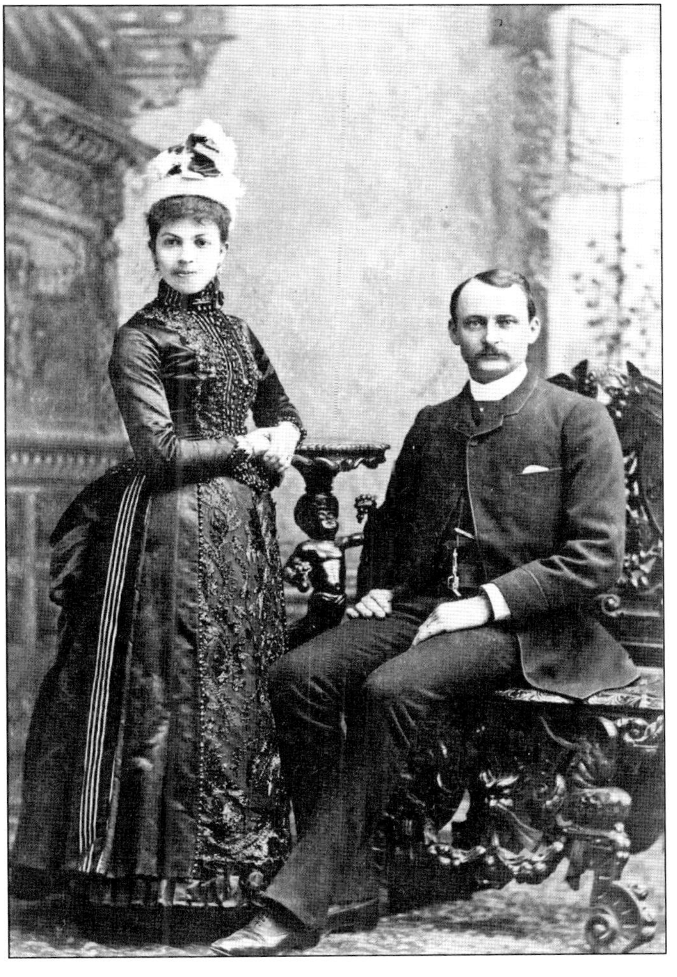

Angelina Yorba and Samuel Kraemer, who were married in September 1886, are the parents of Adella Kraemer Muckenthaler. Like the Muckenthalers of Kansas, Daniel Kraemer, Samuel's father, emigrated from Germany to the Midwest and finally to Anaheim. He bought 3,900 acres and a dirt-floor adobe (built in 1837) from the Ontiveros family in 1865. The Ontiveros were a land grant family who were also in-laws of the Yorbas (Angelina's grandmother was an Ontiveros). The Yorbas were one of the oldest and most influential families in California. Adella had seven siblings (of which she was the oldest girl)—Samuel Peter, Arnold Ruperto, Angelina, Gilbert Ulysses, Lawrence Prudencio, Geraldine, and Louis Thomas. (APLHC.)

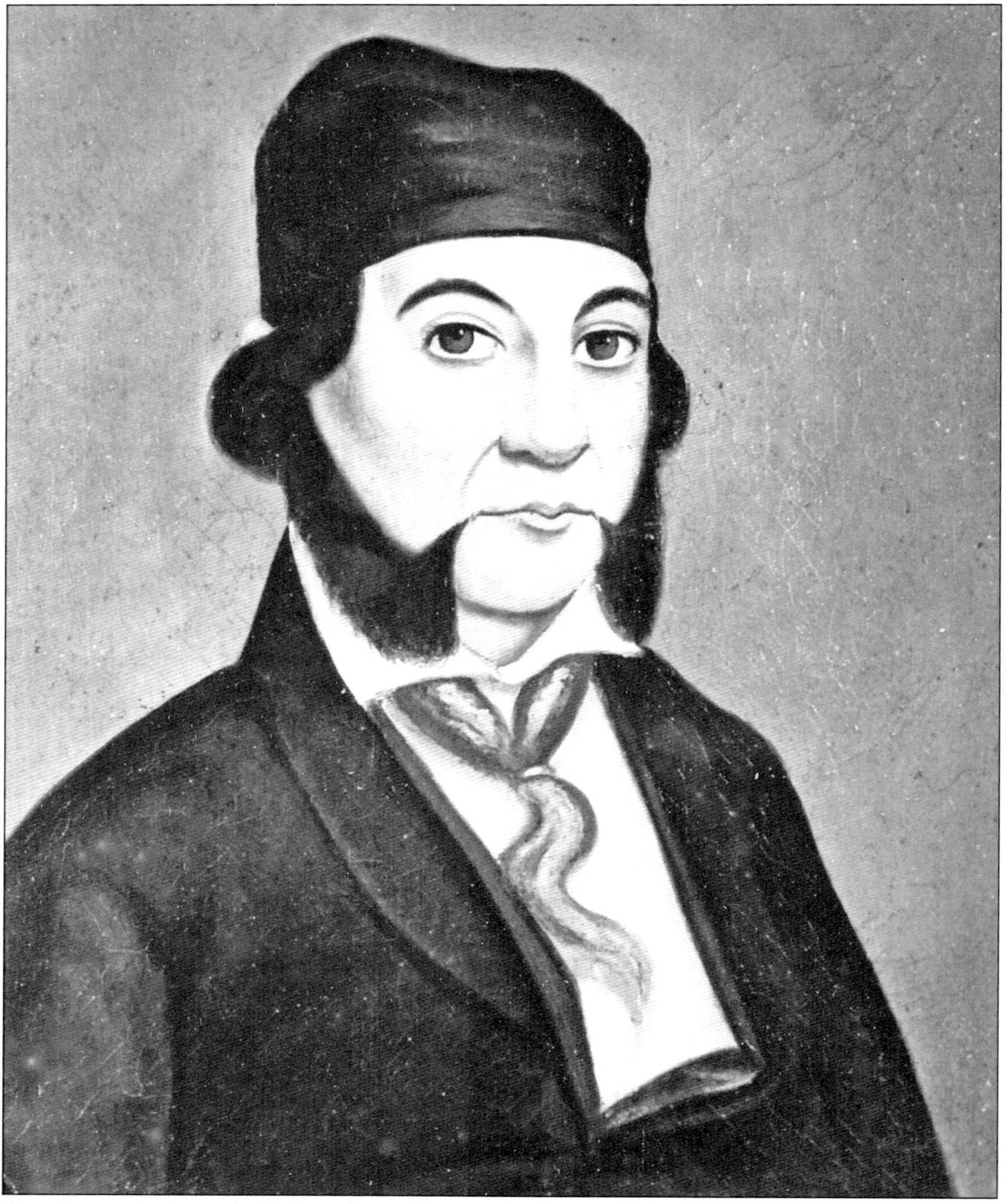

Don Bernardo Antonio Yorba inherited acres of what would become the cities of Yorba Linda and Anaheim from his father, José Antonio Yorba. His lineage was that of a Spanish adventurer. José Antonio was a Spanish volunteer soldier and became captain of the guard on Fr. Junipero Serra's mission to Alta California. He fought against the pirate Hippolyte Bouchard at San Juan Capistrano. He was rewarded with a Spanish land grant in present-day Orange County. His 17 children would marry into most of the other land grant rancho families and help to shape Southern California history. When Bernardo's son, Prudencio, married Maria de los Dolores Ontiveros, the two rancho families united. Angelina Yorba was Prudencio's daughter. (Courtesy of First Title Insurance.)

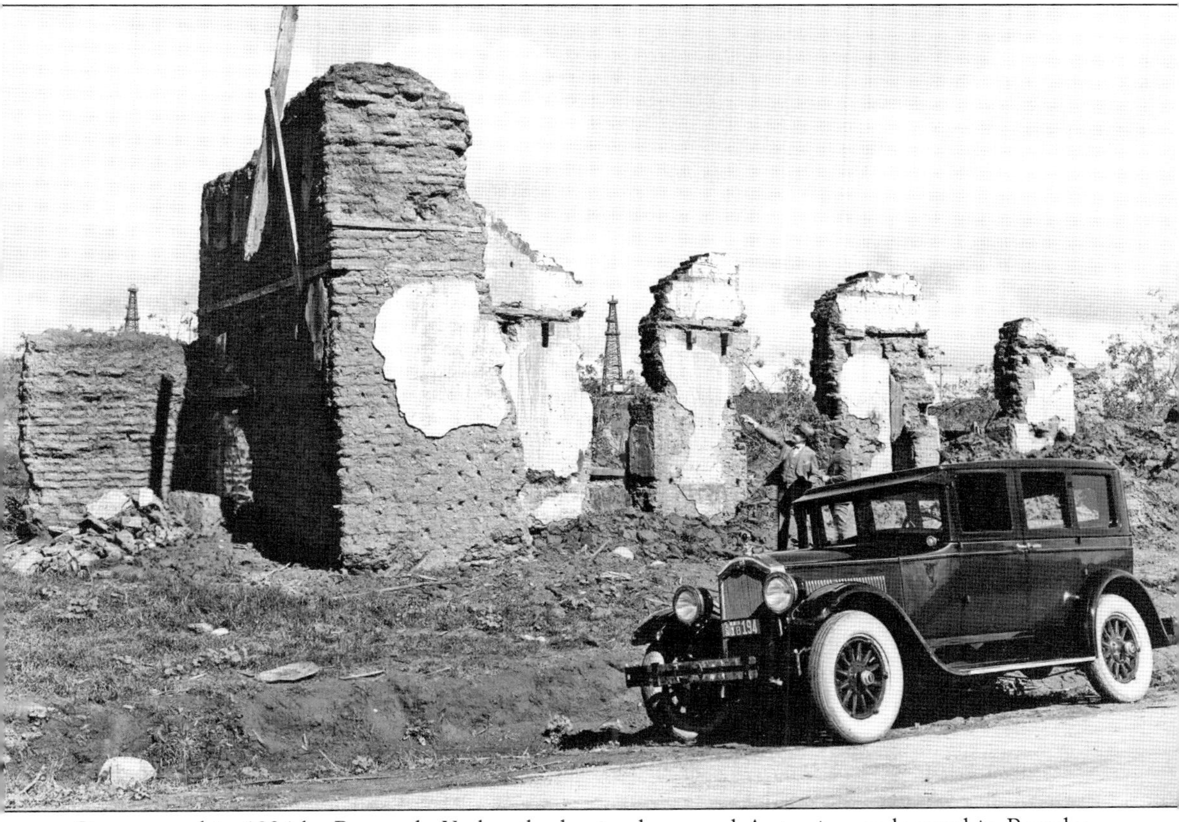

Constructed in 1834 by Bernardo Yorba, the hacienda named Antonio was located in Rancho Cañón de Santa Ana (now Yorba Linda) and was the headquarters of a 35,000-acre ranch that stretched to the Pacific Ocean to the south and the foothills to the north. The residence had two stories and more than 30 rooms. Samuel Kraemer had the ruins of the building demolished in 1926. Even though the rancho land grant families are gone, their descendants (like the Muckenthalers) still have small holdings, existing in the form of mini-malls and commercial centers. (APLHC.)

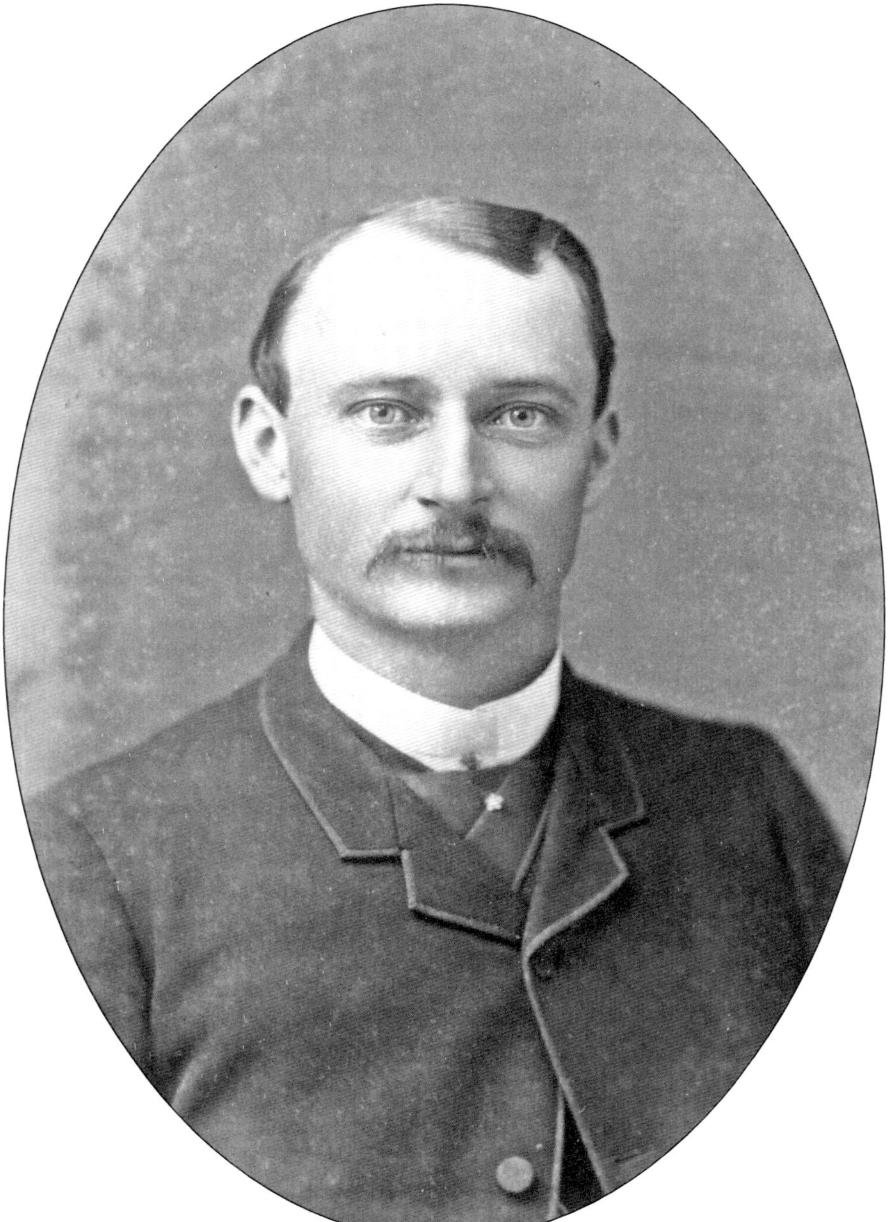

Samuel Kraemer was the son of Daniel Kraemer and Eleanora Schraw, who had immigrated to the United States from Germany in the 1850s. Samuel helped bring the railroad through Placentia by donating the land for the depot. He helped organize the Placentia National Bank in 1911 and was on its first board of directors. He also built the first high-rise for the bank, located on the northeast corner of Bradford and Crowther Avenues, and the first orange packinghouse in Placentia. He donated a lot on the northeast corner of Murry and Ramona Streets to start the first Catholic church in Placentia, known as St. Joseph's Mission Catholic Church, built in 1926. The Kraemers were active in St. Boniface Catholic Church in Anaheim. They had always been respected as a friendly, industrious, civic-minded, and generous family. (APLHC.)

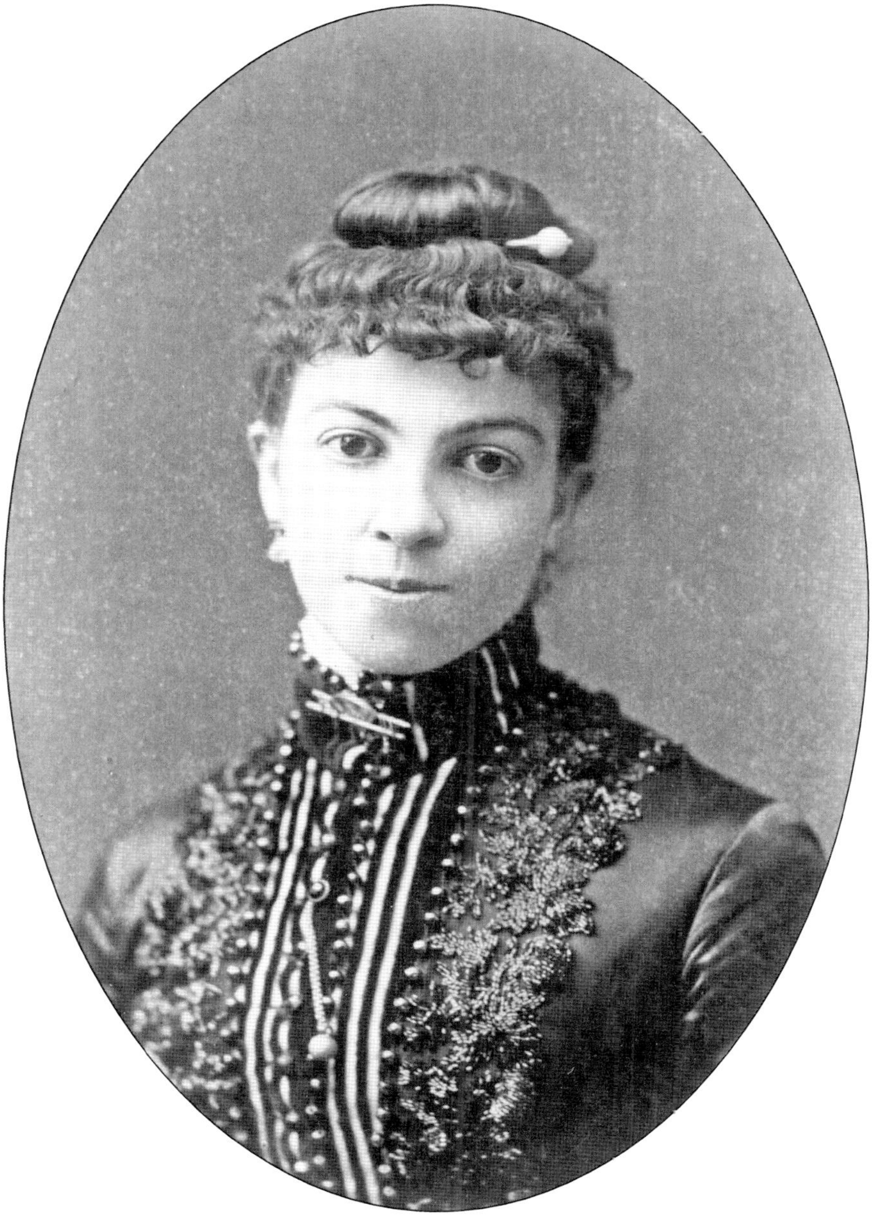

Angelina Yorba was the daughter of Maria de los Dolores Ontiveros and Prudencio Yorba. Both the Yorbas and the Ontiveros were important land grant rancho families. Unlike the Yorbas, whose land grant came from the King of Spain, the Ontiveros family received their grant from the Mexican government in exchange for exploring Alta California (upper California). Their land grant was in the Santa Maria Valley, north of Los Angeles. Angelina, of direct Spanish descent, came from the earliest Mexican American families in the region. Prudencio increased his lands through marriage, a tradition with these rancho families, which often had more than a dozen heirs. Angelina spoke with a Spanish accent at the time of her marriage to Samuel Kraemer. Samuel had learned to speak Spanish, making him an invaluable intermediary between the Kraemers and the largely Spanish-speaking population in the area. (APLHC.)

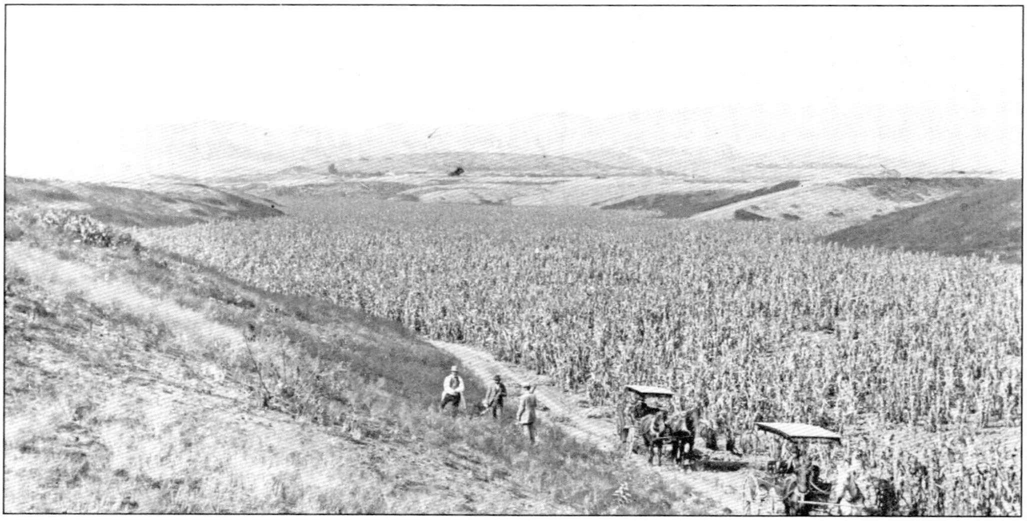

By the time Angelina and Samuel Kraemer were married, Samuel had already been given 500 acres of his father's expansive ranch in what was then northern Anaheim. Samuel's father, Daniel Kraemer, had originally purchased 3,900 acres for $4.60 per acre. Samuel experimented with Valencia oranges, eventually planting more than 60 acres of trees in addition to 130 acres of walnuts. Their land was eventually incorporated into the city of Placentia, which he helped found in 1876. Samuel and Angelina Kraemer raised their children, named Arnold, Samuel P., Angelina, Adella, Gilbert, Louie, Lawrence, and Geraldine. (Above, APLHC.)

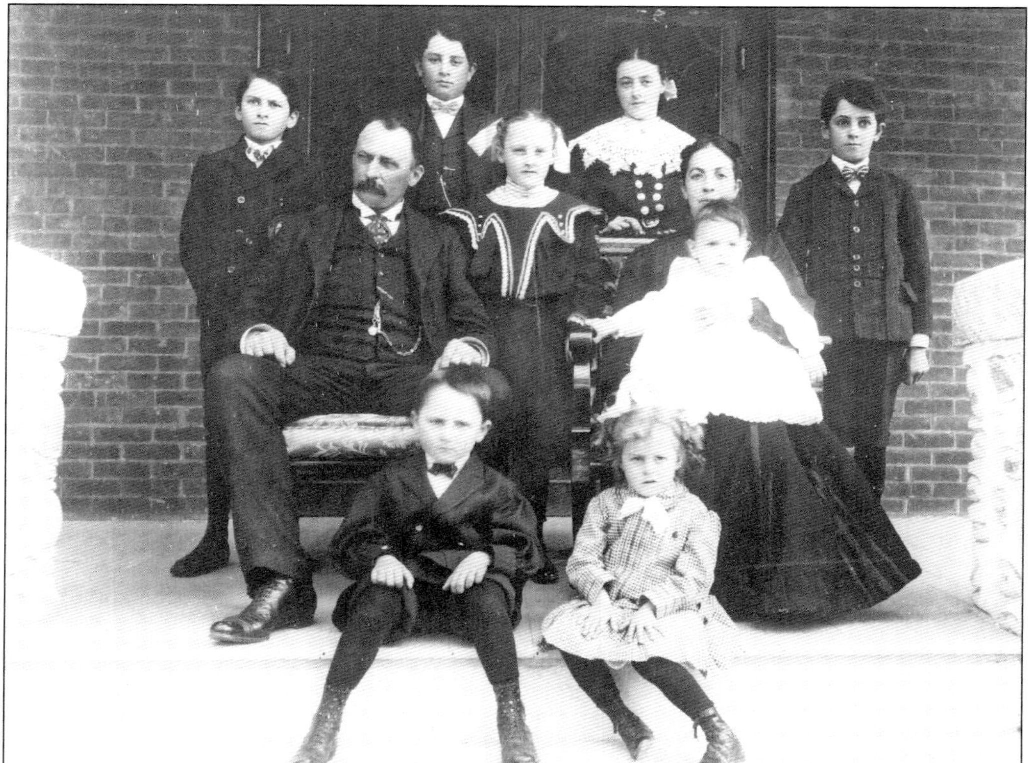

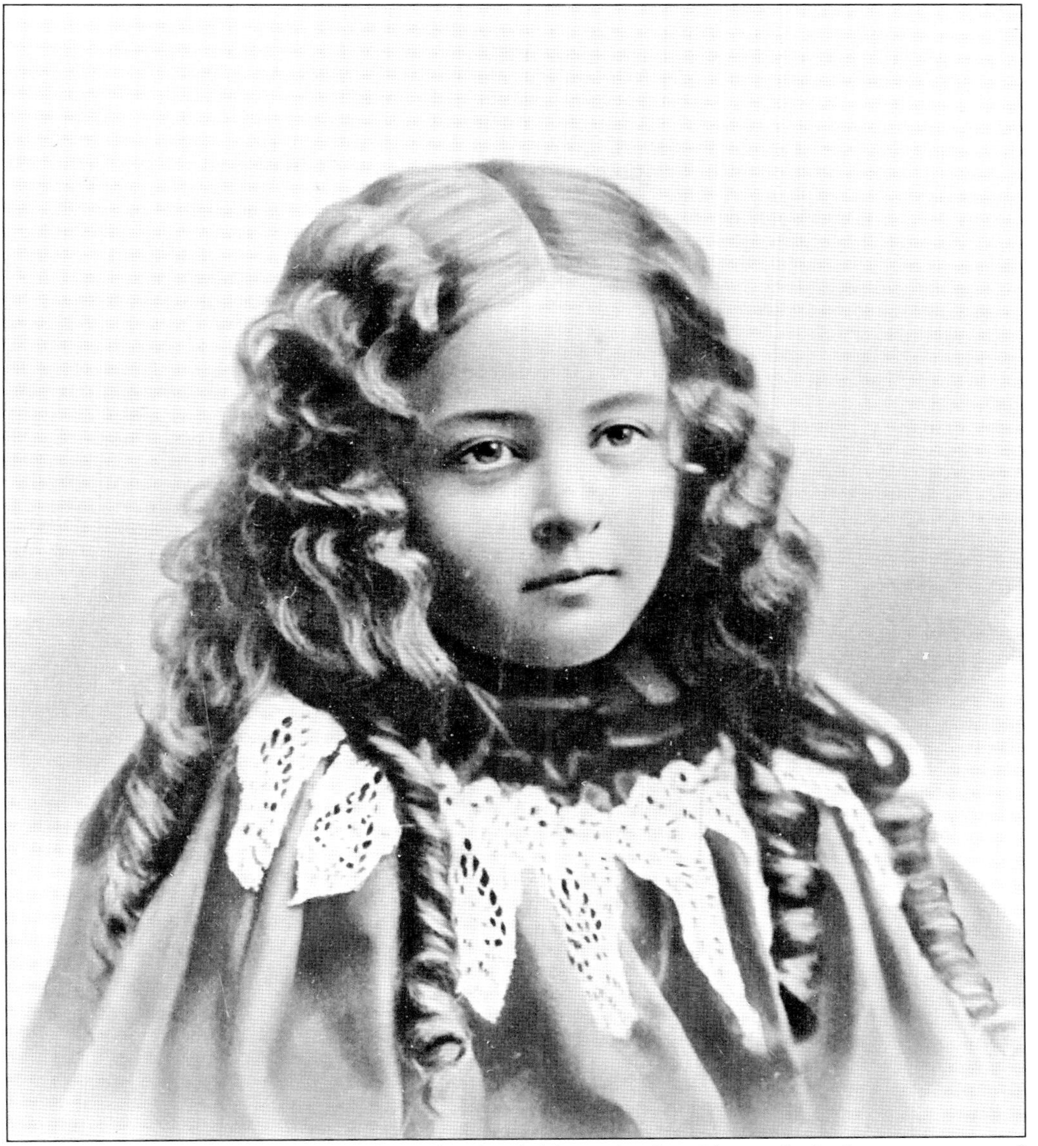

Adella Kraemer was the second oldest of eight children. As the oldest girl, she became a second mother to her siblings, even taking over the management of the household when her mother was ill. She was devoutly Catholic, often leading the family in the rosary. Adella pursued her education through the eighth grade. Most of her free time was spent with her family or at church, where she would meet her future husband. She was a vibrant, cheerful young woman who loved the outdoors and spending time with friends when not helping her mother.

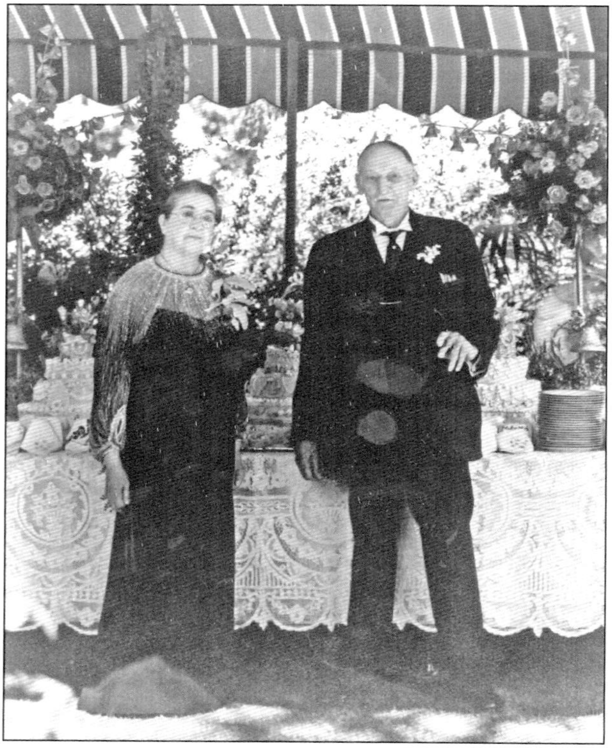

Samuel and Angelina Kraemer celebrated their 50th wedding anniversary on September 30, 1936. Their journey from Illinois to Orange County was typical of many German American families, but their ingenuity and industriousness over a lifetime helped to define the region as a land of oil and oranges. The generosity and guidance of the elder Kraemers helped to make the Muckenthaler estate possible, and the Kraemers took the Yorba legacy to the next generation. Like the Yorbas before them, who helped shape Yorba Linda, they brought Anaheim, Placentia, and—through Walter and Adella—Fullerton into the 20th century.

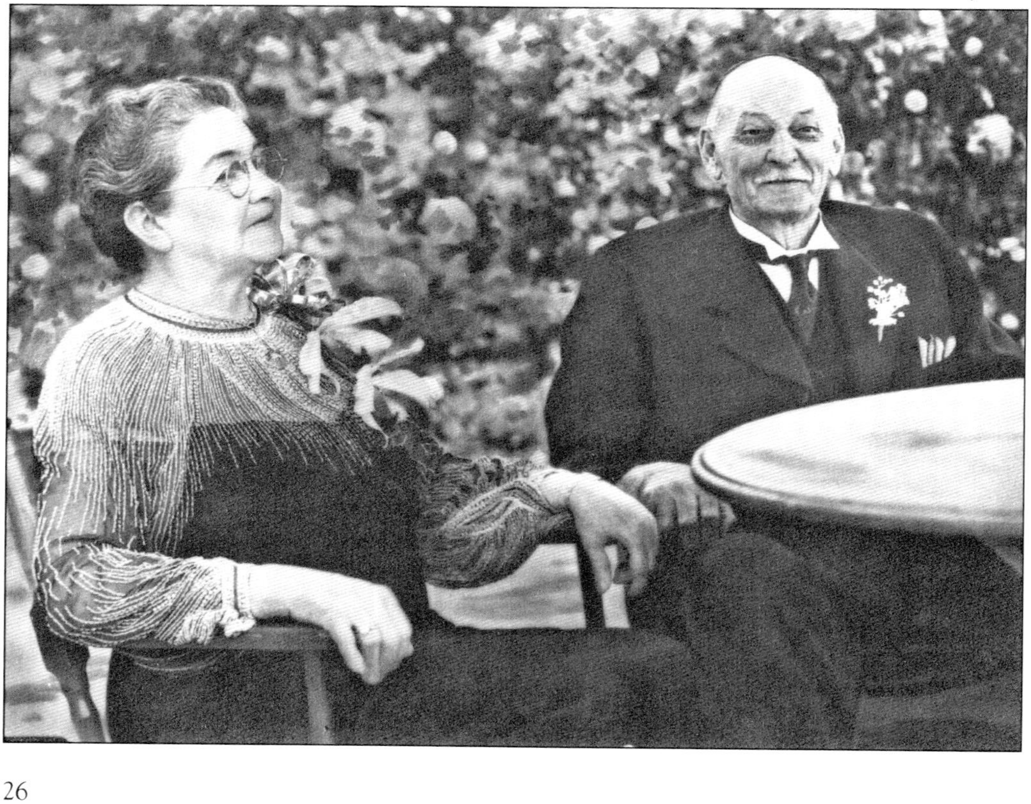

Three

Walter and Adella

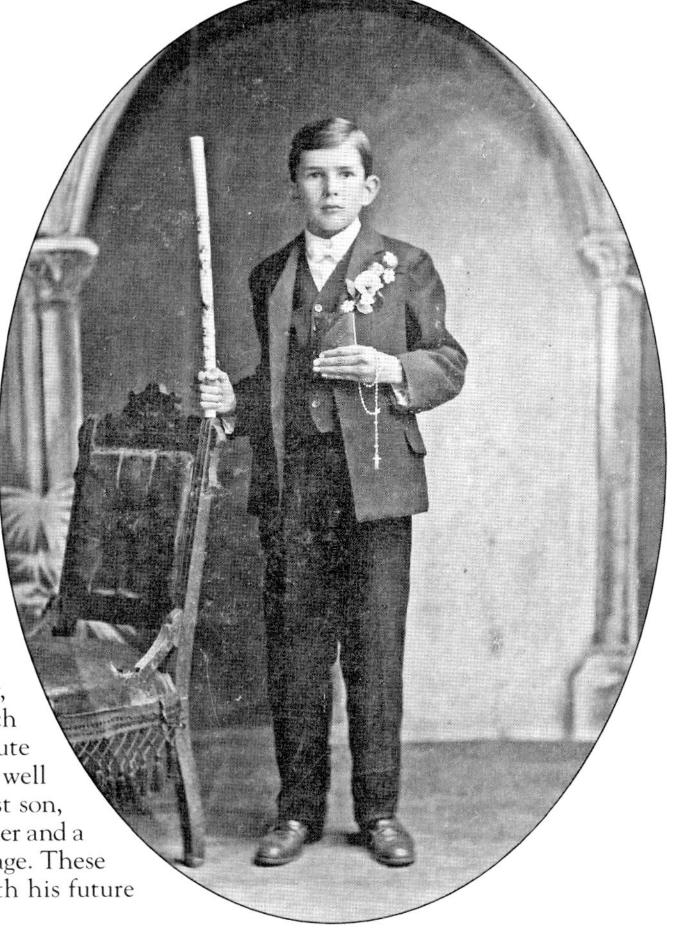

Walter Muckenthaler received his First Communion in 1902 in Paxico. Religion was at the center of the German immigrant community and shaped young Walter's character. Catholicism is a fundamental element of western rancho life and made it easier for the German families to integrate into new towns made from ranchos. The candle, rosary, and missal he holds are examples of a childhood filled with heartland values of honesty, respect, and industriousness, which forged a fair-minded and resolute character that would serve him well throughout his life. As the eldest son, he learned how to be a hard worker and a good family member at an early age. These are qualities he would share with his future wife, Adella Kraemer.

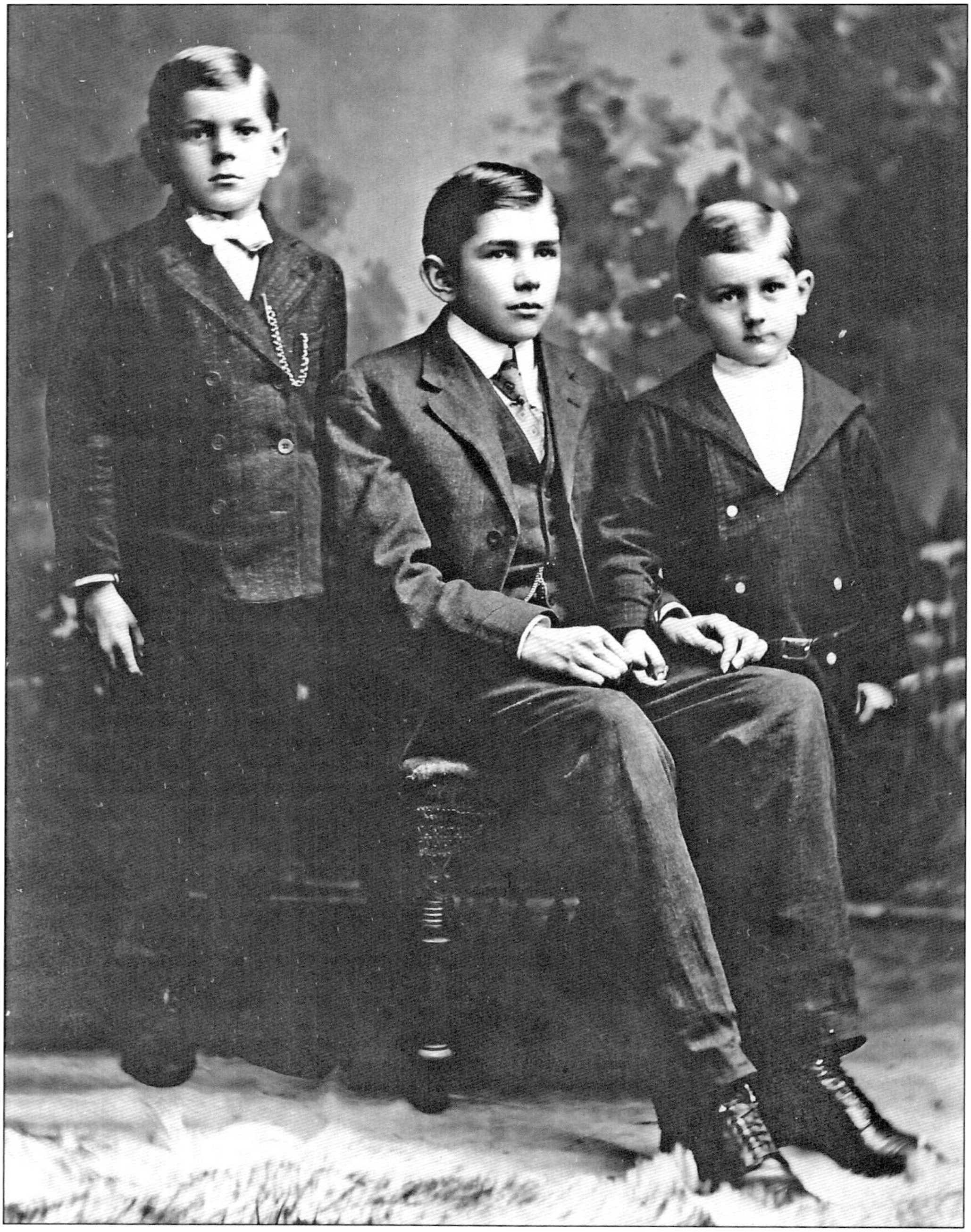

A 14-year-old Walter is pictured with his 8-year-old brother, Lawrence, and 5-year-old brother, Martin. The Muckenthaler children were educated by Benedictine nuns at Sacred Heart Church in Anaheim. Strict curriculum required that biblical lessons be recited in German, though the language had long since given way to English in the Muckenthaler home. The brothers would stay close their whole life and often helped each other in business and during family trials. Walter was also very close to his sisters. Pioneer families, who endured many hardships as a group, would often stay very close.

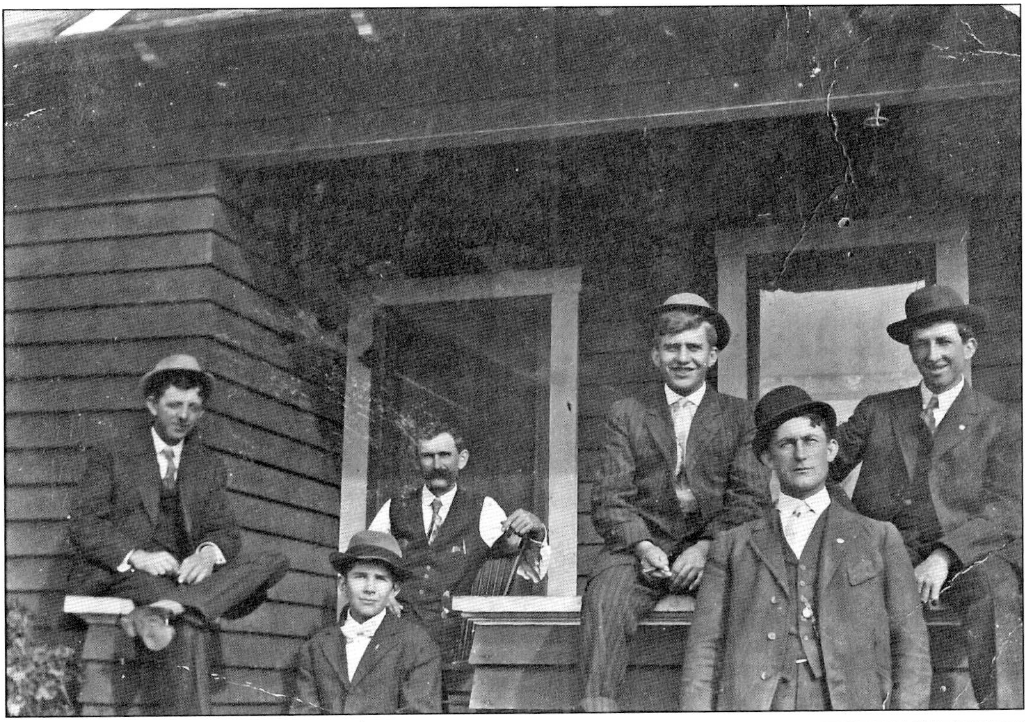

Albert and his boys relax in Anaheim on the front porch of their home with friends on a Sunday morning while waiting for the girls to go to church. The adjustment to Anaheim was an easy one in some ways. The freezing winters of Paxico gave way to the mild climate of Southern California, where the family put their farming and business skills to good use. From an early age, Walter (right) demonstrated a capacity for leadership. During the two years that the family operated Anaheim's Boston Bakery, they learned they could rely on Walter as an able supervisor of others. Anaheim was a small, tight-knit community of German Americans and Mexican Americans who lived and worked together to forge a new future and gain the prosperity promised by the American dream.

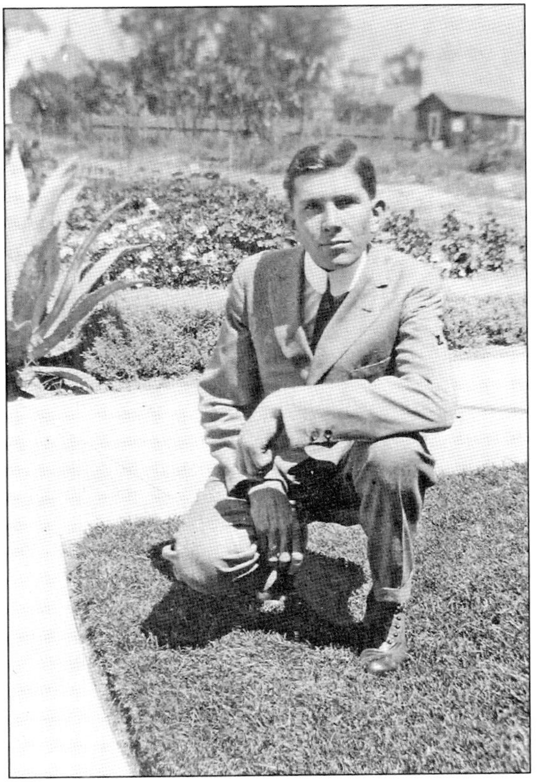

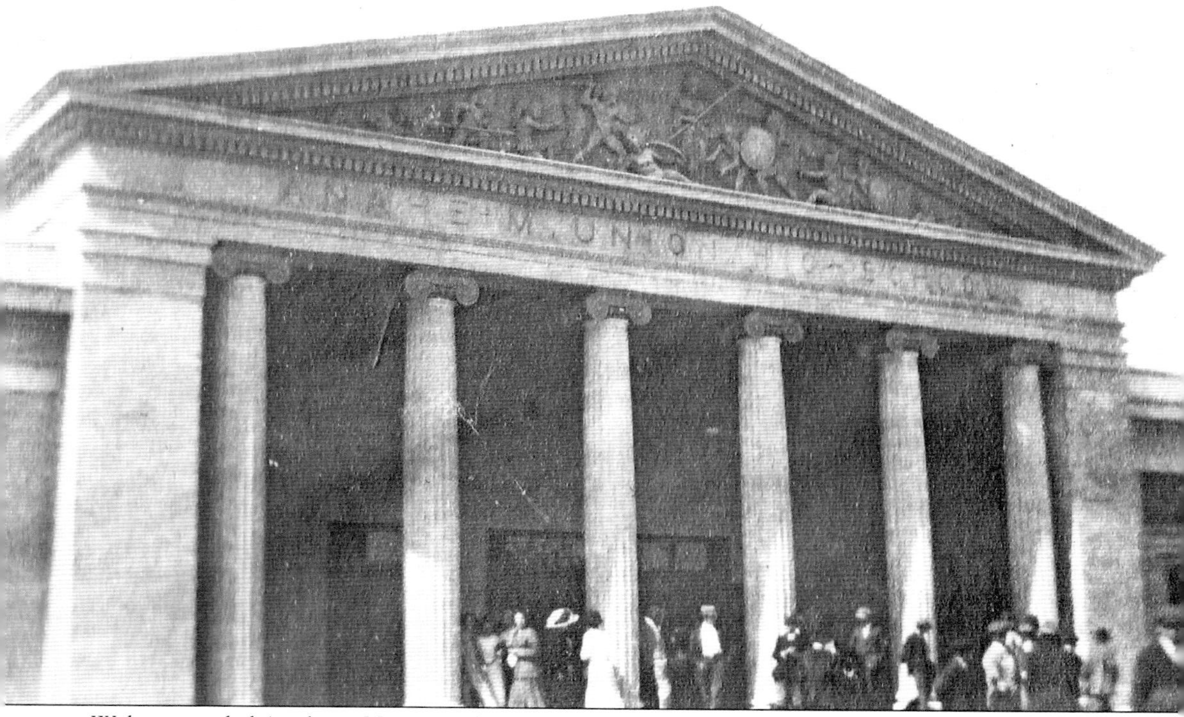

Walter attended Anaheim Union High School as a freshman in 1911. The campus, since demolished, opened in 1898 as the third high school in the county. Attending Anaheim Union High School opened up a whole new world of social activity with new friends for young Walter. He enjoyed his four years there, growing from a young freshman to a tall, slender young man, one of 30 members of the graduating class of 1914. His social skills and theatrical talents would serve him well in his future career as a public servant on the Fullerton City Council. (Walter's son, Harold, would attend Fullerton Union High School, the county's second-oldest high school campus.)

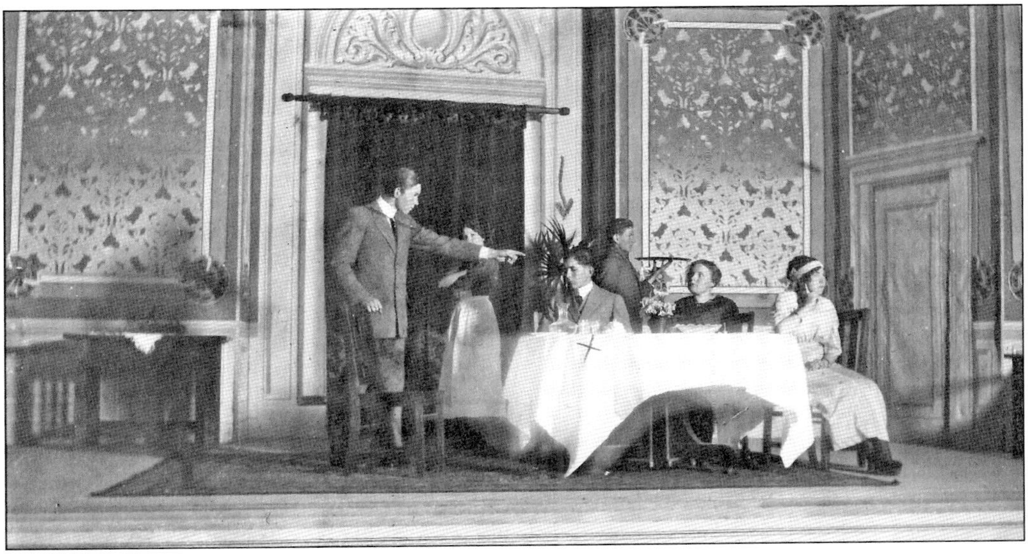

Walter performed in a German play titled *Stubbornness* in March 1913. He played Alfred, husband of Emma (above). He was also selected to play the lead character in the school's production of *Esmeralda*. In this image, Walter rehearses with his drama group in what seems to be a play about a dentist (below). He had a strong interest in drama. These early experiences in the arts led to a lifelong love of theater, music, dance, and art that culminated in his family insisting that the Muckenthaler Cultural Center be used for the arts rather than preserved as a historical museum. The sign in Spanish shows that even in a German immigrant community, the Spanish language is an important part of Southern California. In 1914, California had only been part of the United States for 66 years.

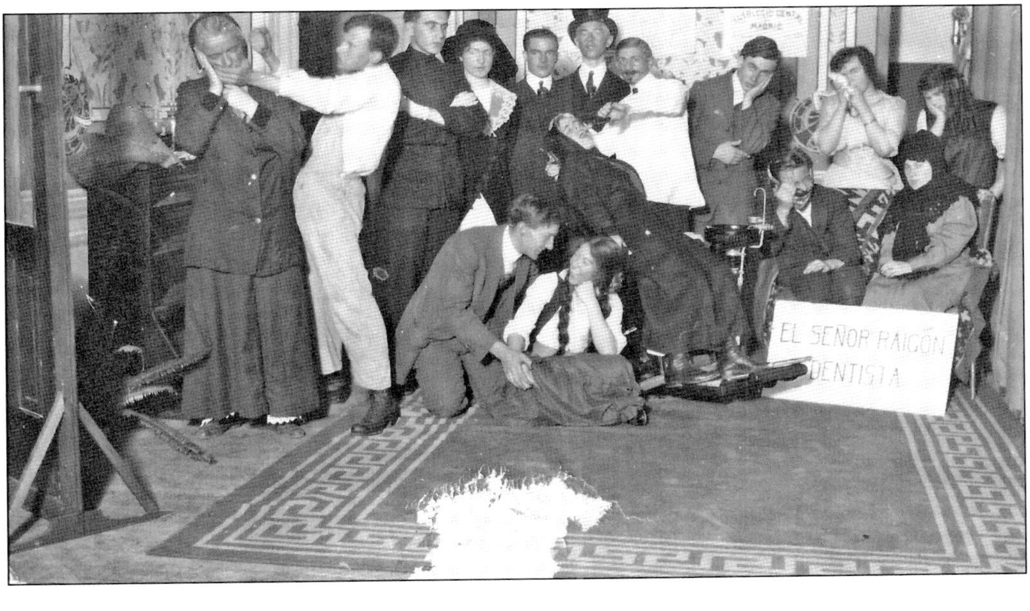

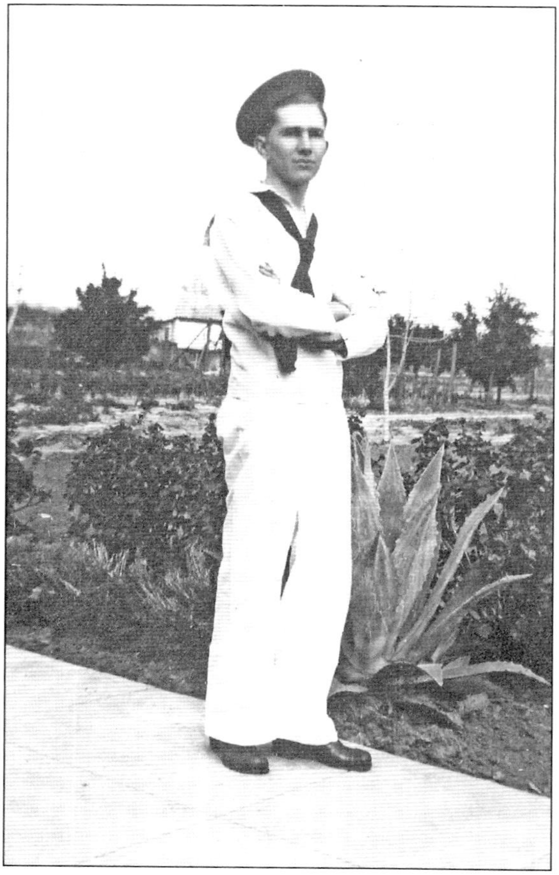

Walter's granddaughter Peggy speculates that this suit was a costume for his appearance in *H.M.S. Pinafore*, but it is also possible that it comes from his Navy stint during World War I. Set to begin his training at North Island in San Diego, doctors discovered that Walter had an undiagnosed heart murmur. He was disappointed to return home. Two decades later, he was proud when his son joined the Navy in World War II.

Adella Kraemer did not attend high school, but she often visited her sister Geraldine at Fullerton Union High School, where Geraldine was among the first to attend the new campus, opened in 1911 at its present location. This photograph includes the two sisters and their friends at a picnic before a football game.

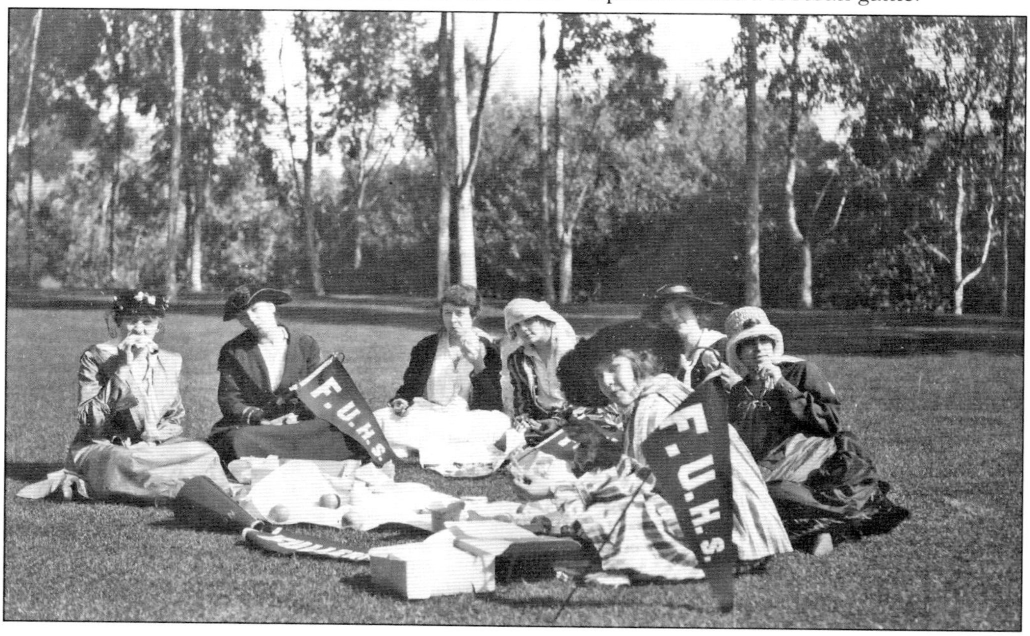

The Muckenthaler siblings embraced the opportunity to operate a bakery on their own. Handling a business for their successful father was a welcome challenge at such a young age. They had fun being bakers but also understood the importance of a good work ethic and sound business sense. Baked goods were very important to German immigrants. *Kaffee und Kuchen* (coffee and cake) is very similar to the English teatime. German cakes include *quarkkuchen* (cheesecake) and *Schwarzwälder Kirschtorte* (Black Forest). Usually, the cakes and pastries were accompanied by a steaming hot cup of coffee or tea. Breads were served with every meal and provided good energy for a day working an orange grove or an oil derrick.

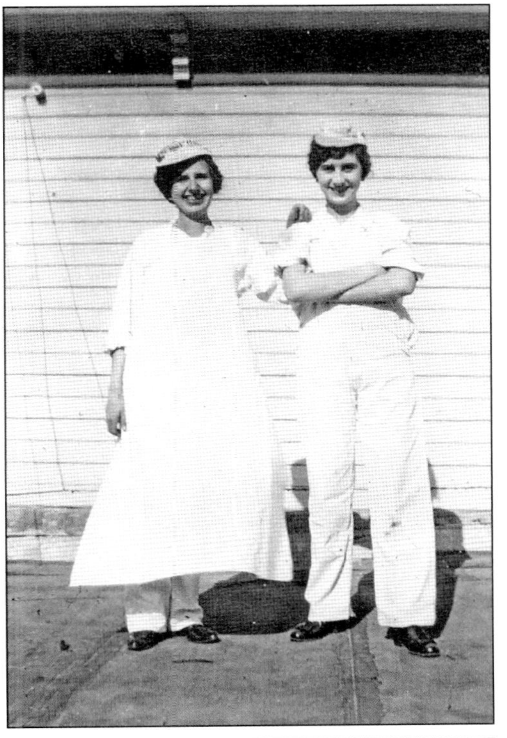

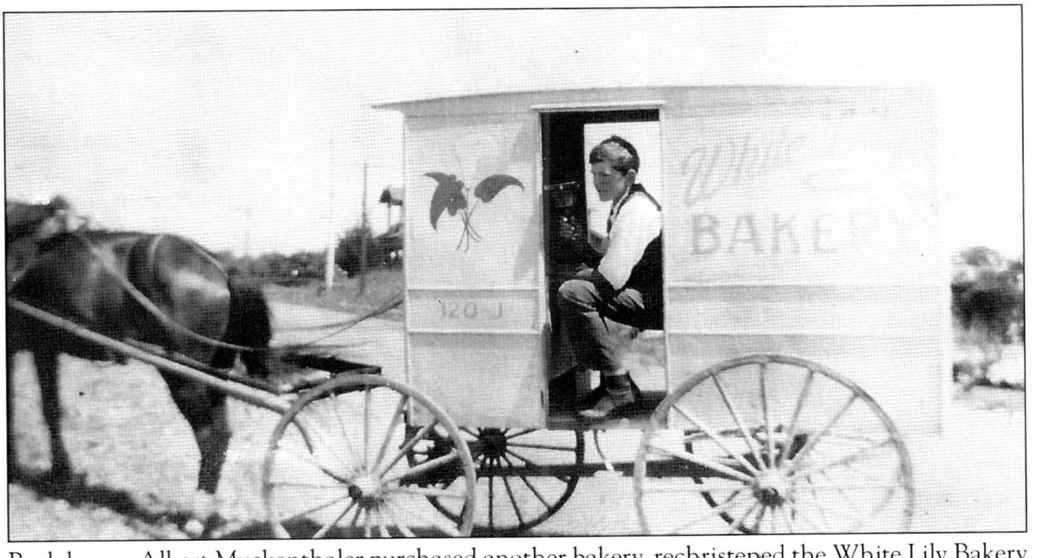

Back home, Albert Muckenthaler purchased another bakery, rechristened the White Lily Bakery by his son Walter. The white lily is a Catholic symbol of purity and the Blessed Virgin Mary. Walter was dedicating his new business venture to Mary while also alerting his customers to the purity of his ingredients. The white lily is also a design motif throughout art history and the basis for the fleur-de-lis. With Vi acting as salesperson and younger brother Lawrence making deliveries, Walter pitched in with youngest brother Martin to operate the business. Though the venture was successful for a time, inflation and competition from more modern facilities led them to sell the business to an acquaintance of Albert's, though they did make a small profit on the sale.

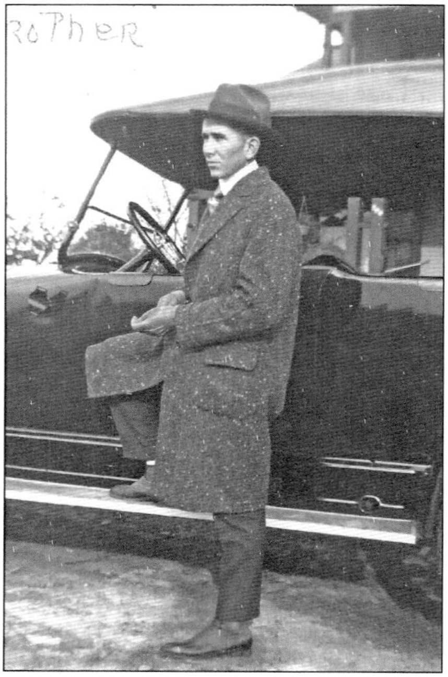

In his early 20s, Walter earned enough money to purchase a black Dodge sedan, and he began to think more about a young lady named Adella Kraemer. His family had known the Kraemers for years through St. Boniface Church. Dodge cars first rolled off the assembly line in 1914, and this vehicle was produced during the first years of the brand. They were great cars and quickly soared to second place in the automobile race with Ford for supremacy. Dodge pioneered or made standard many new features, such as all-steel bodies, 12-volt electrical systems, and sliding-gear transmissions. They were more upscale than Ford's Model T.

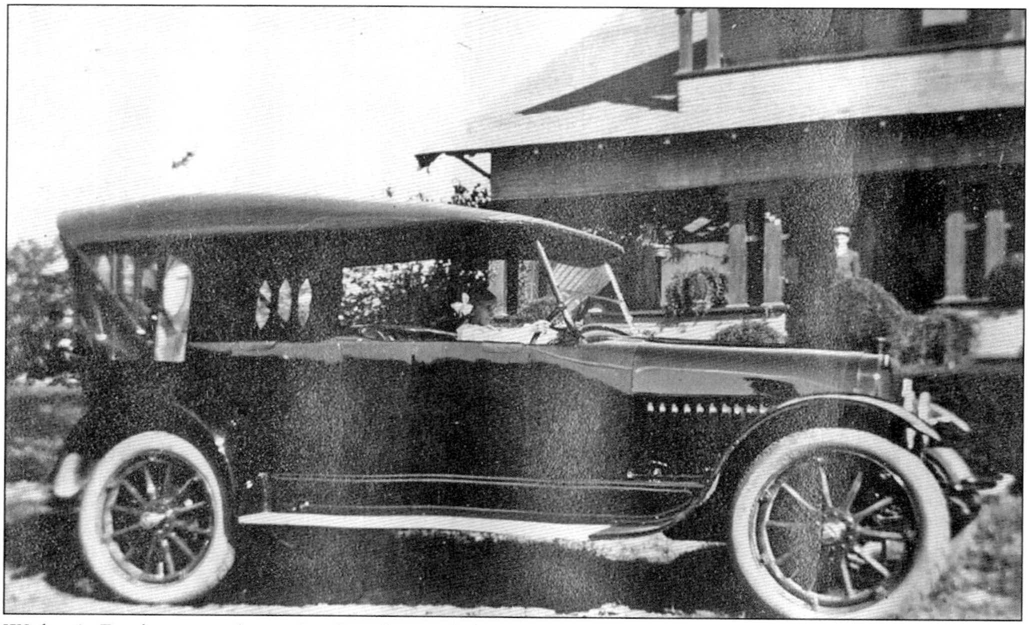

Walter's Dodge gave him the freedom of the open road, which no doubt came in handy for transporting himself to Hollywood, the nearby canyons and beaches, and other popular destinations. Very few people his age enjoyed the luxury of an automobile, as not many who were so young managed a business. Walter obviously loved cars. He took more pictures of his cars than he did his house. He would have been proud that after his home became a cultural center, the foundation started a classic car show in 1993 as a fundraiser. The Muckenthaler Motor Car Festival, now in its 16th year, is a major fundraiser for the center. On the third weekend in May, it features a hot-rod show on Saturday and a best of classic automobiles show on Sunday.

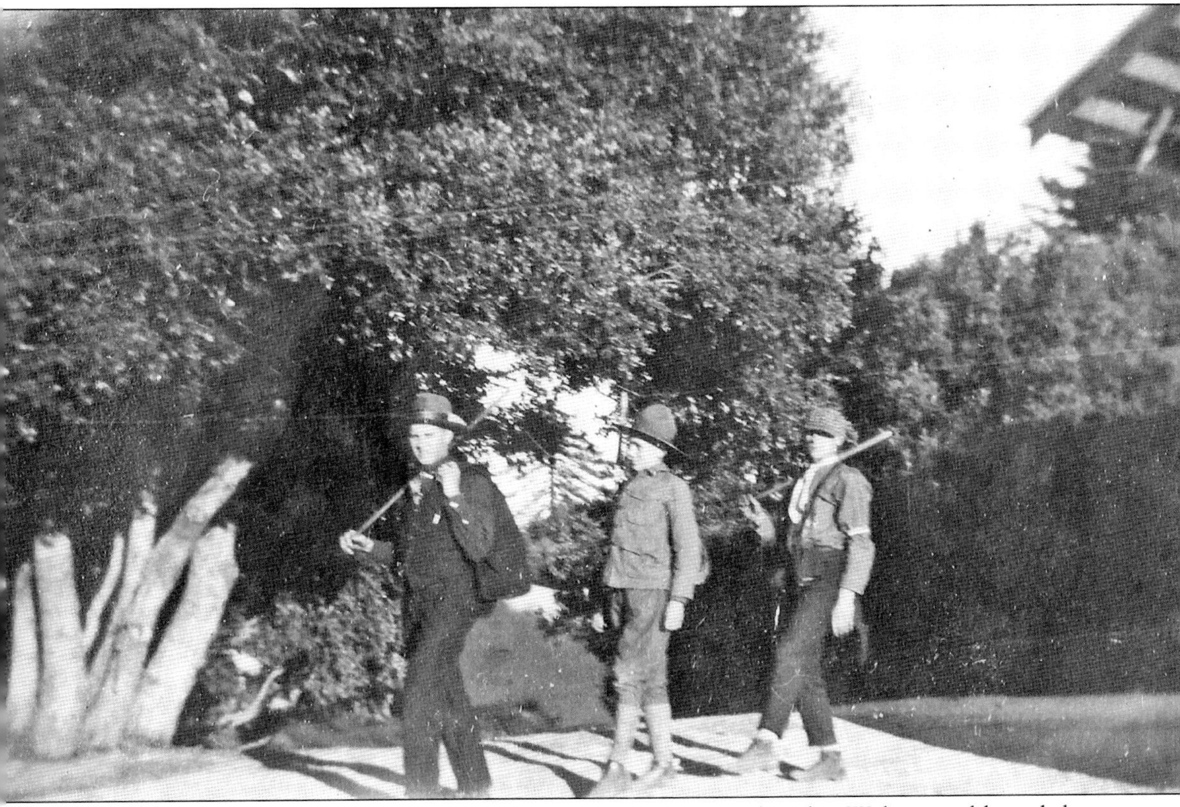

The men enjoyed many pastimes, including fishing at Mammoth Lake. Walter would teach his son to fish and enjoy the mountains as much as he did. Later, Harold bought a cabin at Big Bear, and the family spent many happy weekends in the mountains on fishing trips.

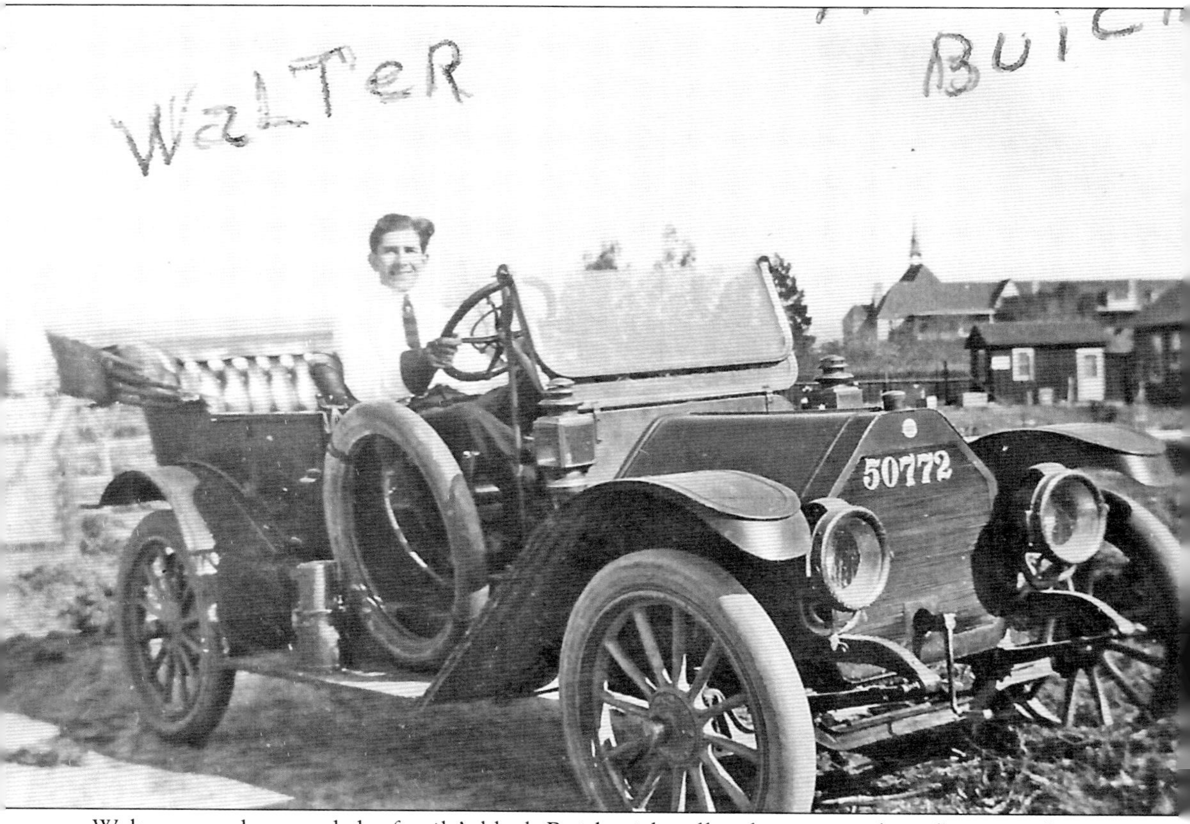

Walter once decorated the family's black Buick with yellow bunting and sunflowers to honor his home state of Kansas in an Anaheim merchants' floral parade. With Walter at the wheel and his sisters Abbie and Vi and their friends waving from the passenger seats, the design won second place.

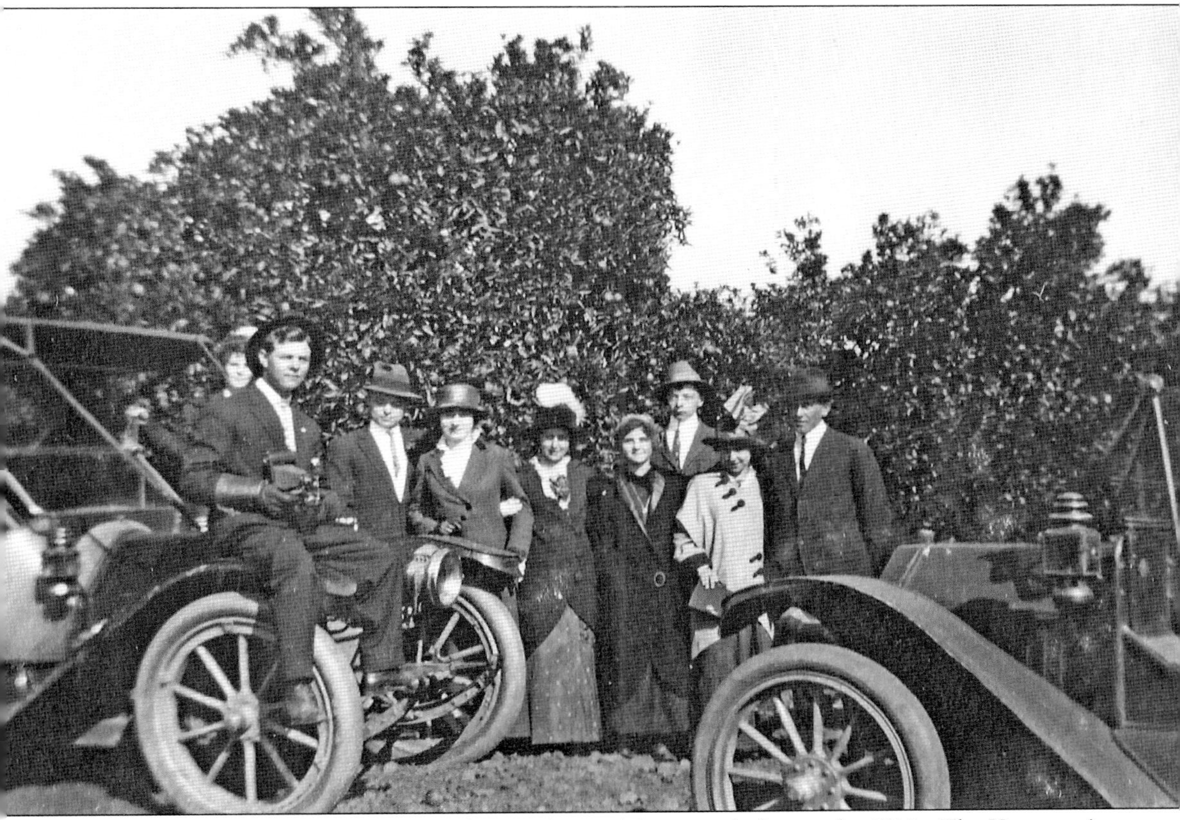

In this image, the Kraemer family gathers in front of their ranch during the 1910s. The Kraemers' orange groves once covered the city of Placentia, where the Valencia variety was commercially planted in the 1880s. There are several stories claiming the Valencia comes from China or India. Both Irvine Ranch and Riverside claim to have first cultivated the variety here. Whatever the origins, the Valencia would play an important part in Walter's future. Southern California Valencia oranges became known the world over as the standard of quality, thanks to organization among the growers. The Southern California Fruit Exchange in Claremont helped shape the industry and became the Sunkist Cooperative in 1908. Currently, Sunkist has more than 6,000 grower members.

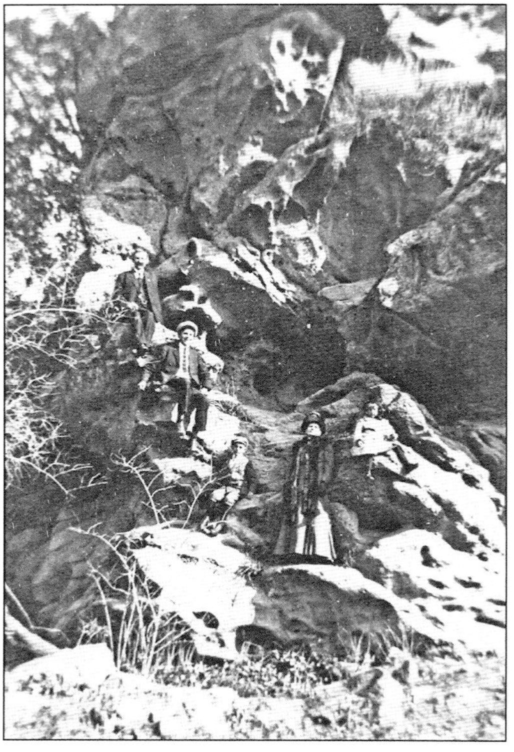

There were many places to visit and explore in Southern California. Wherever Walter went, he seemed to have a camera with him. He kept a record of his travels in a small black album, providing captions in elegant white script below each photograph. His caption for this image read, "Rocks in Santiago Canyon near Orange County Park, Orange County, California."

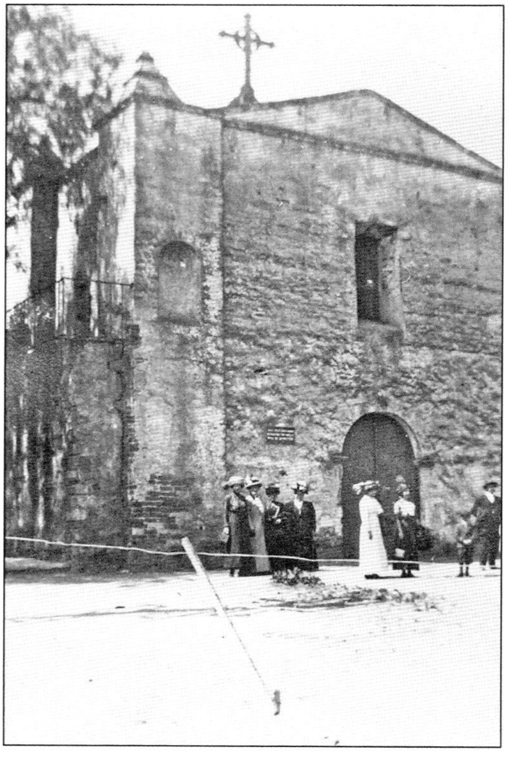

Several of Walter's photographs are of the San Gabriel Mission. The front view is shown here. He was very impressed with the architecture when he visited the landmark in 1913. Mission-style architecture was very popular in California, following the examples set by the Mission Inn in Riverside and the Panama-California Exposition buildings in San Diego's Balboa Park. Walter later incorporated elements of these styles into his own home.

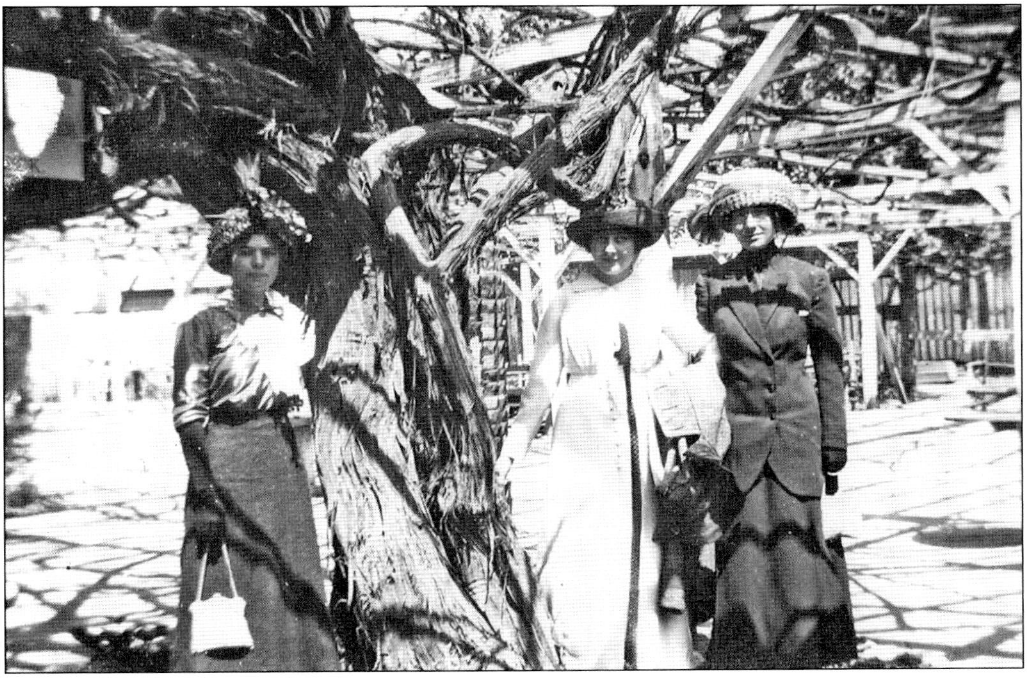

The tree-lined background in this photograph is actually a giant grape vine in the San Gabriel Mission. It covered 9,000 square feet. The famous mission grapevine might have inspired Walter to plant his own grapes over an arbor on the west side of the rear patio of the Muckenthaler villa years later. This giant vine still exists, but Walter's vines are gone. He also took this photograph of the mission bells in San Gabriel, California. Walter's visit would have been just a few years after the arrival of the Claretian Missionary Fathers, who began restoring the structure in 1908. The San Gabriel Mission was built by Joseph Chapman, an ancestor of Fullerton's Charles Chapman and a prisoner of the pirate Bouchard.

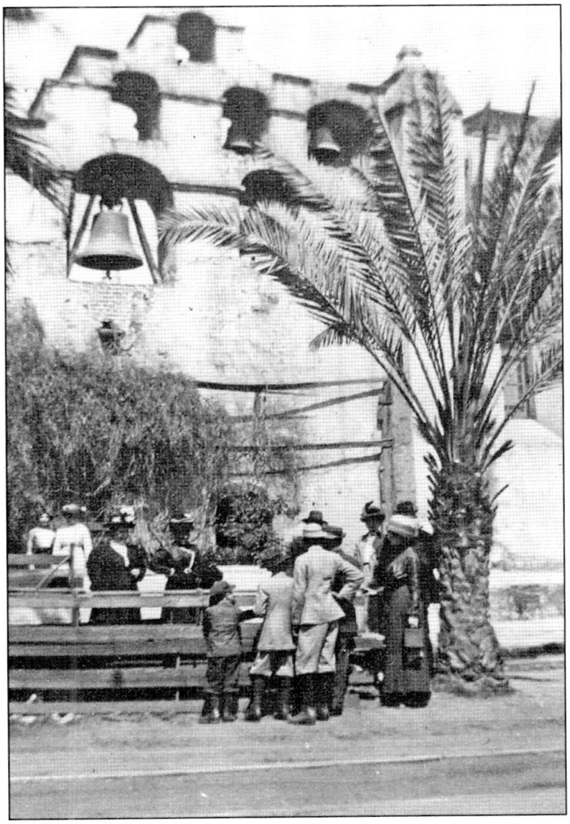

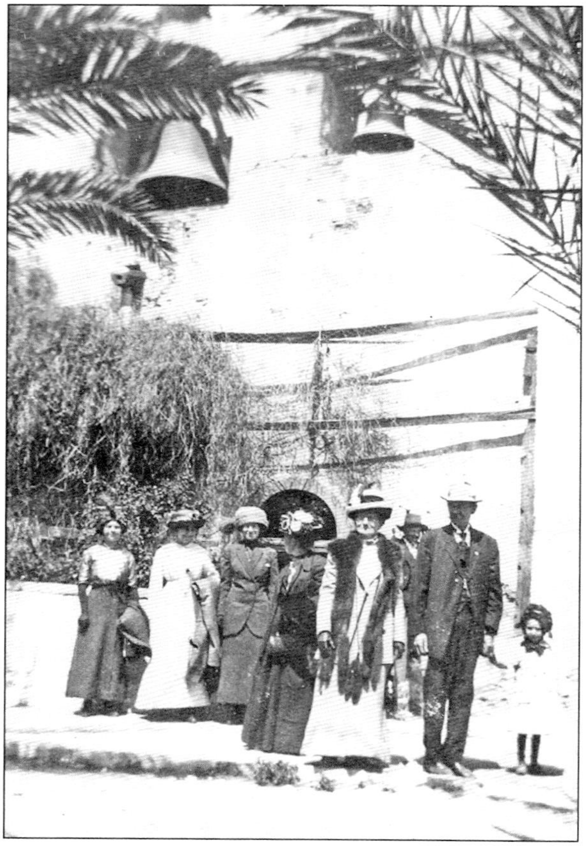

This photograph was taken in 1913 during a mission play party in San Gabriel, California. Reenacting mission life and stories became a big part of early California theater, inspiring romantic characters like Zorro, created in 1919. The Yorbas, soon to be Walter's in-laws, were part of mission history.

Walter's sister, Vi, poses at Coronado Beach in this photograph. Though the site of Walter's future home was to be approximately 20 miles from a beach, it was the first hill north of the ocean across the flood plain of north Orange County. Sea breezes still keep the property five degrees cooler than surrounding areas.

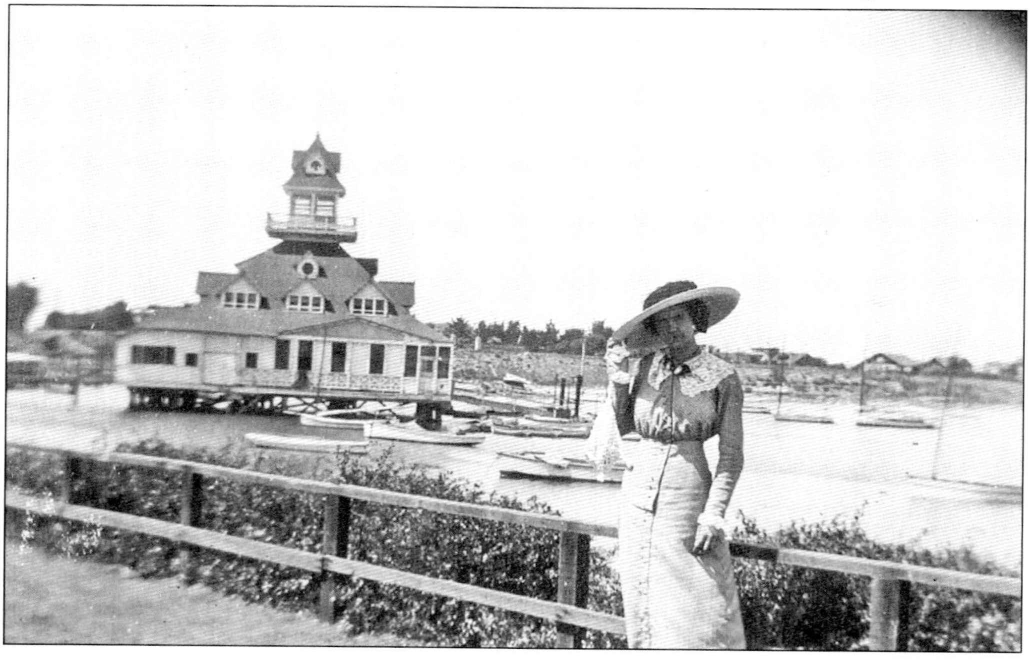

Walter stands on the rocky cliffs of Santa Catalina Island. Just a few years later, Catalina Island boasted great steamships that transported visitors to the island, where they could gamble and see shows at the grand casino. Although development by the Wrigley family would soon make it a popular honeymoon destination, it was then enjoyed primarily for its ocean views and unspoiled landscape.

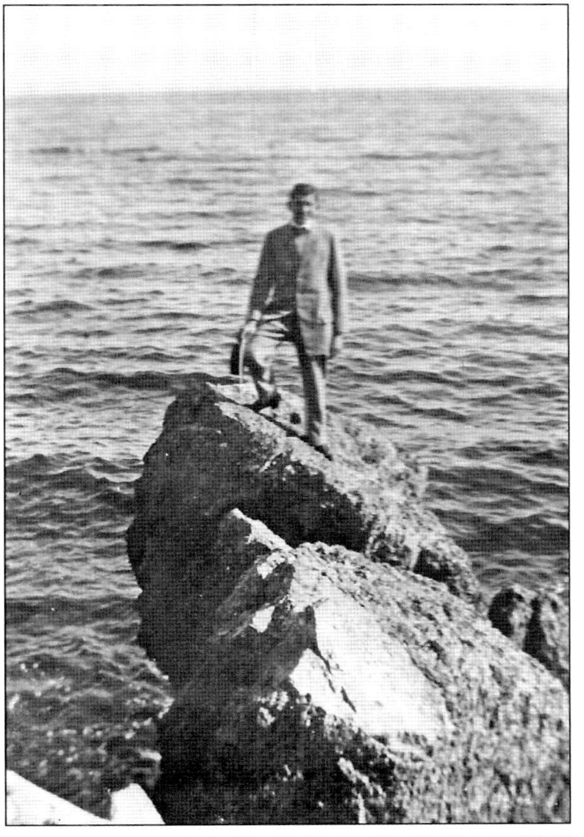

"A rose between two thorns" is how Walter described his sister Vi in this photograph, flanked by himself (left) and family friend John Glotzbach near the vacation island's tent city. The tents, which could be rented for $7.50 per week, would soon be replaced by cottages and the island's famous casino.

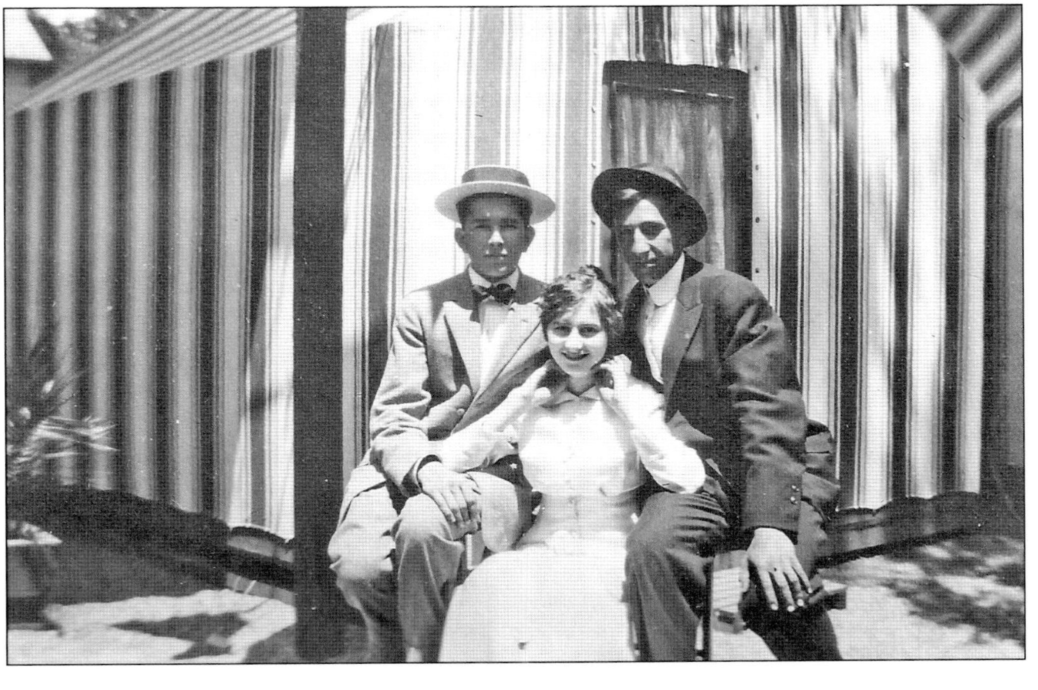

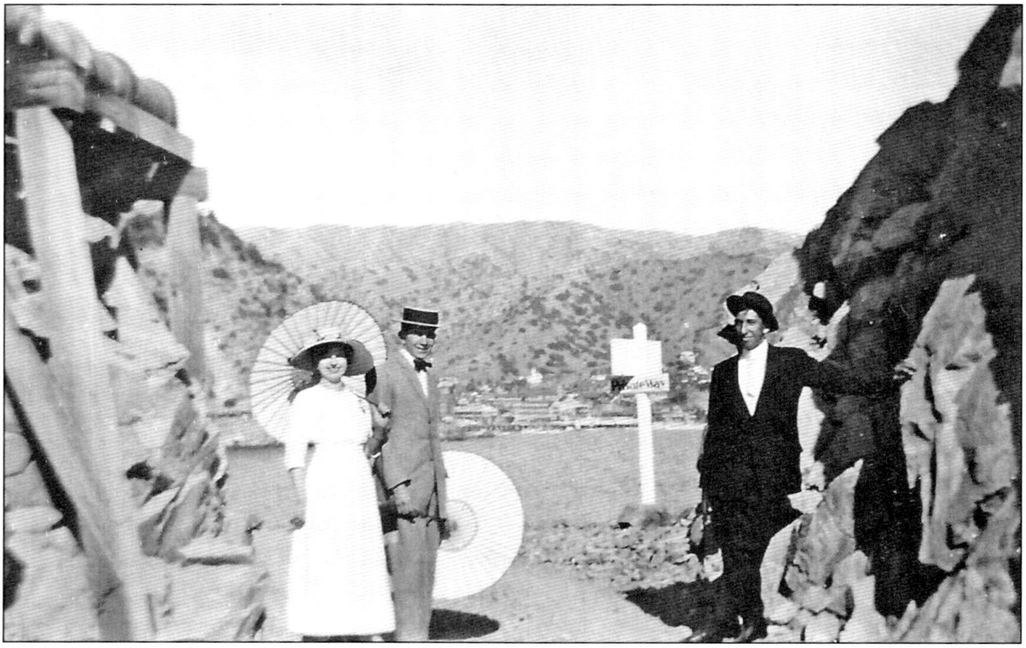

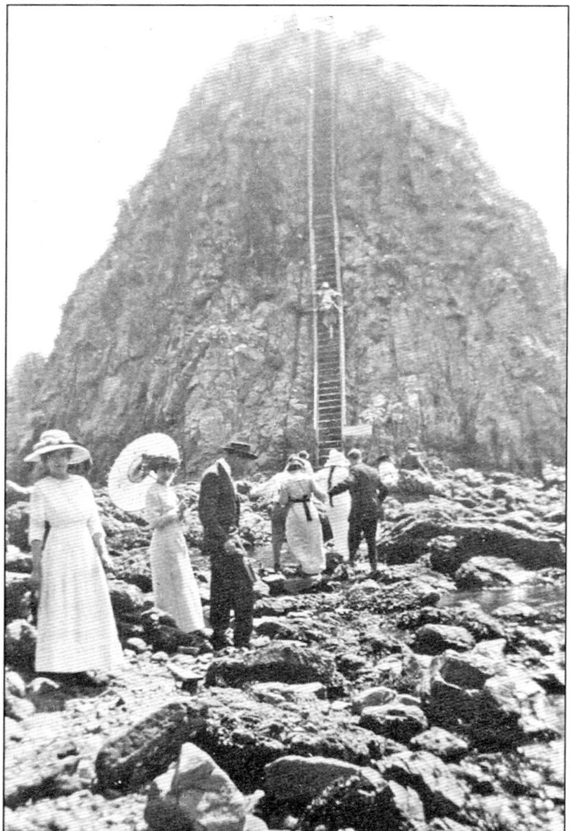

Cousin Ida Ebert and John Glotzbach pose on Lovers Lane. The city of Avalon on Santa Catalina Island is visible in the distance. The photograph was most likely taken by Walter's sister Vi. Before its freewheeling casino days in the 1920s, Catalina was a sport fishing capital; it had become a destination for tourists when Avalon was developed in the 1890s. Photographs of men catching fish twice their size at the Tuna Club brought curiosity seekers by the droves. It was a dusty, 30-mile drive through orange groves to Long Beach, and then a 30-mile steamboat trip to Avalon. At left, Walter took a photograph of the stepping-stones at the foot of Sugarloaf Rock on Santa Catalina Island. His camera preserves a view of Sugarloaf a decade before it was blasted away to provide a better view of the famous casino.

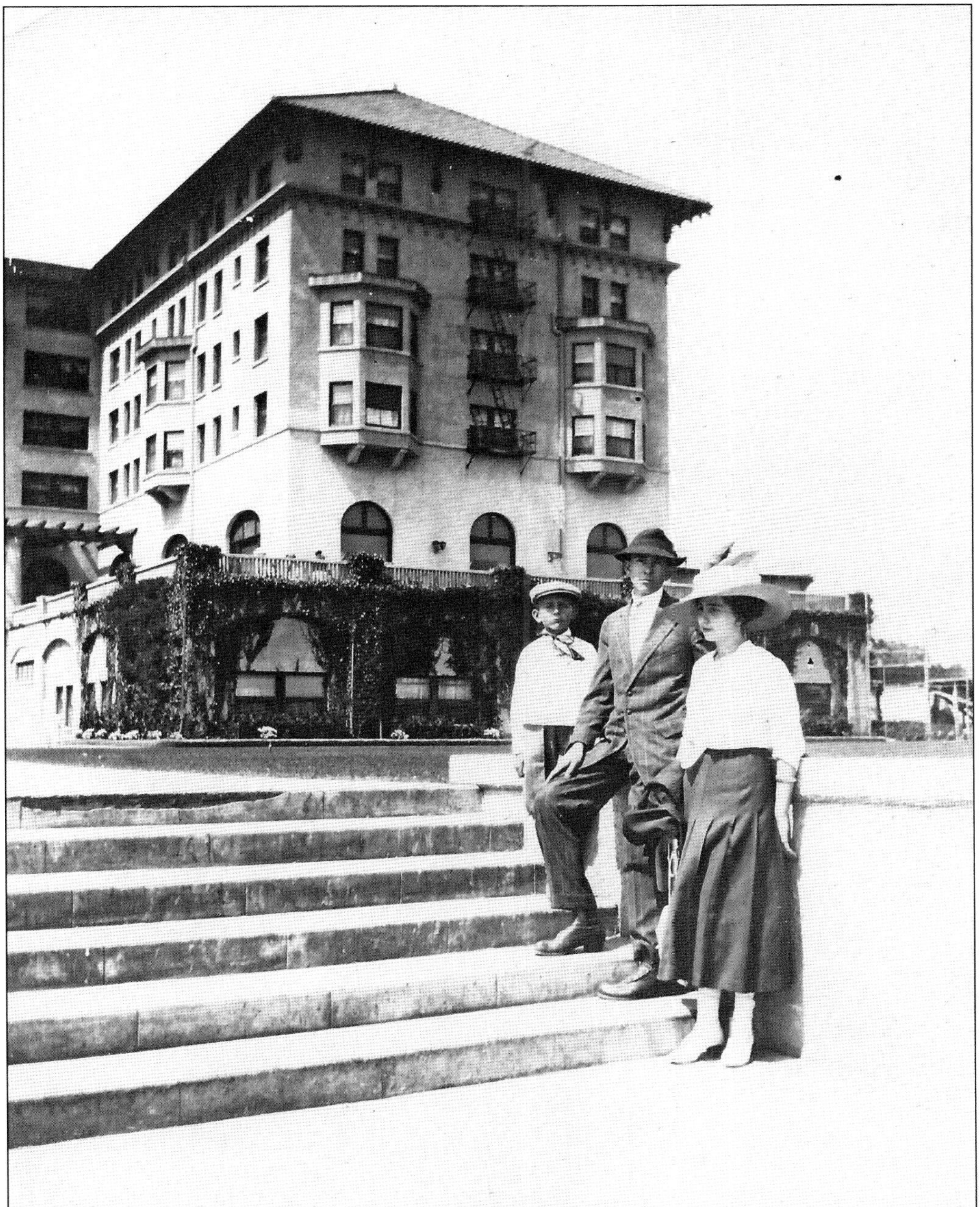

Walter, Martin, and Vi visit the Virginia Hotel in Long Beach. The hotel was known for its marble columns and grand staircase. A drive from Anaheim to Long Beach may have taken an entire day, traveling on dirt roads in a horseless carriage. A night spent in Long Beach would make the trip to or from Catalina much easier. The Virginia Hotel was built by Col. Charles Drake, who was responsible for bringing water to Long Beach and developing much of its downtown. The hotel was at the Pike, Long Beach's own resort spot, the biggest attraction in Southern California before Disneyland. A trip to Long Beach and Avalon was a whole week's worth of adventure in 1914.

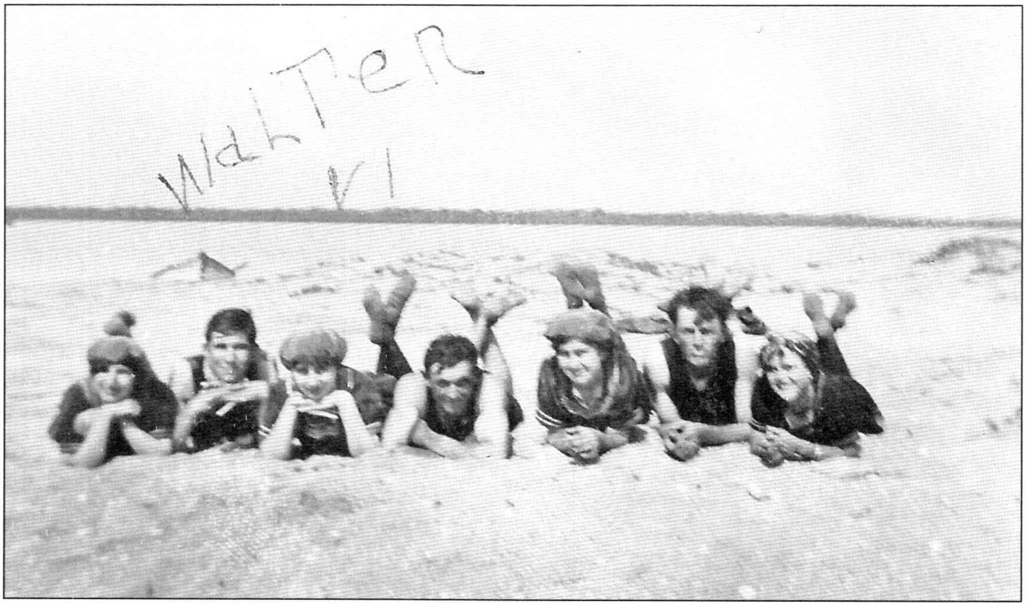

Walter Muckenthaler and his friends pose at Anaheim Landing (Seal Beach) in 1910. The beach was a popular place to meet friends and a cool alternative to hotter inland temperatures in the summer. Boating in the surf of Anaheim Landing was a favored activity. Young men and women sported the latest swimwear fashions. Men wore shorts and sleeveless bathing tops while women often wore ruffled bathing suits that covered them to below the knee. Because Anaheim Landing was built by Anaheim's German community, they felt especially comfortable there. In 1915, the name was officially changed to Seal Beach, and it was designed as a vacation spot, much like Catalina was. Seal Beach had the longest pier south of San Francisco at the time.

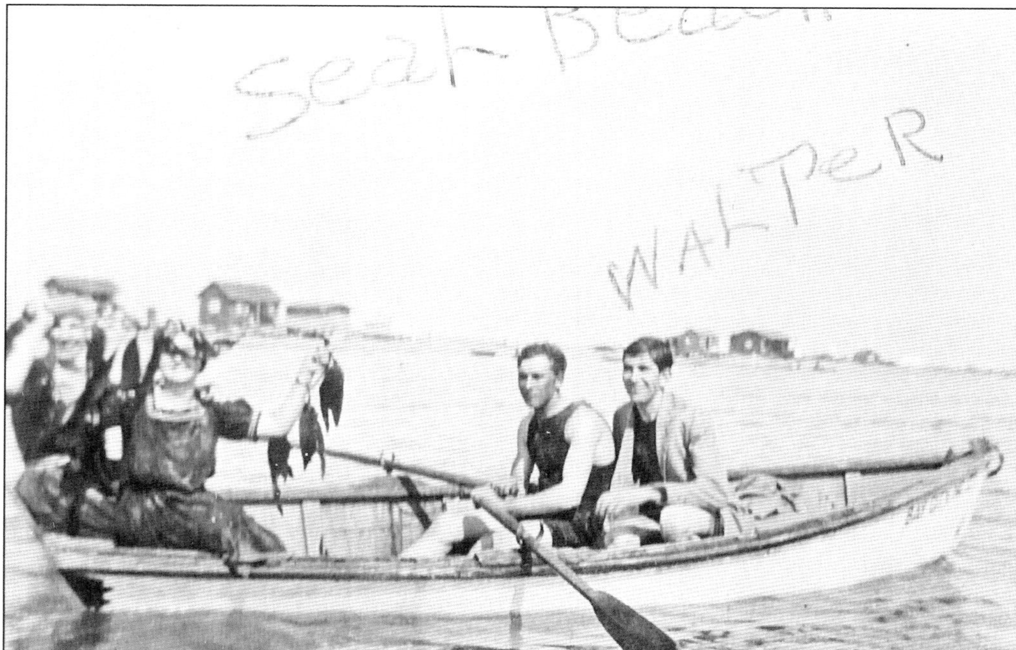

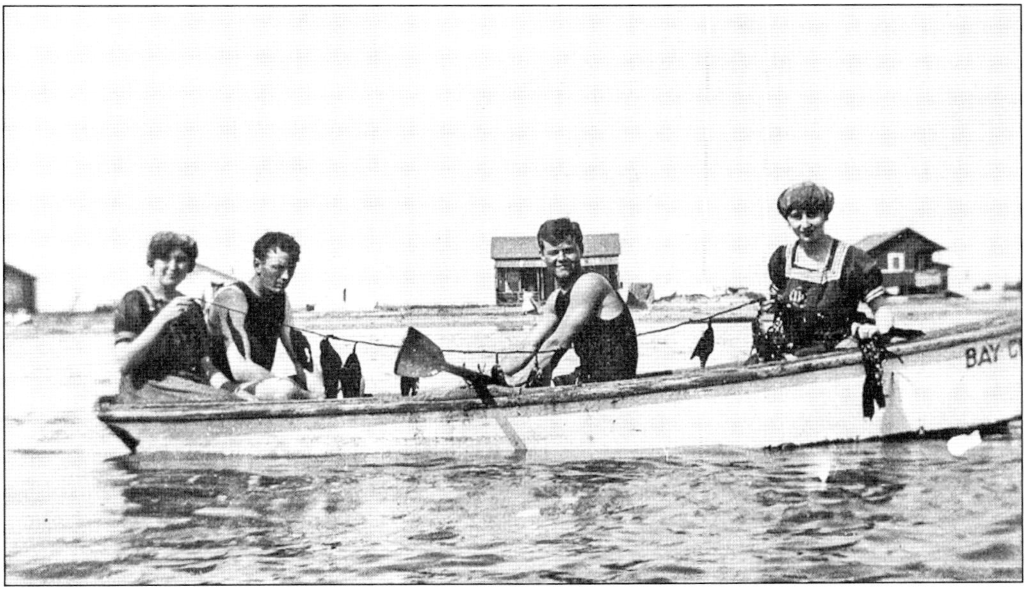

Anaheim Landing attracted the sportsman in Walter and many others. It got its name because the German immigrants of Anaheim needed a port to load goods. With the Red Cars of the Pacific Electric Railway, it was no longer needed as a port, and it became a beach where German residents could relax. They also called it Bay City, which by the 1910s became a city of tents. The wide, uncrowded beaches and relatively calm waters allowed for swimming and rowing in the surf, but the drive was 15 miles. Getting there could mean a flat tire from running over horseshoes or other debris. Walter had a fondness for the ocean from the first time he saw it in 1909. Each of his siblings would eventually purchases cottages by the beach, and though Walter never did, his son, Harold, did.

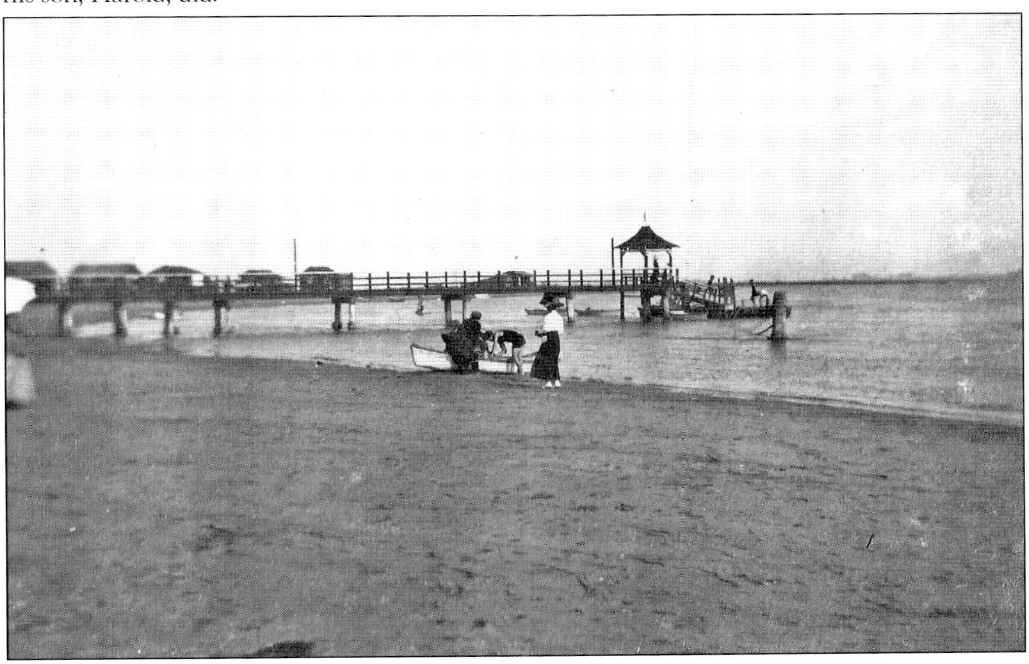

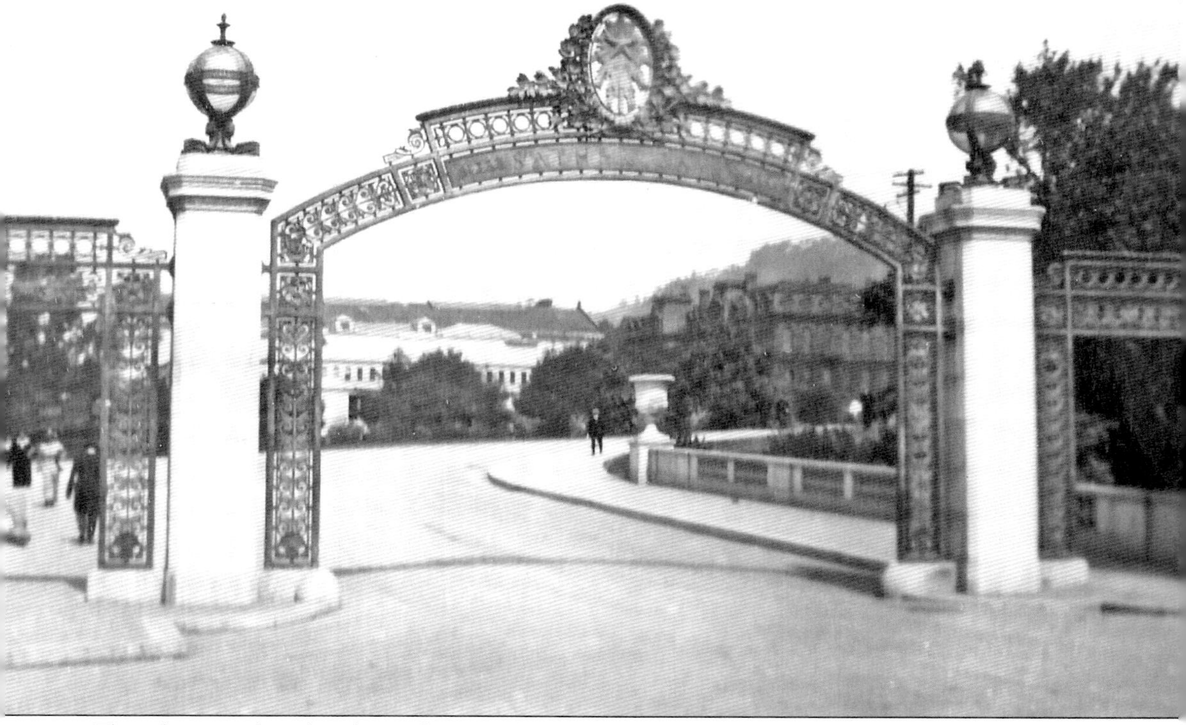

This photograph, taken by Walter as a freshman, shows the University of California–Berkeley's Sather Gate. Walter put away enough money from working at the Boston Bakery to pay his expenses for a year at Berkeley. In 1916, he enrolled in the university's School of Architecture and Design with the goal of becoming an architect. He was the first of his family to attend college. Walter's college education happened during Berkeley's golden period of growth, in which Berkeley was moving to the forefront in civil engineering education and playing an important part in training engineers to build the West. Civil engineering was an important part of Berkeley's architecture program at the time, and this may have contributed to Walter ending up in civil engineering for the railroad and later for the city of Fullerton.

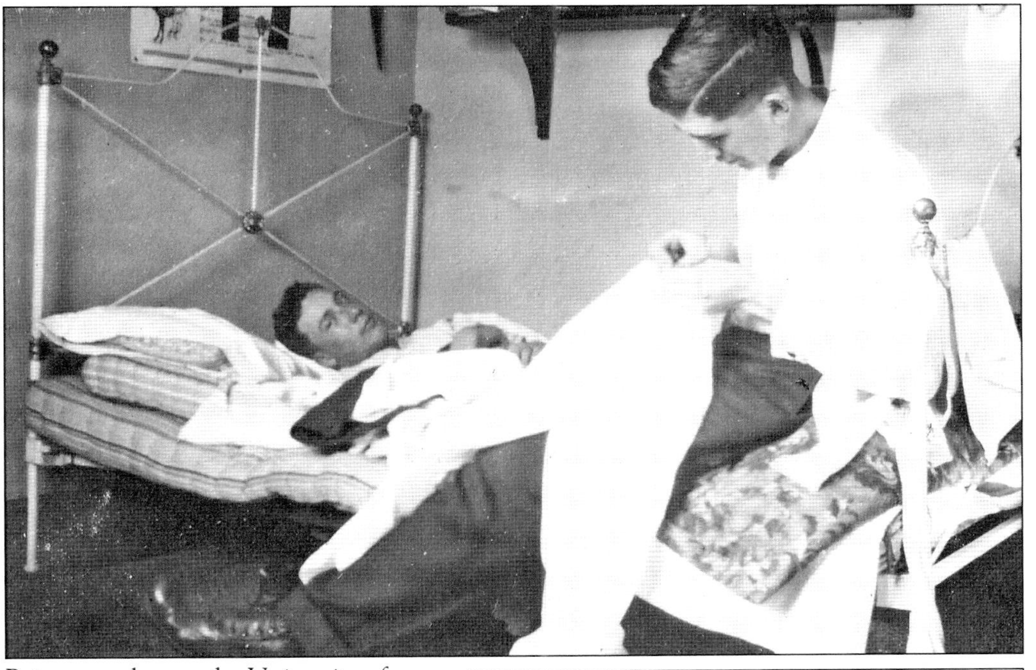

Being a student at the University of California–Berkeley helped Walter to become a more independent young man. He thoroughly enjoyed his time at the school, but finances and World War I would interrupt his academic career. One of the university's most recognizable symbols, Sather Tower, was caught by Walter's camera in 1916. The Sather Tower is colloquially known as the Campanile because of its resemblance to the Campanile di San Marco in Venice. Walter's keen interest in architecture no doubt led to his appreciation of such landmarks on the campus.

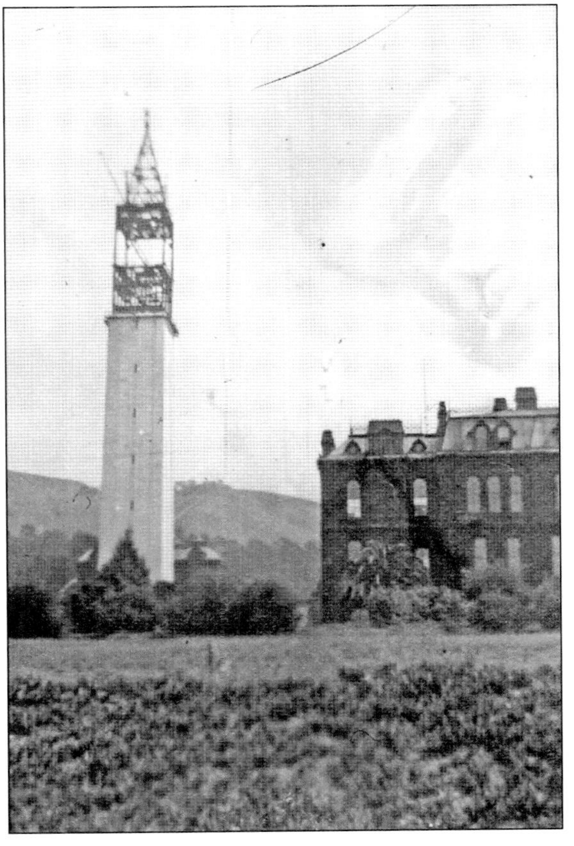

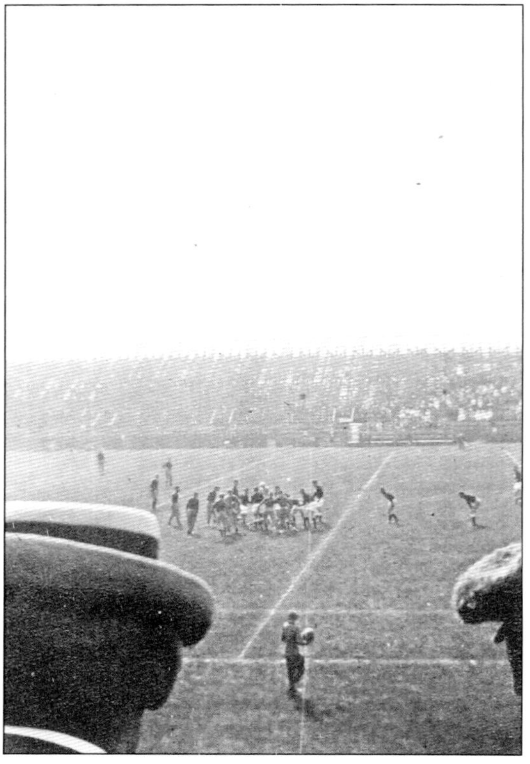

Walter relished his time at the University of California–Berkeley, finding enjoyment in the many facets of student life. Sports have an illustrious tradition at the University of California's oldest campus. This snapshot is of a university football game in 1914. Walter served in the ROTC while studying at Berkeley. By the end of his year at school, America was at war against his father's homeland of Germany. There was a strong patriotic sentiment among German Americans during the world wars. There was a great onus on immigrants to show their patriotism to their adopted country, even though they had close relatives in the old country, and Walter was disappointed that he could not do so.

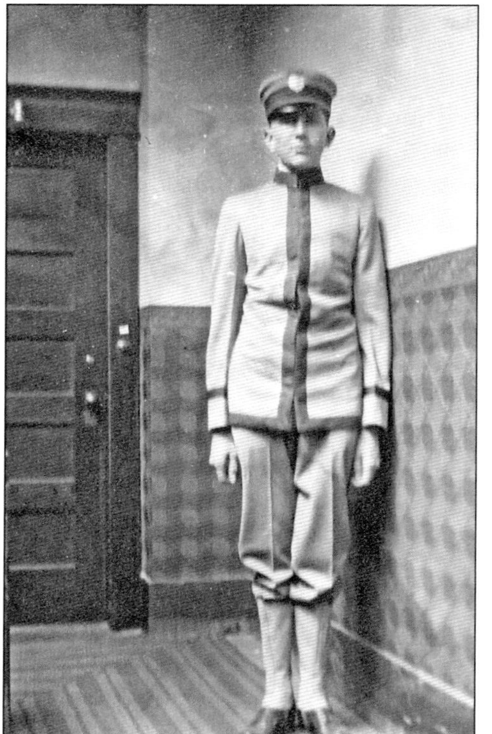

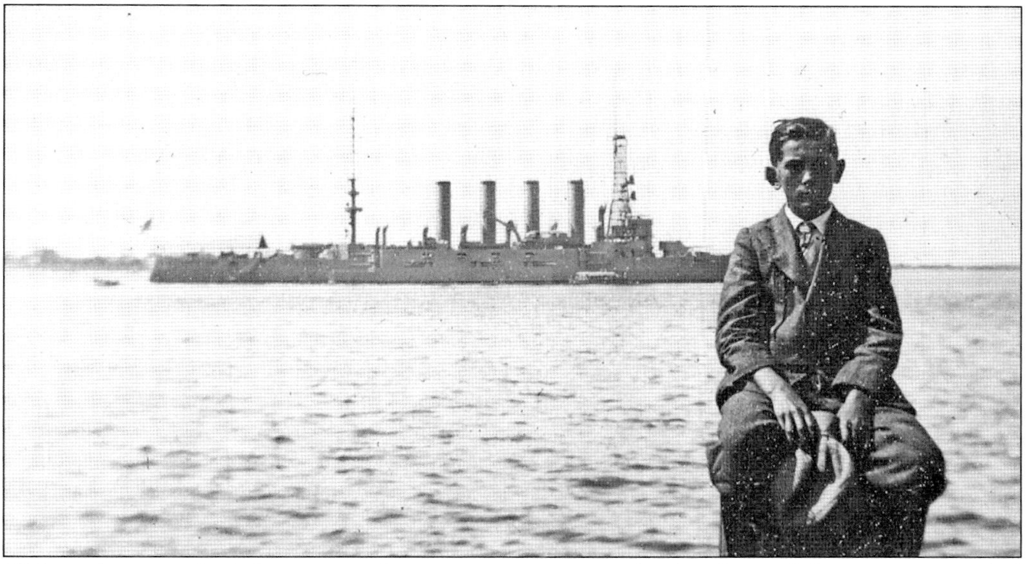

Walter photographed ships more than once, suggesting that his love of the ocean extended to a yearning for exploration and travel. Although he would never pilot one himself, he did eventually travel by ship across two oceans with his family. Walter joined more than 18 million others who visited the famous San Francisco Panama-Pacific International Exposition in 1915. He photographed many of the extraordinary Beaux-Arts buildings there. His own home would eventually reflect the architectural style of the San Diego Panama-California Exposition, held that same year. It was the San Diego exhibition that created Balboa Park, causing a fascination with Mission-style architecture that lasted for more than 20 years.

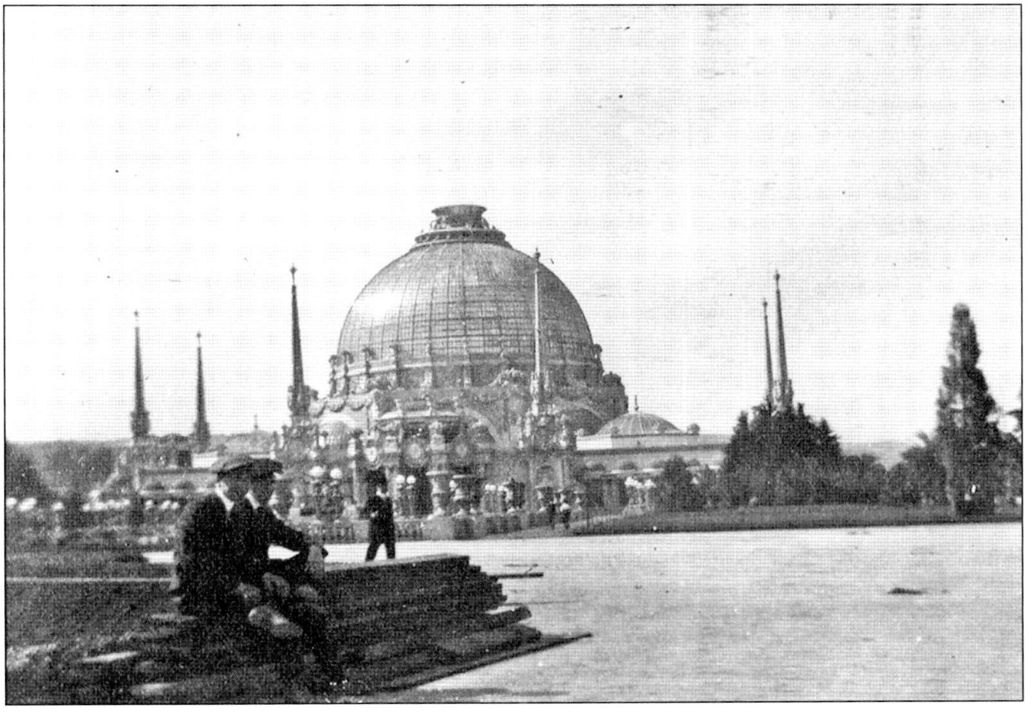

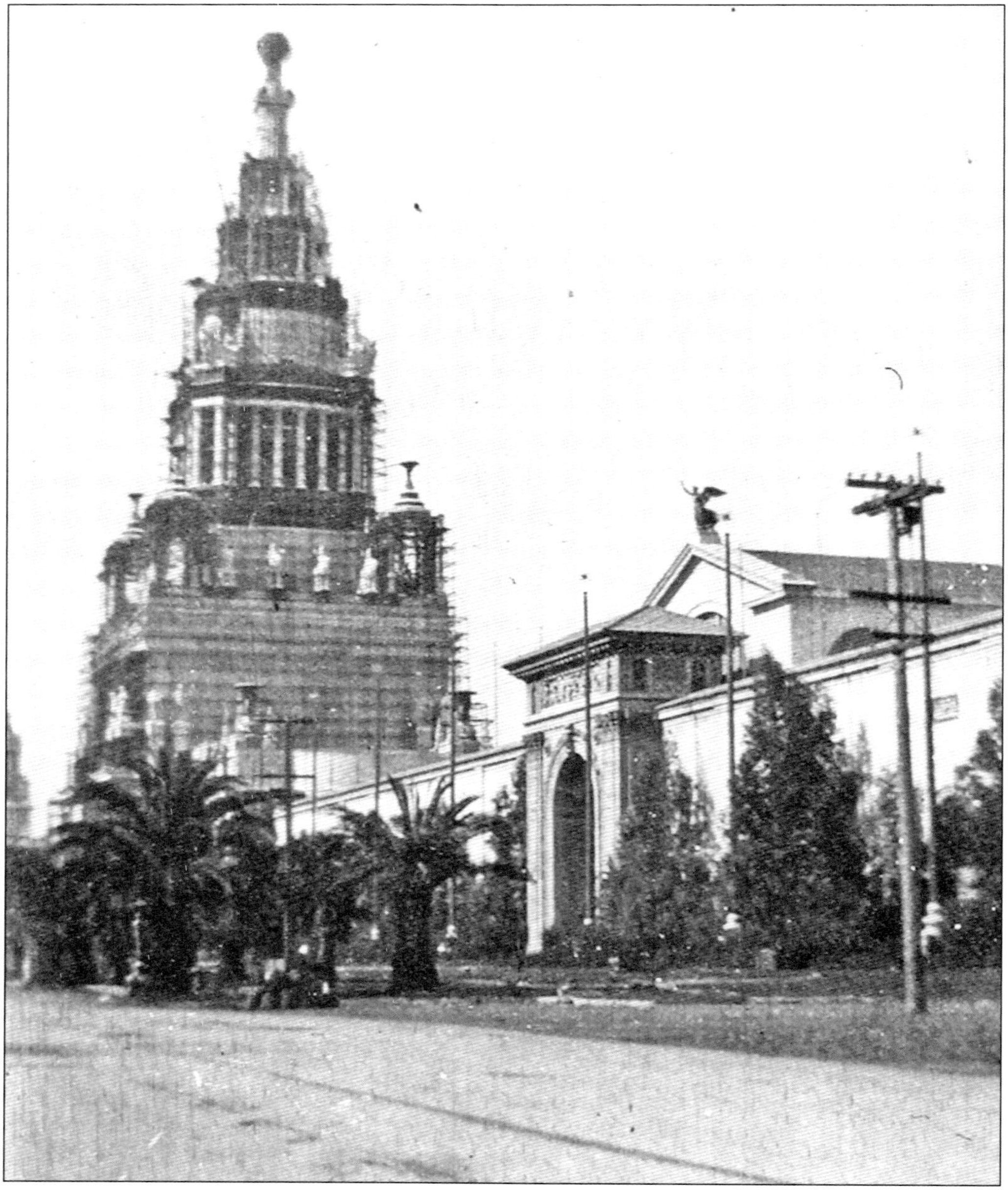

One of the 1915 San Francisco Panama-Pacific International Exposition's main attractions was the Tower of Jewels, a 435-foot temporary structure covered with more than 100,000 glass gems. The 3/4- to 2-inch colored gems sparkled in sunlight throughout the day and were illuminated by more than 50 powerful electrical searchlights at night. In front of the tower was the Fountain of Energy, flanked by the Palace of Horticulture on the west and the Festival Hall to the east. The arch of the tower served as the gateway to the Court of the Universe, leading to the Court of the Four Seasons to the west and the Court of Abundance to the east. These courts formed the primary exhibit area for the fair. The exposition showed that San Francisco had completely recovered from the 1906 earthquake. Architectural curiosities and historical landmarks alike both appear with some frequency in Walter's photograph album.

Descended from the Yorbas, Adella Kraemer (right) retained the refined Castilian features of her ancestors. Her beauty and grace were obvious to young Walter Muckenthaler, who also appreciated her sense of adventure. As a rancho girl, she raised cattle, horses, and chickens. She helped her mother to care for her seven siblings. Her faith in her church and her family was matched only by Walter's. She grew up with strong determination and a pioneer spirit from a lineage that tamed California (from her mother's side) and traveled halfway across the world to find a dream (from her father's side). Her story is the story of California. Raised in what was then rural North Orange County, Adella Kraemer was quite adept at riding horses, an activity she loved (below). Walter is never pictured riding horses; he loved cars and mechanical things. Although there were no stables at the Muckenthaler estate, Fullerton had a number of stables, a few of which remain to this day. Horseback riding along the foothill desert trails of Coyote Hills must have been as much fun then as it is today.

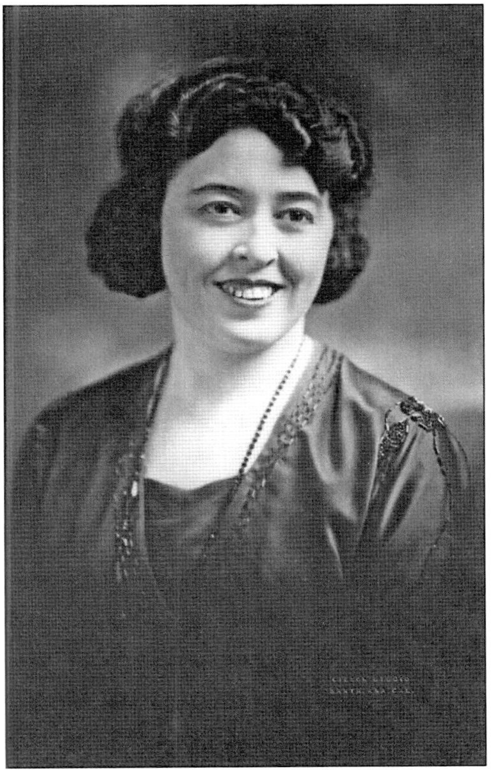

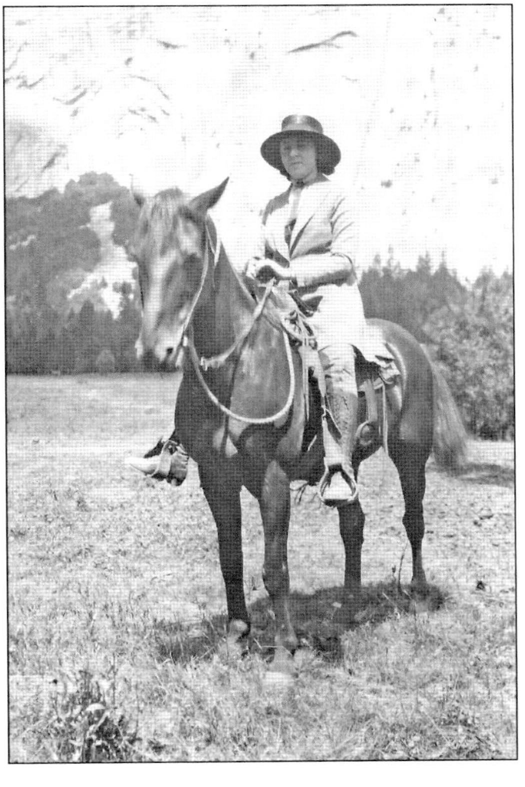

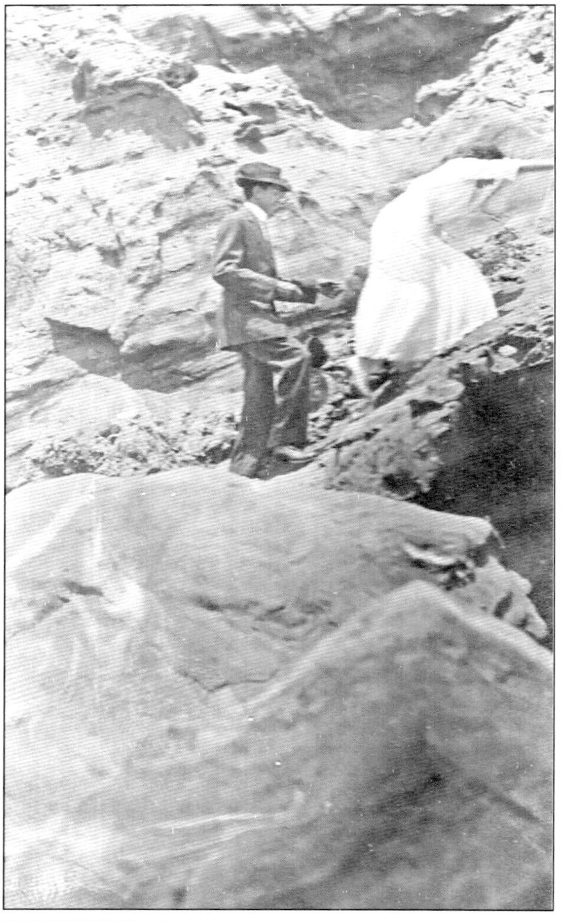

Walter and his friends enjoyed many social occasions together, providing a proper atmosphere for the young couple to get to know one another, such as church picnics and hikes through the rugged territory of the surrounding hills (left). Santa Ana Canyon was a favorite place for Walter Muckenthaler and Adella Kraemer to picnic on group dates (below). They also enjoyed dinners together in Hollywood, where they saw many silent film stars of the day.

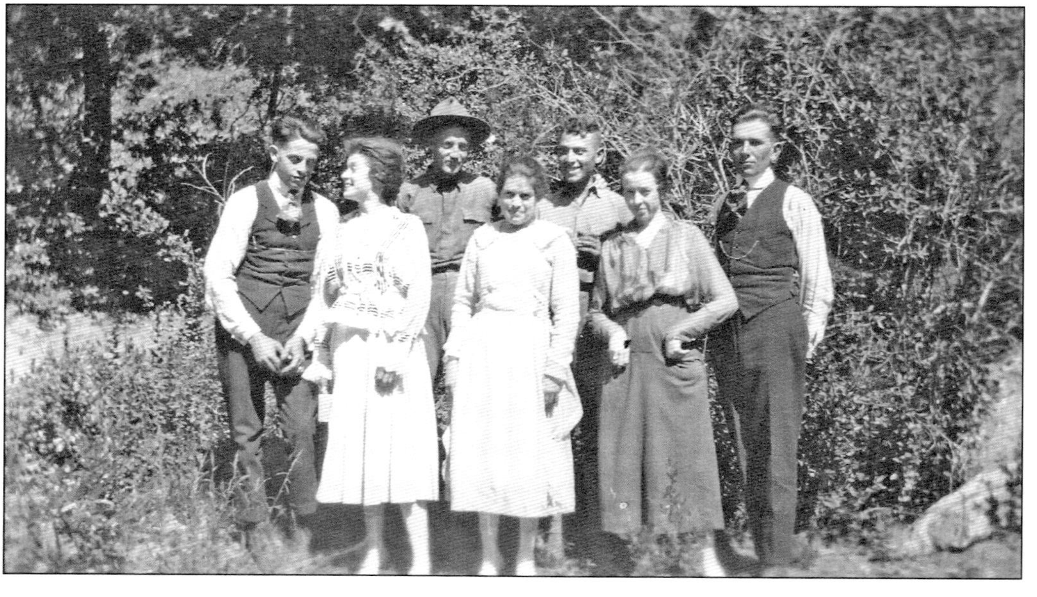

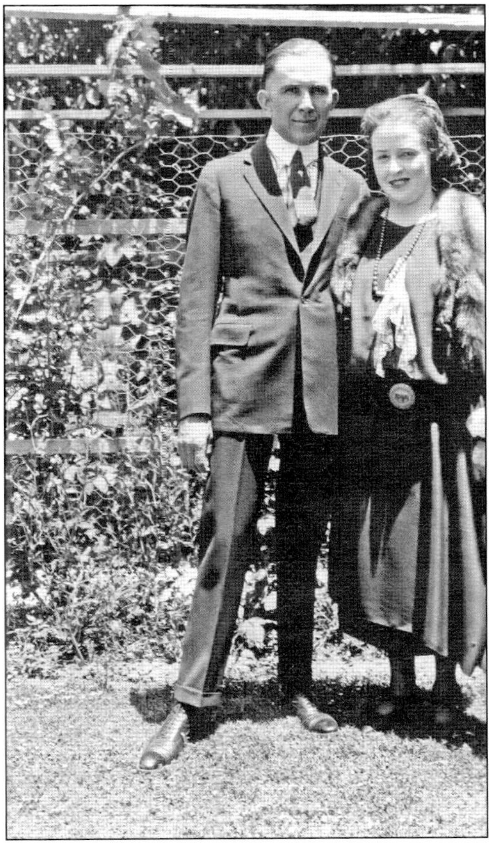

Raised as devout Catholics, both Walter and Adella recognized the seriousness of marriage. Pictured after Walter's proposal, the smiles on their faces seem to promise a future full of promise and opportunity, open to endless possibilities. Below, Adella Kraemer, sister Edna Kraemer, and mother Angelina Kraemer relax at the beach. As her wedding approached, Adella spent time with her mother and sisters. The beach was a favorite place. Even after marriage, Walter and Adella spent nearly every weekend at the beach. As the early 1920s approached, swimwear became more revealing, showing bare knees and shoulders. A few years earlier, this would have been considered scandalous.

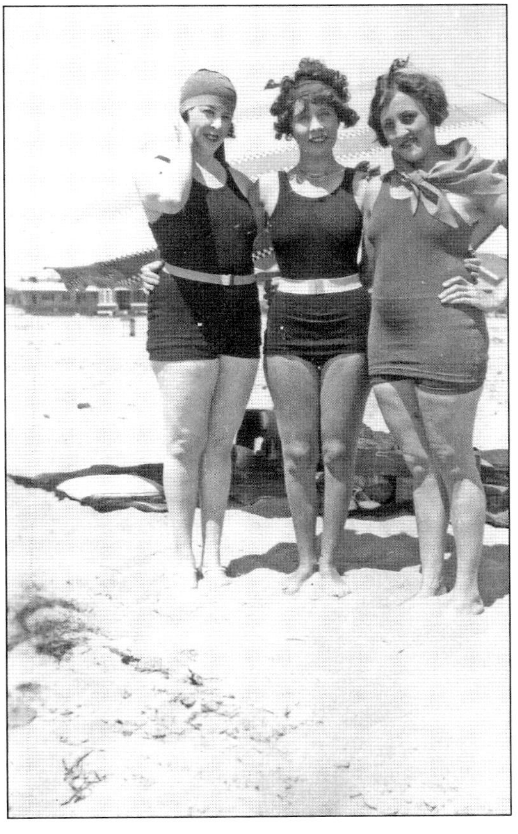

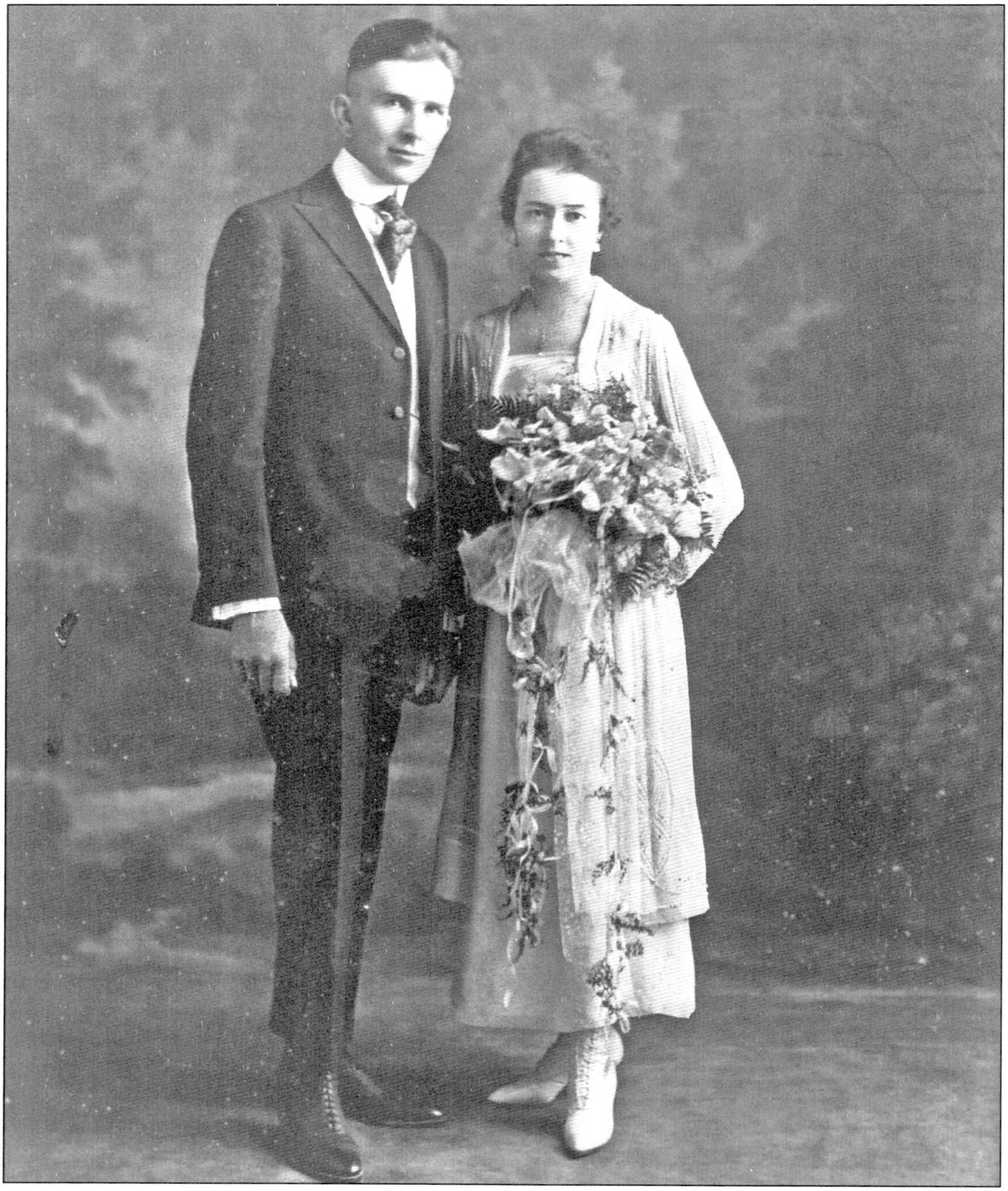

Walter Muckenthaler and Adella Kraemer were married at St. Boniface Church on Lincoln Avenue in Anaheim in 1919. This wedding picture shows that it was a simple but formal wedding. Both families were in attendance. As a wedding present, the Kraemers gave the couple an 80-acre orange grove in Fullerton, but it had no house. They honeymooned at the famous Mission Inn in nearby Riverside, where they enjoyed its mix of Spanish Colonial, Moorish Revival, and Mission Revival architecture. They later incorporated their love of Mission-style architecture in their home. Back in North Orange County, the young couple made their first home in Fullerton in a small apartment on East Whiting Avenue. Midway between Walter's family in Anaheim and Adella's family in Placentia, their new hometown was close to relatives but far enough away to give them a sense of independence.

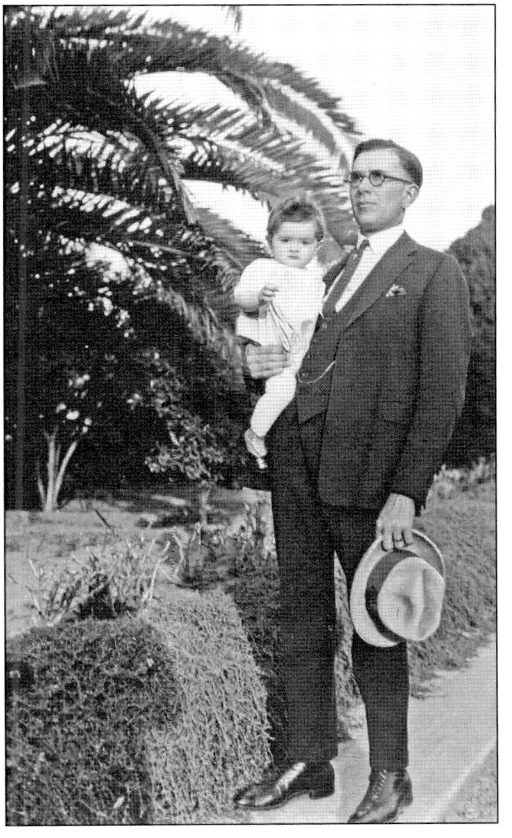

The young couple's first and only child, Harold Walter Muckenthaler, was born on October 1, 1922. By this time, the couple had moved to a small house on the 100 block of East Ash Street, south of downtown Fullerton. Harold would grow up adored by his parents, but he wouldn't be a lonely child. Walter's brother would have 11 children. Harold had plenty of friends and the children of the ranch workers with whom to have adventures. Now 89 years old, Harold remains a top supporter of the cultural center named for his family. He is a man full of life and love for the arts, which he was instrumental in bringing to Fullerton.

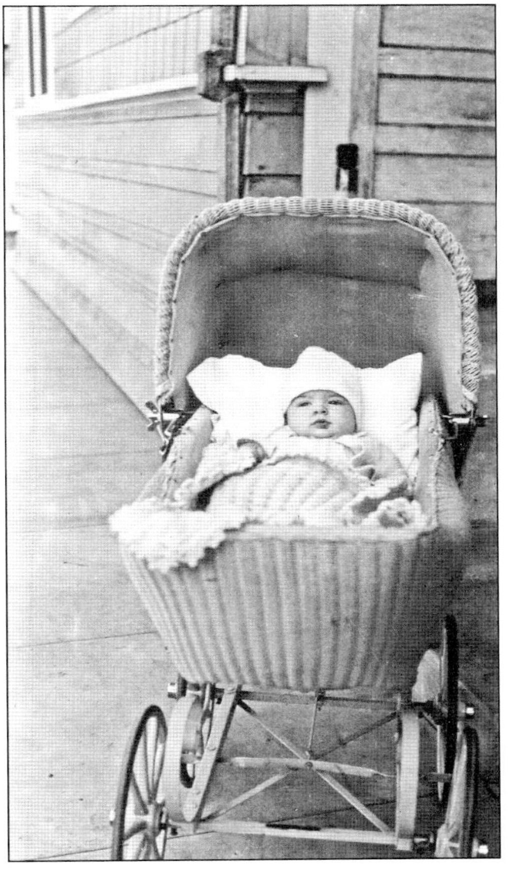

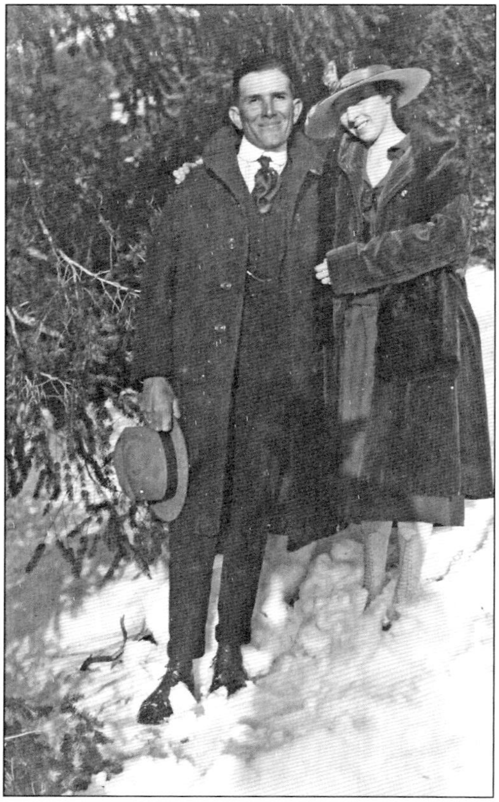

Adella and Walter both loved the outdoors. Even while playing in the snow in the mountains of Crestline, California, they maintained a formal appearance (above). Crestline was designed like an alpine village and was filled with other German immigrants. Walter and Adella were a happy couple with their baby son, Harold. Walter adjusted well to domestic life. His bachelor days long behind him, he now thought seriously of his family's financial future. Even with the gift of a citrus grove from his in-laws, Walter wanted to make a name for himself and support his family on his own.

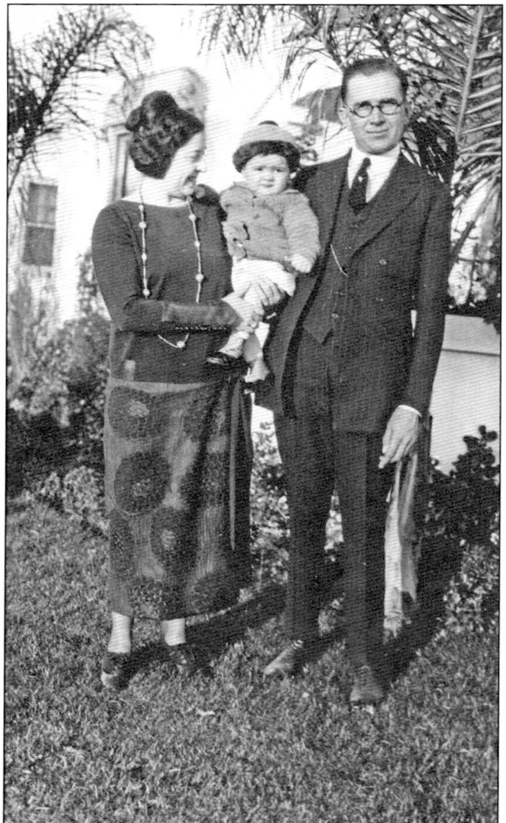

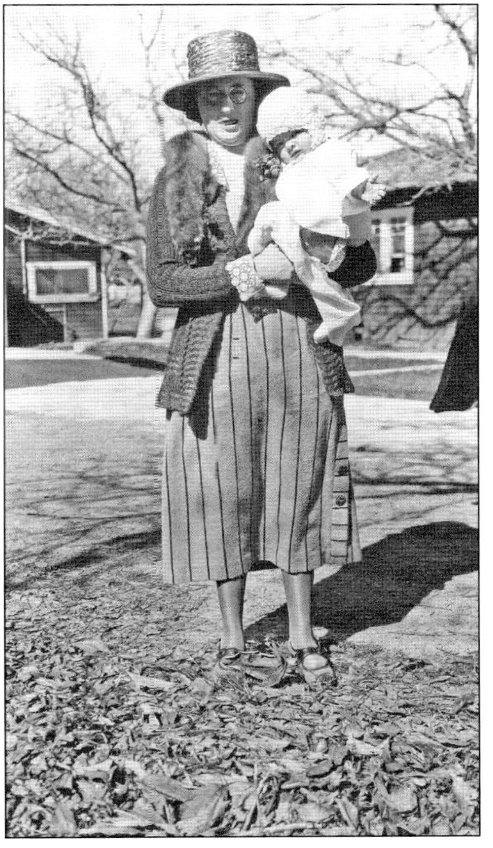

Adella and Harold wait for their father to come home. Walter had little trouble finding employment with the Santa Fe Railroad. His first assignment was to survey a stretch of tracks running along the cliffs between Santa Ana and San Diego (currently the route of the Amtrak *Pacific Surfliner*). The job paid well for the time. As a civil engineer for the Santa Fe Railroad, Walter helped construct a freight route through the Cajon Pass. It led to faster transportation for railcars up the steep grade and was of great importance for commerce in the developing region.

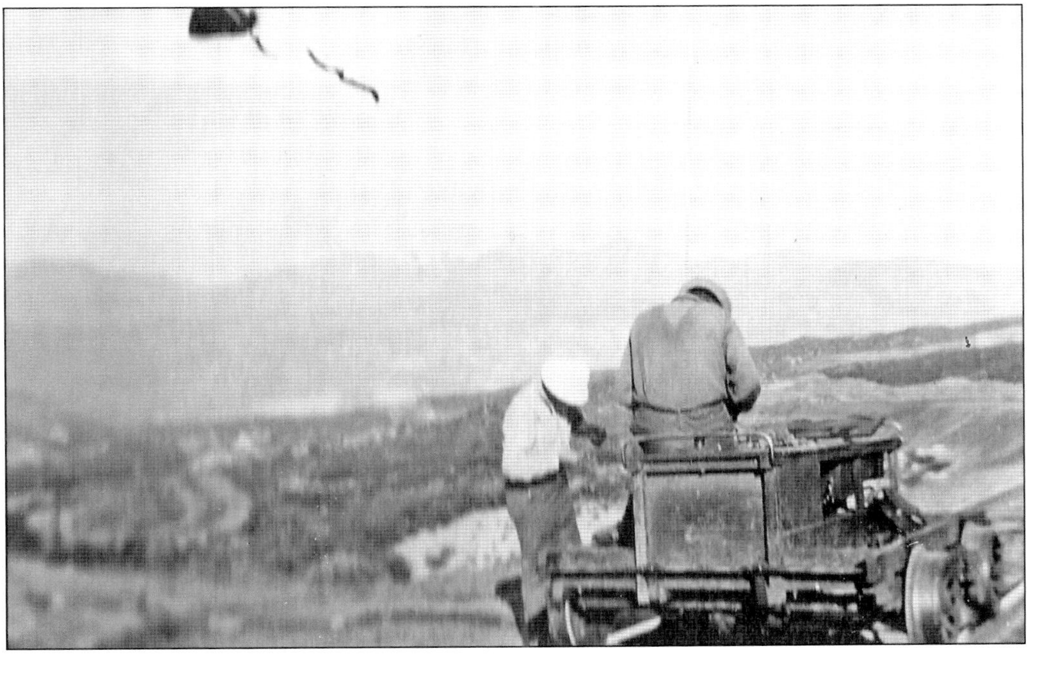

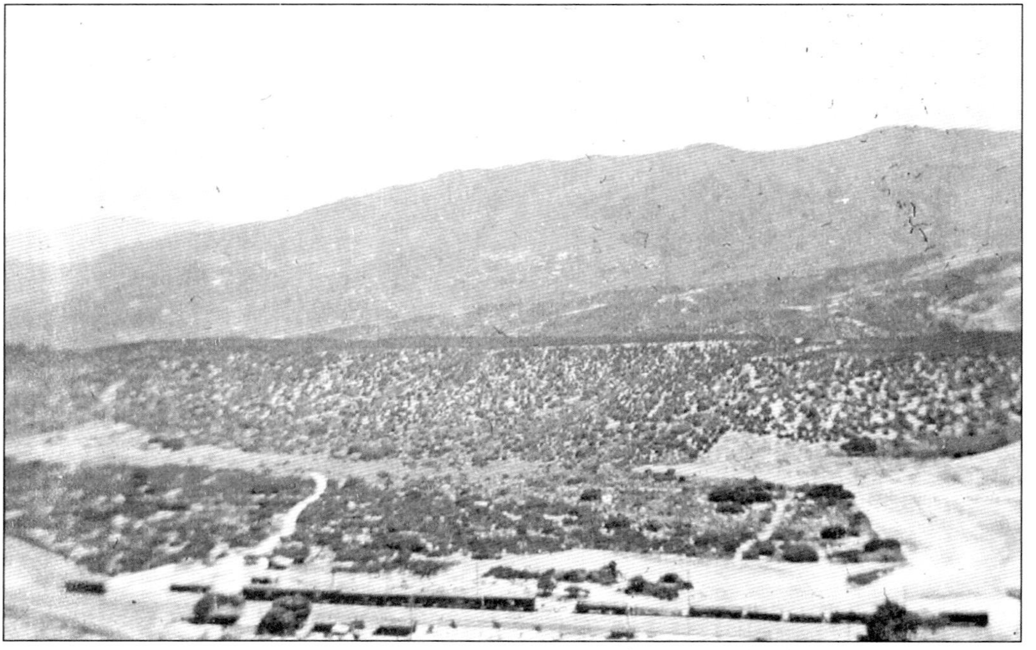

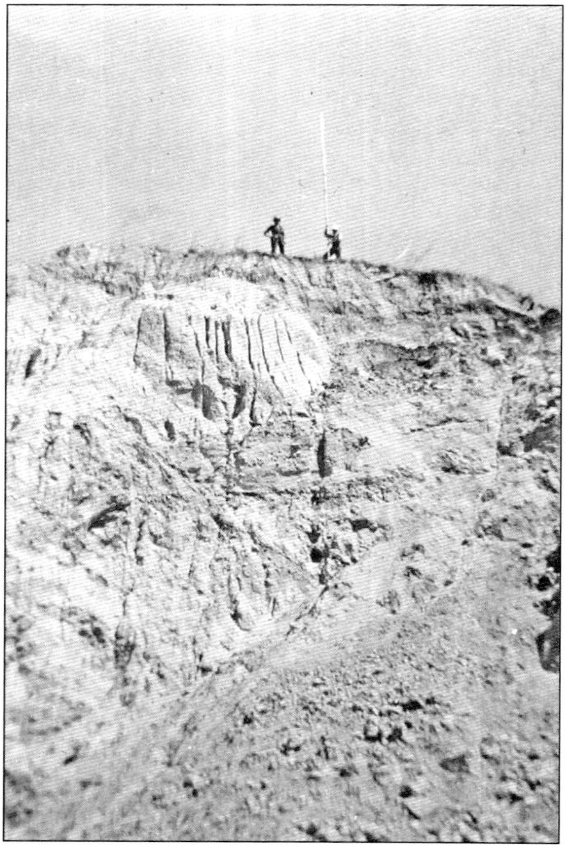

Walter's work for the Santa Fe Railroad took him away from his new bride for as long as a week at a time and as far away as Victorville, California, approximately 80 miles away. Walter's longtime habit of carrying a camera allowed him to record his experiences. This is land that he is surveying for the railroad, believed to be in the Cajon Pass. The photographs are a part of Walter's series from his days surveying for the railroad and are great images of California before urban sprawl. Walter saw every inch of Southern California from the Mexico border through this pass and through the mountains toward the great Nevada desert. Walter loved the peacefulness of the desert, but he missed Dell (Adella's nickname) and his growing son.

Both Adella and her father, Samuel Kraemer, worried about Walter's close proximity to blasting crews. Railroad construction was dangerous work. A derailed car that threw Walter and his crew down a ravine left him hospitalized for days. Through city engineer Herman Hiltscher, Adella's father helped Walter secure a position as city surveyor for Fullerton. The job represented steady, safer employment close to home. It would also be the start of his relationship with the City of Fullerton. Below, Walter surveys the city from a high point. While surveying for the City of Fullerton, he could plan for his family's future with their 80 acres near the Carhart Ranch. The Carharts originally purchased their much larger ranch from the Bastanchury family, who had been Basque sheepherders in Fullerton since the mid-1800s. The Bastanchury ranch at one time took up half of Fullerton. There are streets in Fullerton named for the Bastanchury family and the Carharts. Even the Bastanchury homeland of Basque has a street named for it.

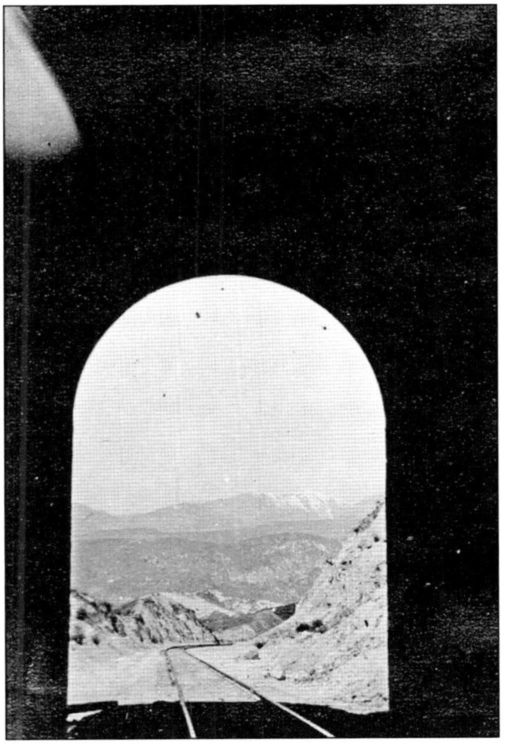

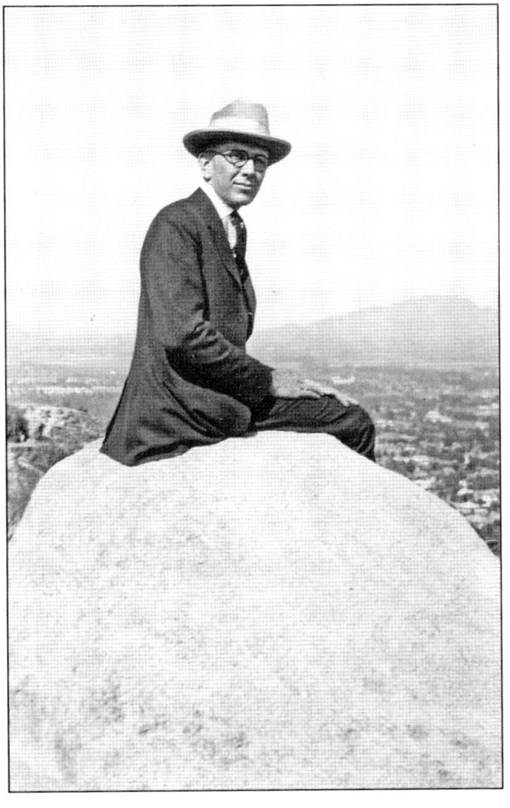

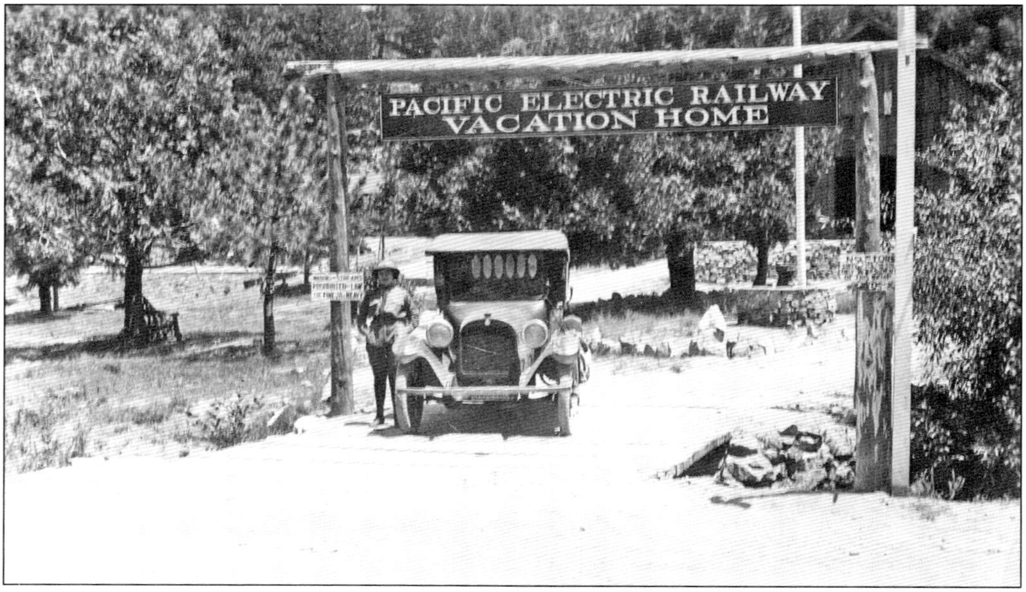

Walter and Adella visited the Pacific Electric Railway Vacation Home. The young couple enjoyed traveling by automobile to places of natural beauty, including Yosemite National Park. The majestic Sequoia National Park drew them in with its giant trees. Walter and Adella were well traveled in an age when much of California was undeveloped and automobile travel was mostly on dirt roads with ruts from oxen carts. Cars were less dependable, and gas stations were farther apart. Hotels were few and far between, and camping gear was much less portable. Traveling the West by car in the 1920s took a great deal of planning and perseverance.

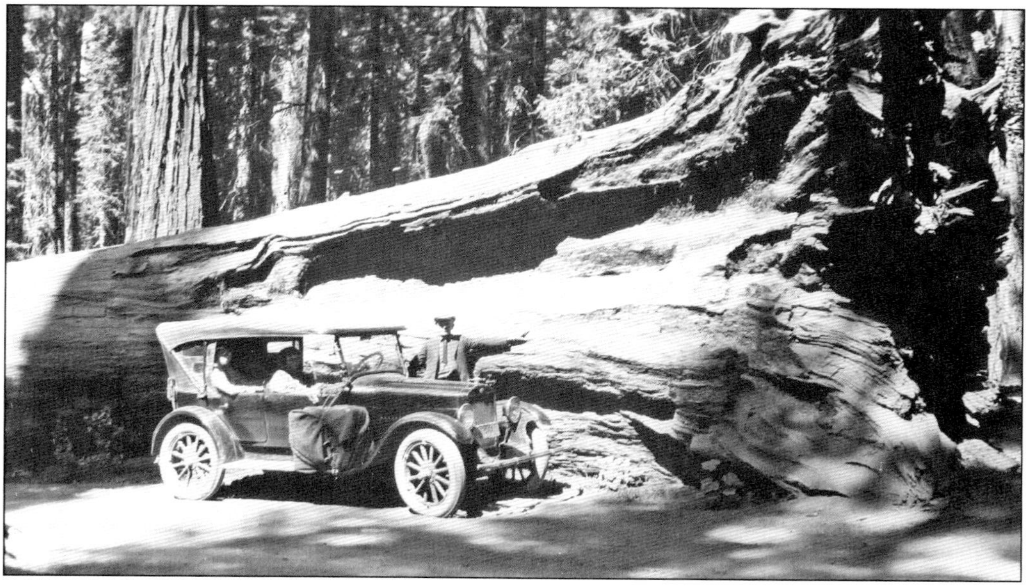

Now that he was home, Walter could attend outings with family and friends. Here, Adella dressed in riding breeches and boots for a picnic with Walter and friends in Santa Ana Canyon. Below, sister-in-law Vi and Adella sit proudly on an early oil tanker car with their friend Anna Pember. Ranchers in Brea discovered oil on their property. It was literally oozing from the grounds (*Brea* is Spanish for "tar pit"). When the Union Oil Company explored south of Brea in 1919, oil was eventually discovered on Samuel's ranch, and he became quite wealthy. He and his neighbor Charles Chapman became the first to build high-rises in the area—Samuel in Anaheim and Charles in Fullerton. Kraemer Avenue in Placentia is named after Samuel for his family's many contributions to the area.

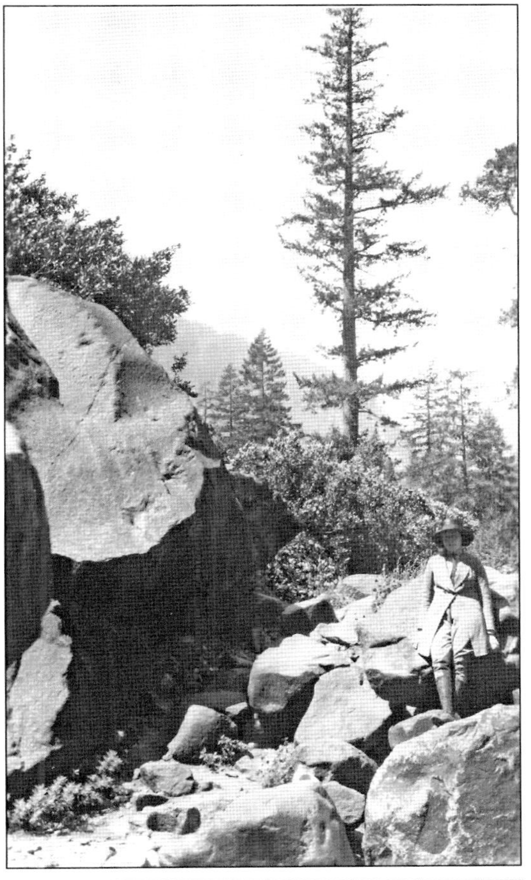

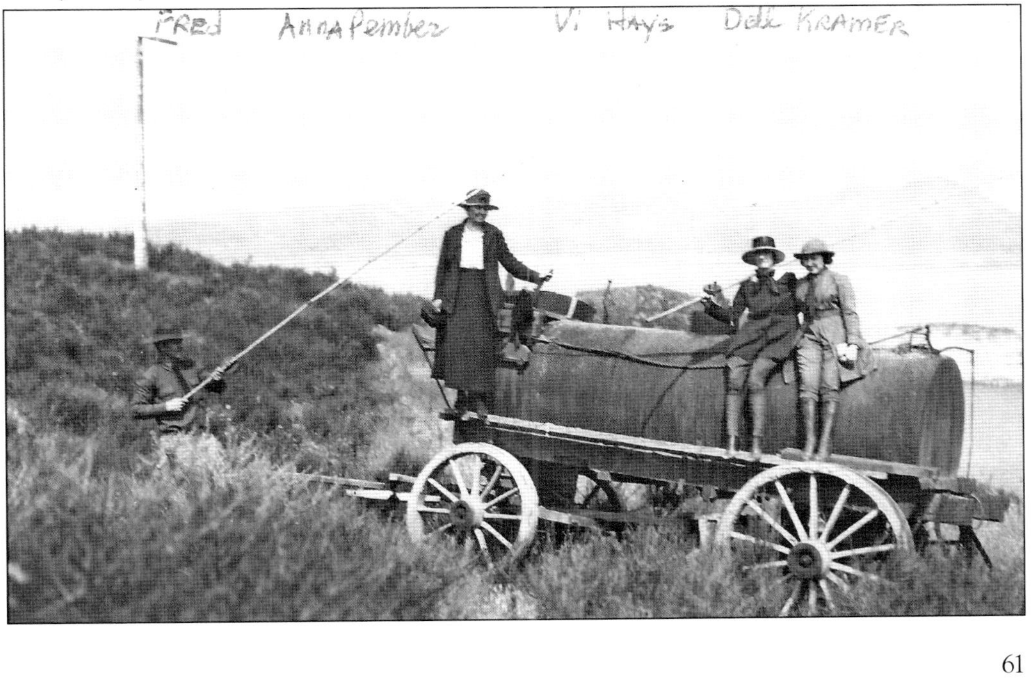

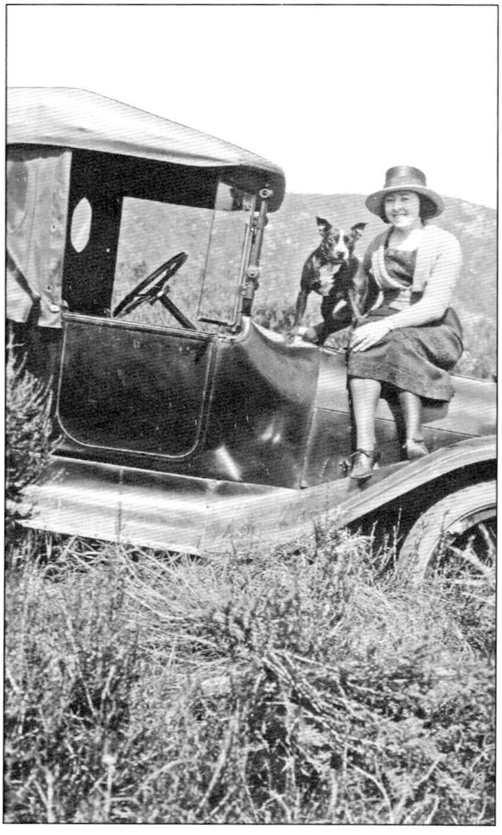

Adella sits on Walter's Dodge with the family dog as they survey what will be their future orange grove. In 1920, just one year after Walter and Adella's marriage, Samuel Kraemer followed Charles Chapman's example of allowing oil drilling on his property. So much oil was discovered that Samuel and Angelina shared their bounty with their children, including their eldest daughter, Adella, who was given one of the leases. The royalties from the oil lease provided the funds needed for Walter and Adella to turn their 80 acres into citrus groves, which were located on Euclid Avenue between Commonwealth and Malvern Avenues northwest of downtown Fullerton. They purchased an additional 8.5 acres of lemon trees just north of Malvern Avenue as a site for a new home. With this steady income, Walter and Adella were free to plan a dream home for their new ranch. Below, Walter sits with young Harold in his grove during construction.

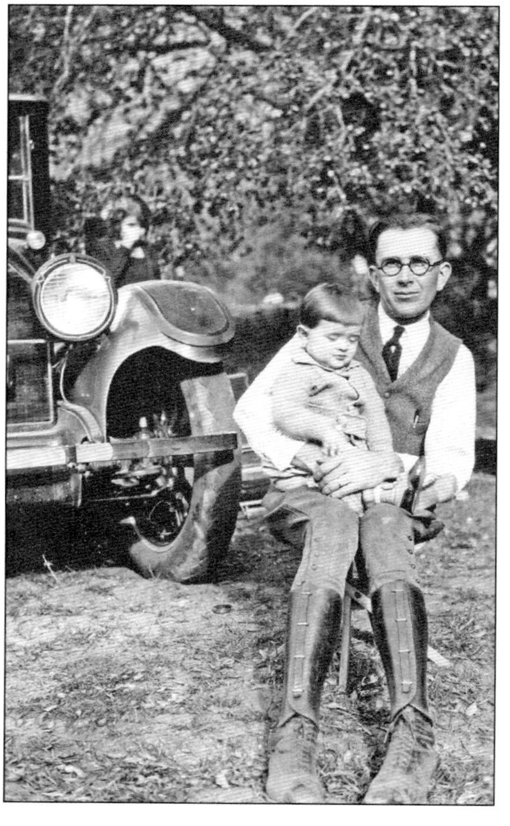

Four

The Villa

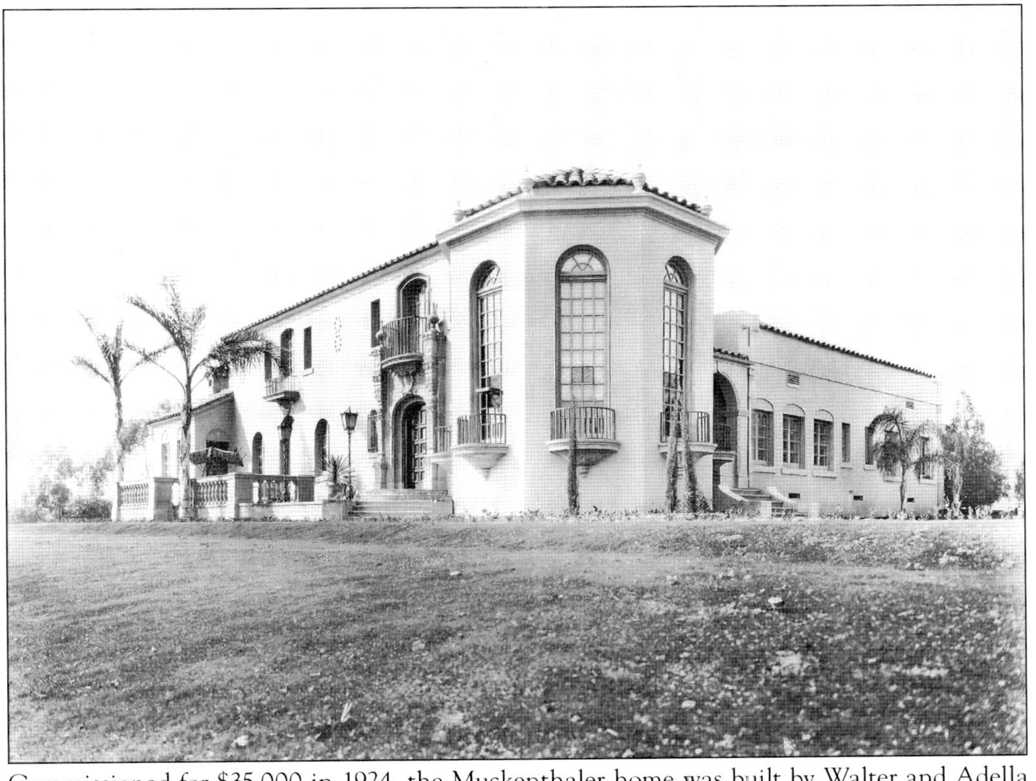

Commissioned for $35,000 in 1924, the Muckenthaler home was built by Walter and Adella Muckenthaler in the Golden Hills area of Fullerton. The 18-room villa was designed by architect Frank Benchley and reflects Walter's interest in Mission-style architecture and Italian villas. Benchley also designed several other distinctive Fullerton buildings, including the California Hotel (now the Villa del Sol) and Pomona Bungalow Court. The villa was built by E.J. Herbert, who also constructed Fullerton's historic Santa Fe Depot. All of Walter's interest and study of architecture came to bear in guiding this work. The home would far exceed the design of a normal ranch house with its spectacular architectural details, including the solarium and the front of the house. This showplace's location on the hill overlooking the ranch has spectacular views that helped to make it special.

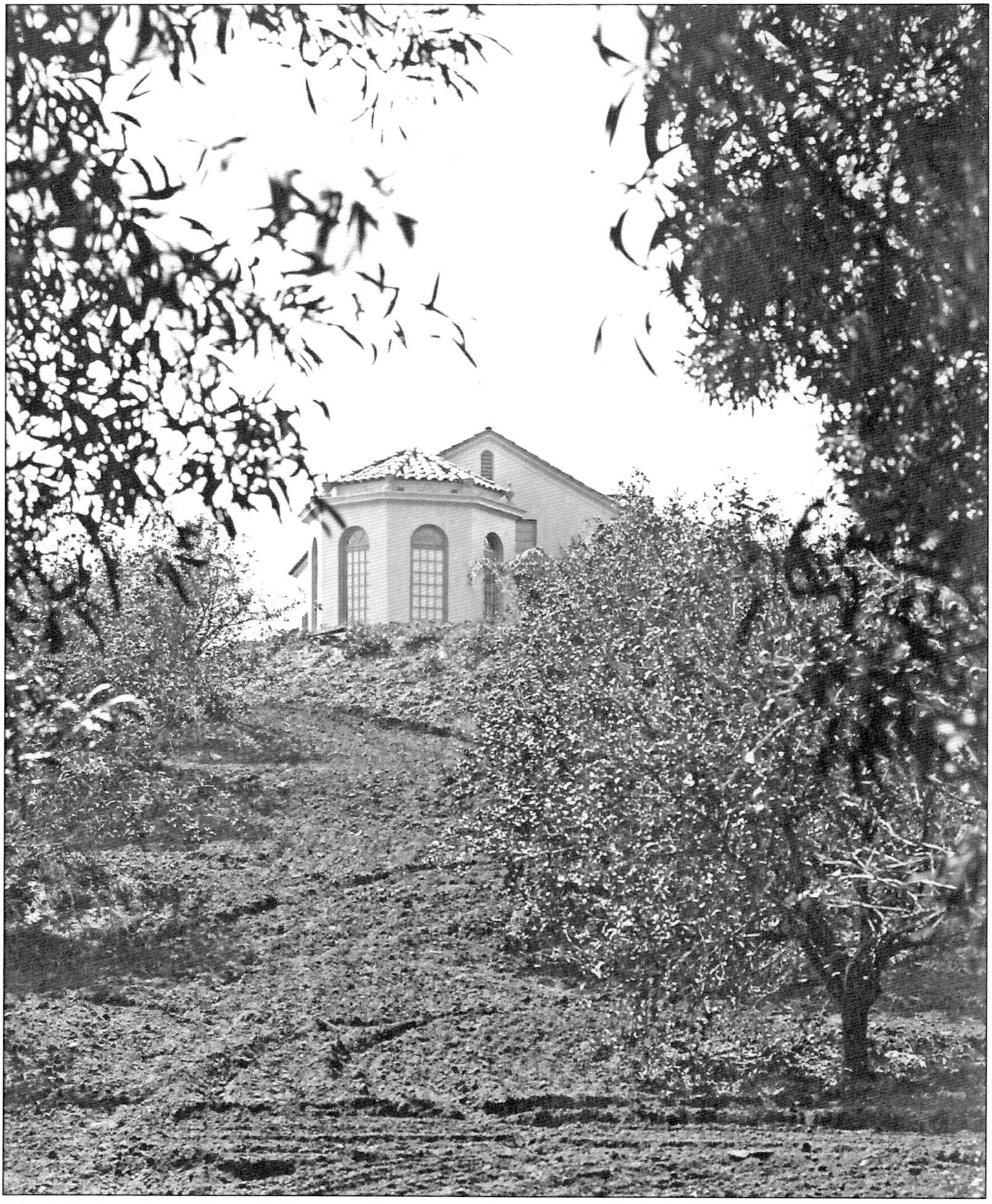

The Muckenthaler home's iconic solarium peaks over the hill from the east near Buena Vista Avenue. Although the walls were built one foot thick at the bottom, the home took only six months to complete. The irrigation pond and the orchards are located at the bottom of the hill, just out of this photograph's frame, to the left. This shot was taken soon after the completion of the house but before the landscaping was done. Within a few years, this land would contain a babbling stream, a jungle of plants growing along the stream, and the stone gazebo. In an ingenious bit of civil engineering, the Muckenthalers bought a half acre on top of the ridge behind them and drilled a well. The water was gravity fed to the stream and pond and then on to the grove. Visitors to the villa would see this as their first view when coming up the hill to the driveway.

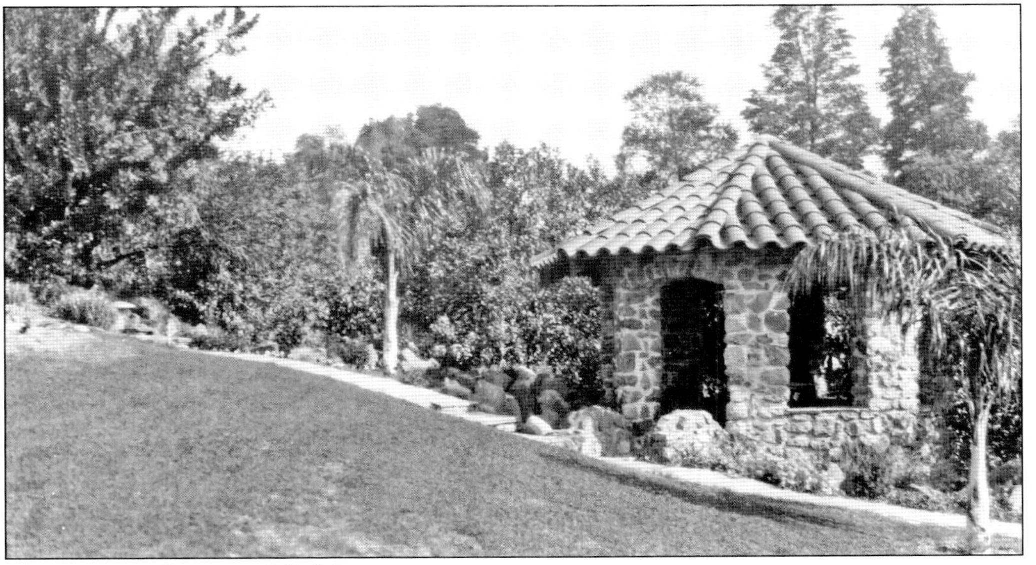

The reservoir that once filled the southeast corner of the Muckenthaler estate was fed by an artificial stream that ran alongside the steps leading down the hill. The concrete-lined pool was frequented by ducks and swans, which Walter fed from a barrel of food kept nearby. The gazebo was a cool spot for resting during hot summers. Harold has fond memories of playing with friends in the reservoir, which was fitted with a small bridge and diving board. Today, the gazebo is a favorite spot for wedding photographs.

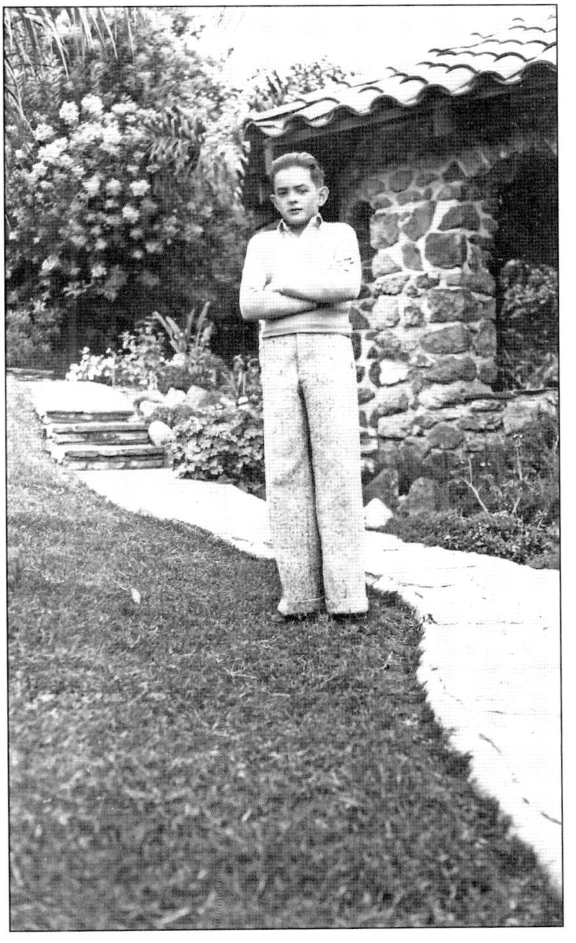

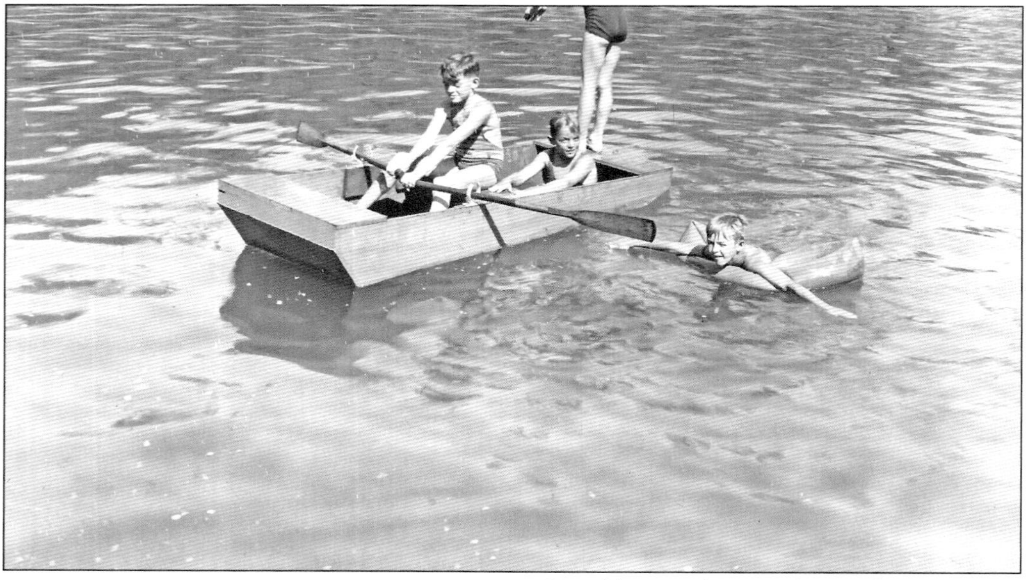

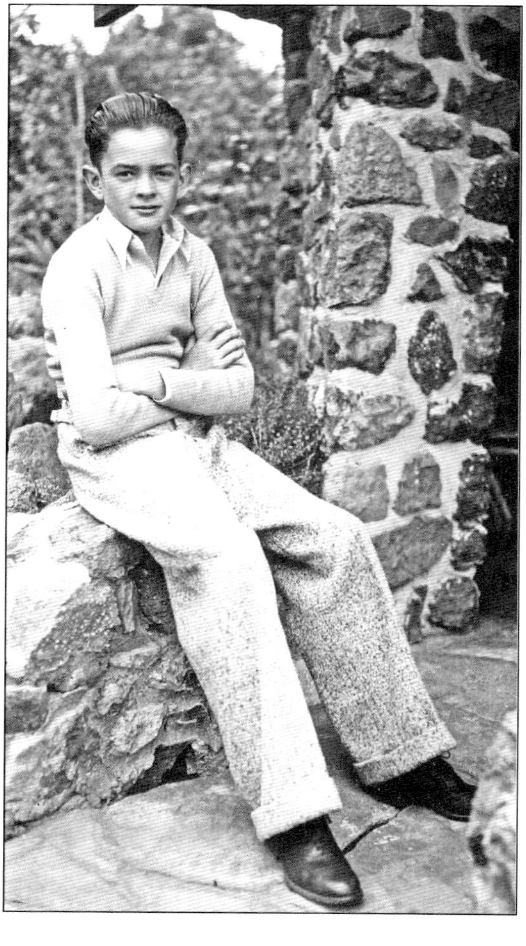

Harold rows a boat in the small irrigation pond that once watered orchards down the hill. The reservoir also served as a swimming pool in hot weather for many of the neighboring children. These ponds were found on every ranch in the area at the time. In the 1960s, a four-year-old child drowned in an old irrigation pond on a neighboring ranch, and the city ordered that all remaining irrigation ponds be filled in. Though a rumor persisted in later years of a drowning at the Muckenthaler estate, no such tragedy ever occurred there. Harold sits in front of the gazebo along the path to the irrigation pond in 1934. Not only do the 75 brides that marry at the Muckenthaler each year take photographs here, but many other wedding parties also come just for pictures in the stone gazebo. It is surrounded by a lush jungle of plants that is still fed from the groundwater left when the stream was dismantled. A stone path still leads to the gazebo from the driveway.

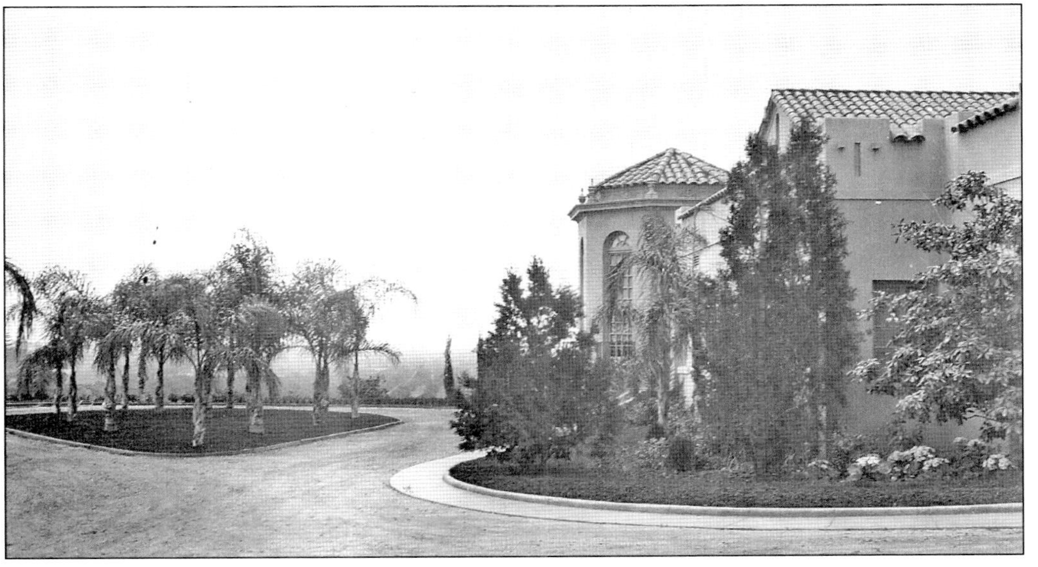

Originally unpaved, the circular driveway led from Buena Vista Avenue to the east side of the house (above). Automobiles could be driven directly to the porch adjacent to the solarium. The small palm trees now tower over the island lawn. In the cultural center's early days, an artist used the palms for a site-specific art piece in which he put bicycle wheels in the trees. No one ever took them down. Today, the trees have grown over the wheels, and it appears as if bicycles are growing out of the trees. Driving up toward the side porch and newly paved entrance, motorists would see the entire 80-acre ranch to the south (below). The driveway also served to cover pipes feeding the irrigation pond from a well a half-mile up the hill near Fern Drive—another civil engineering feature of the house.

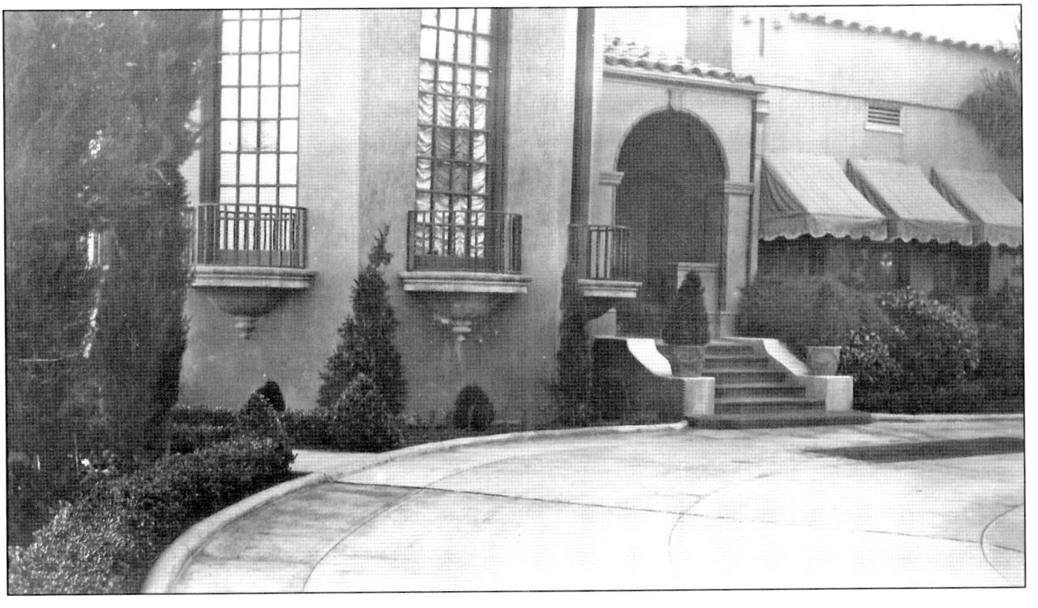

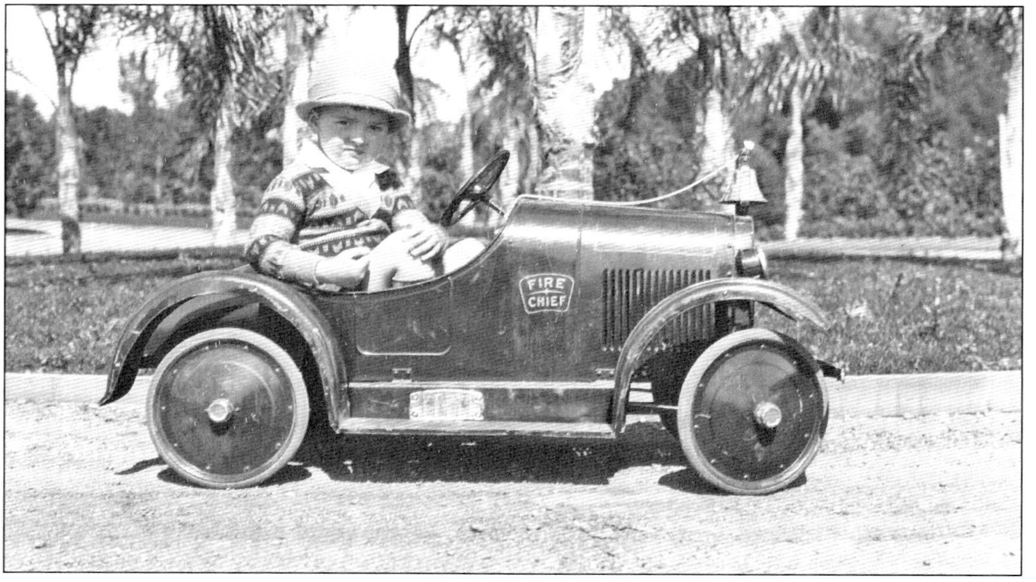

Harold drives his pedal fire engine on the circular driveway in the 1926 photograph above. Home movies of the period show that adult cousins enjoyed driving the little engine around the driveway, too. Notice how small the palm trees are in the background. Today, these trees tower more than 30 feet in the air. Walter was photographed below in 1926 as he drove the family's new Cadillac along the circular driveway. At this time and for many years to come, Cadillac was the symbol of the best a car could be. When someone had a Cadillac, that person had made it.

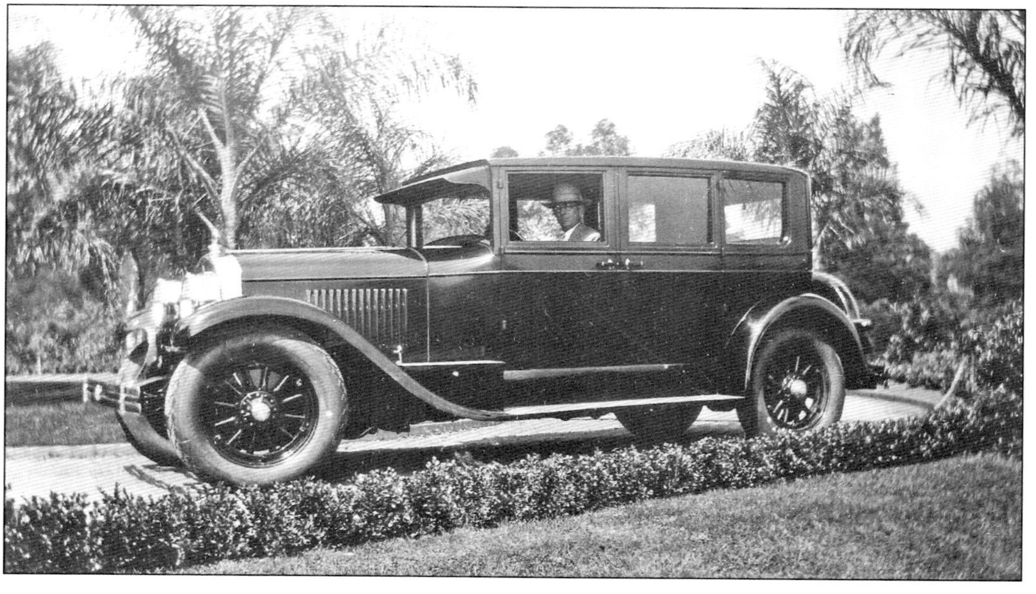

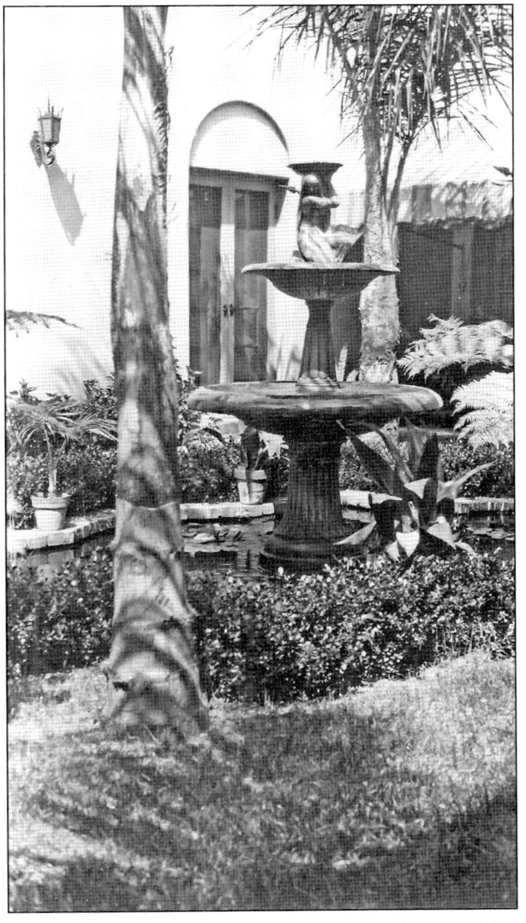

Surrounded by the plants that Walter loved, the home's large open-air atrium was another place to enjoy cooler temperatures in the summer. The fountain was a central element of the Mediterranean estate. A balcony looked down from Walter and Adella's bedroom. A tropical-themed mural once graced the south wall under the arches. Relatives from both sides of the family loved to visit the home, including Walter's niece Geraldine Chambers (daughter of his eldest sister, Abigail). This atrium was enclosed in the 1950s. Though the sunroof in the interior courtyard was originally designed to be opened when desired, it was permanently closed during the renovation in the 1980s.

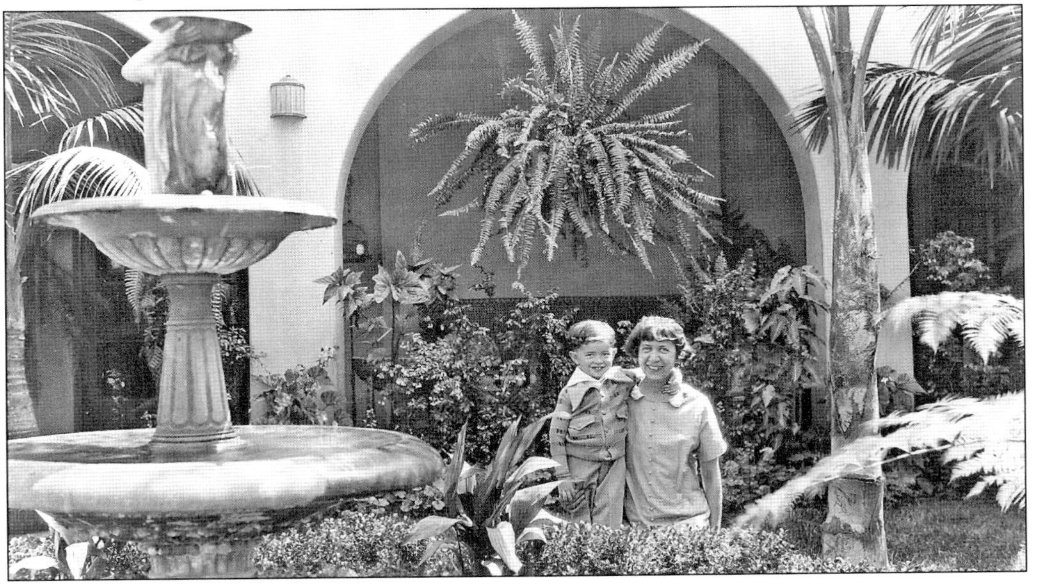

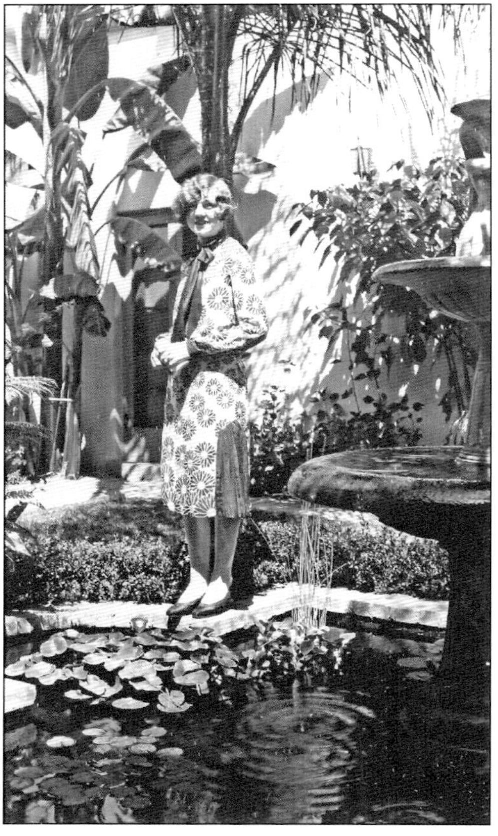

Cousin Rita Guth, visiting from Kansas, stands on the edge of the fountain in the open atrium in the summer of 1926. Below, Adella and Harold Muckenthaler were photographed in 1926 on the lawn of the atrium patio. French doors, visible in the background, led to the breakfast room, which anchored the east wing of the house. Farther into the east wing are the dining room, library, and kitchen. Today, the dining room and library are as they were then. The kitchen has been upgraded to a prep kitchen for catering the many weddings and events at the estate. The library is used as a gallery for exhibiting small sculptures, and the dining room table serves buffet appetizers during gallery openings.

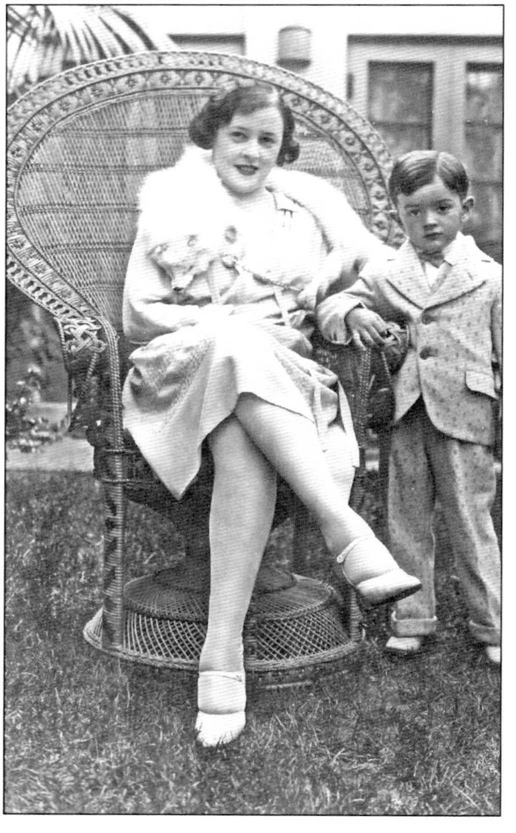

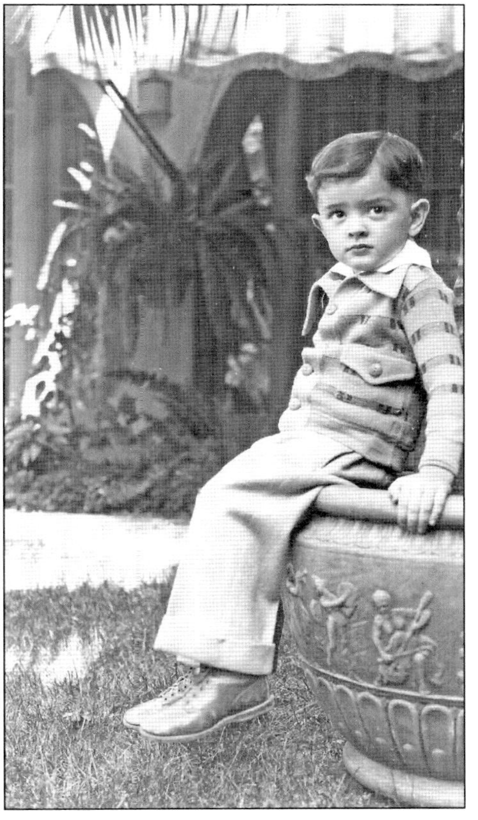

Harold sits on a pot large enough for him to hide inside. Walter loved to find large ceramic pots for his expanding gardens. He and Clark Lutschg visited area nurseries in search of handsome specimens for the rear patio and other areas of the estate. Visitors loved to relax in this rear courtyard, surrounded by the dark stained oak and glass doors and cool shade of the arches. A striped awning in the background shaded more French doors leading into the west wing, which housed the ranch office, a bathroom, and a guest bedroom. Today, the guest bedroom has been converted into the women's restroom. The original bathroom has become the men's restroom. The ranch manager's office, which was used to pay ranch employees and as an infirmary, is now a sculptural art gallery.

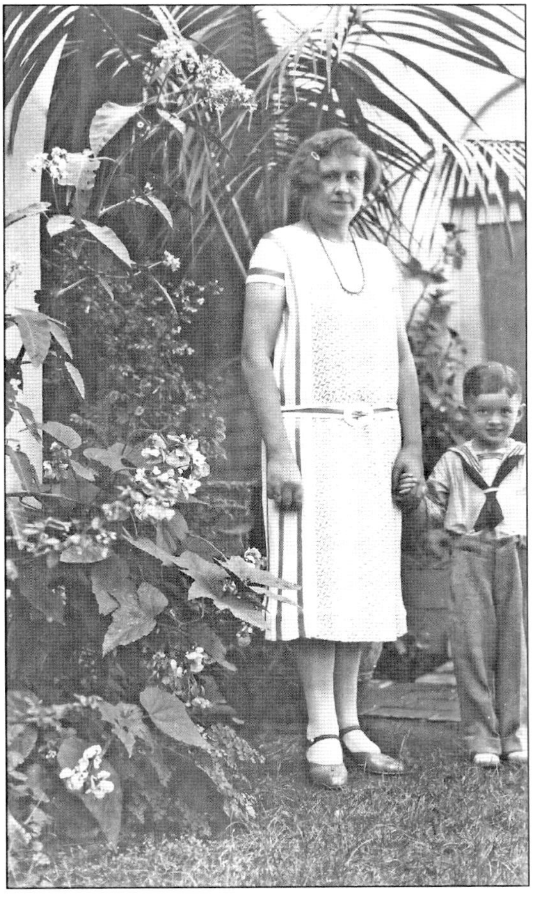

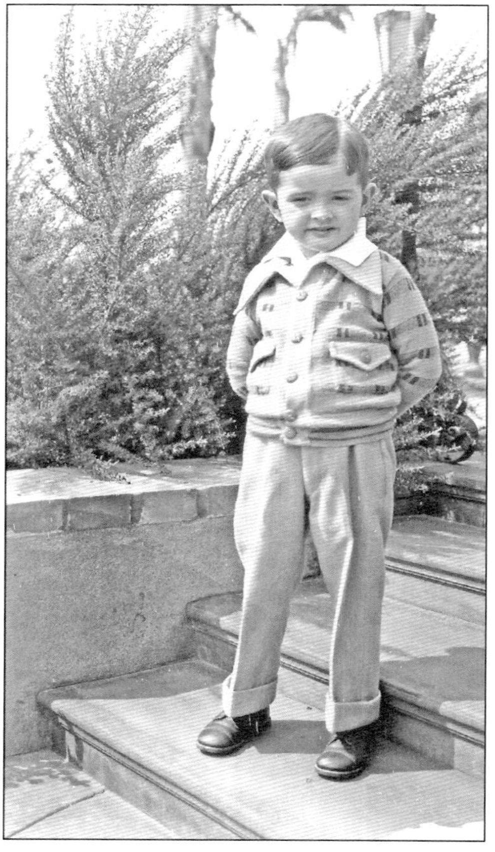

A young Harold is pictured standing on the front porch steps in the mid-1920s (left). Harold had a magical childhood during the Roaring Twenties. It was a time of prosperity across the country, but in California, the possibilities were endless. Harold was an example of the American filled with optimism who had opportunity and seemingly unlimited resources to enjoy. Below, Harold is dressed for cold weather on the front porch with a cousin. His clothes show that he had the best of everything, but a ranch kid could not grow up spoiled. There were endless chores to be done and responsibilities to tend to. Harold would inherit his parents' pioneer spirit and work ethic. Today, he does not live a life of luxury. He drives the same car he has owned since 1973. One is more likely to see him in a flannel shirt than a suit.

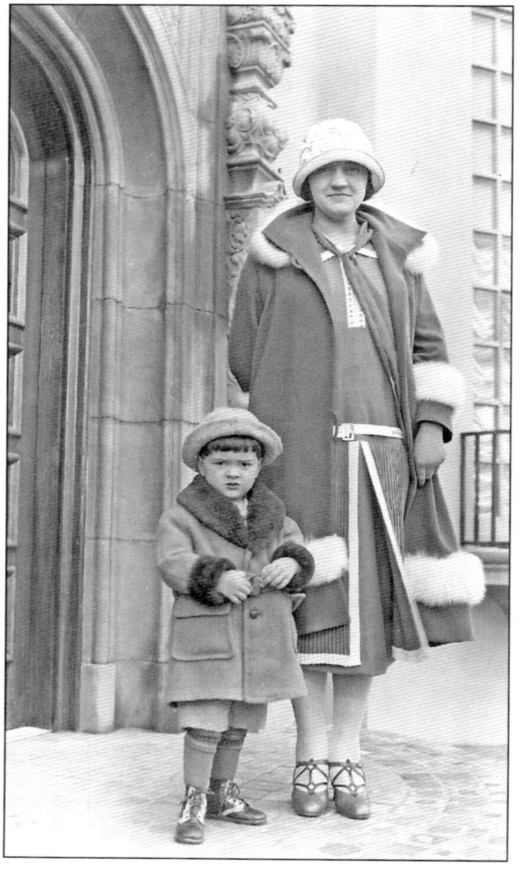

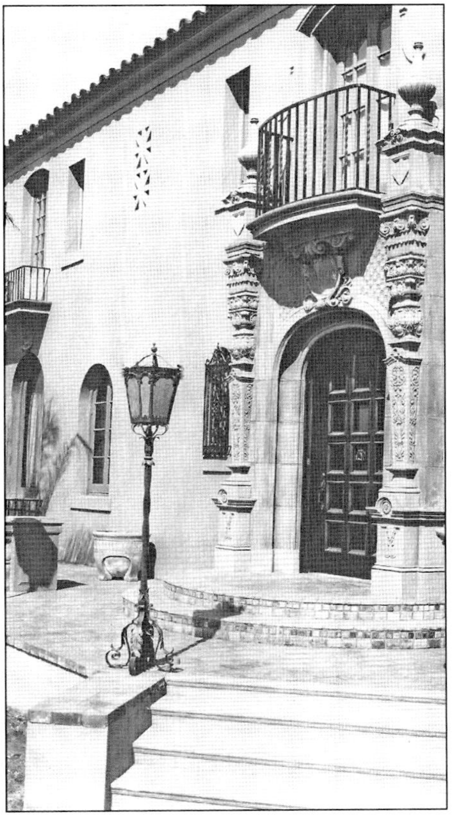

The heavy paneled front door of the home is set into an Italianate cast concrete pediment (right). This concrete was renovated in 2007 through the City of Fullerton and a Getty Foundation grant. In 1927, a young Harold and his father, Walter, posed next to the picturesque sundial at the west end of the Italian Garden. A wrought iron gate surrounded a semicircular goldfish pond, now filled in and covered by brick. The Italian Garden was strategically located to be viewed from the plate-glass dining room window. At different periods, it would feature a trellis, a small reflecting pool, and a sundial. (Right, Launer.)

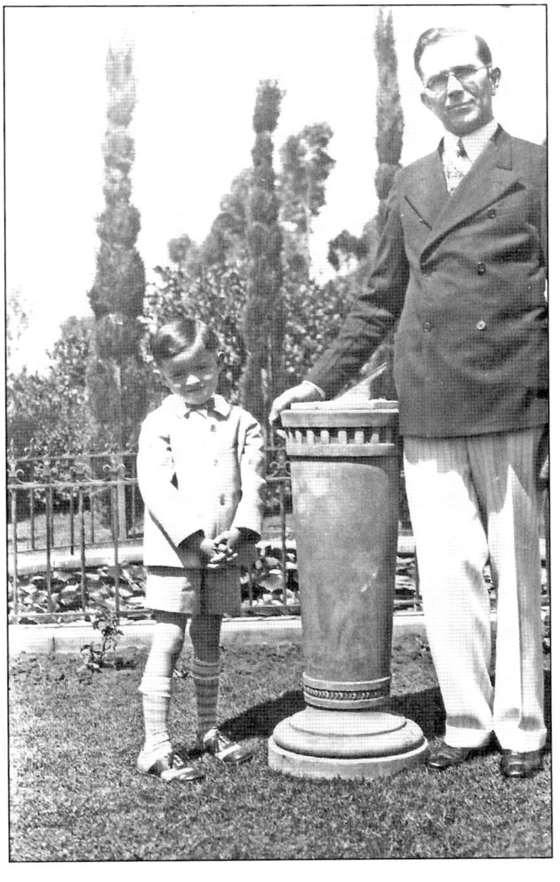

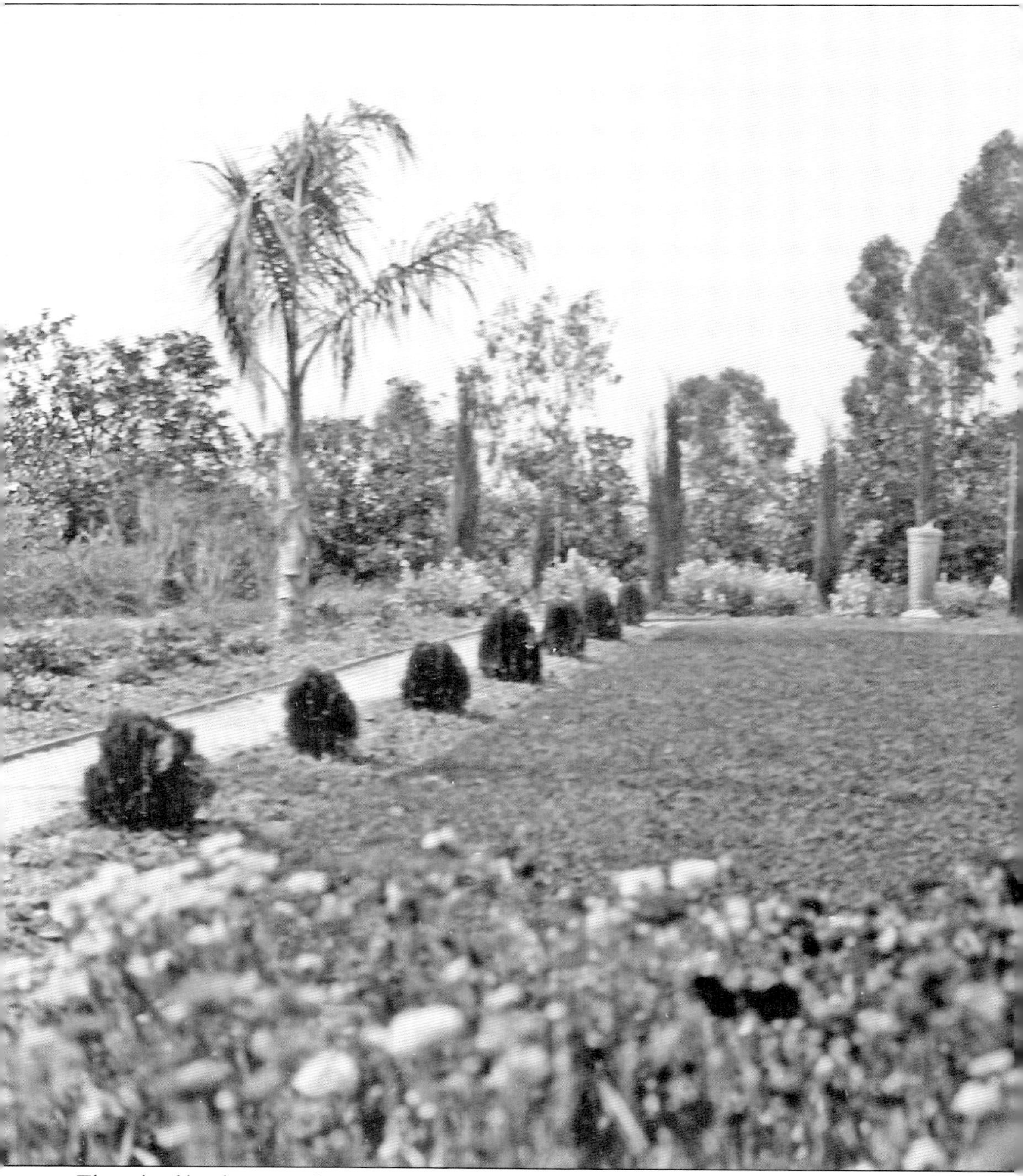

The job of landscaping the estate was originally given to the Howard and Smith Company of Montebello, but the firm left it unfinished. In 1924, Walter Muckenthaler hired Sequoia Nursery's Clark Lutschg, one of California's first registered landscape architects, to complete the project. Three years later, Walter Muckenthaler rewarded Lutschg for his work with a 1926 Ford Roadster. The Italian Garden now hosts more than 75 weddings each year. They are hosted by

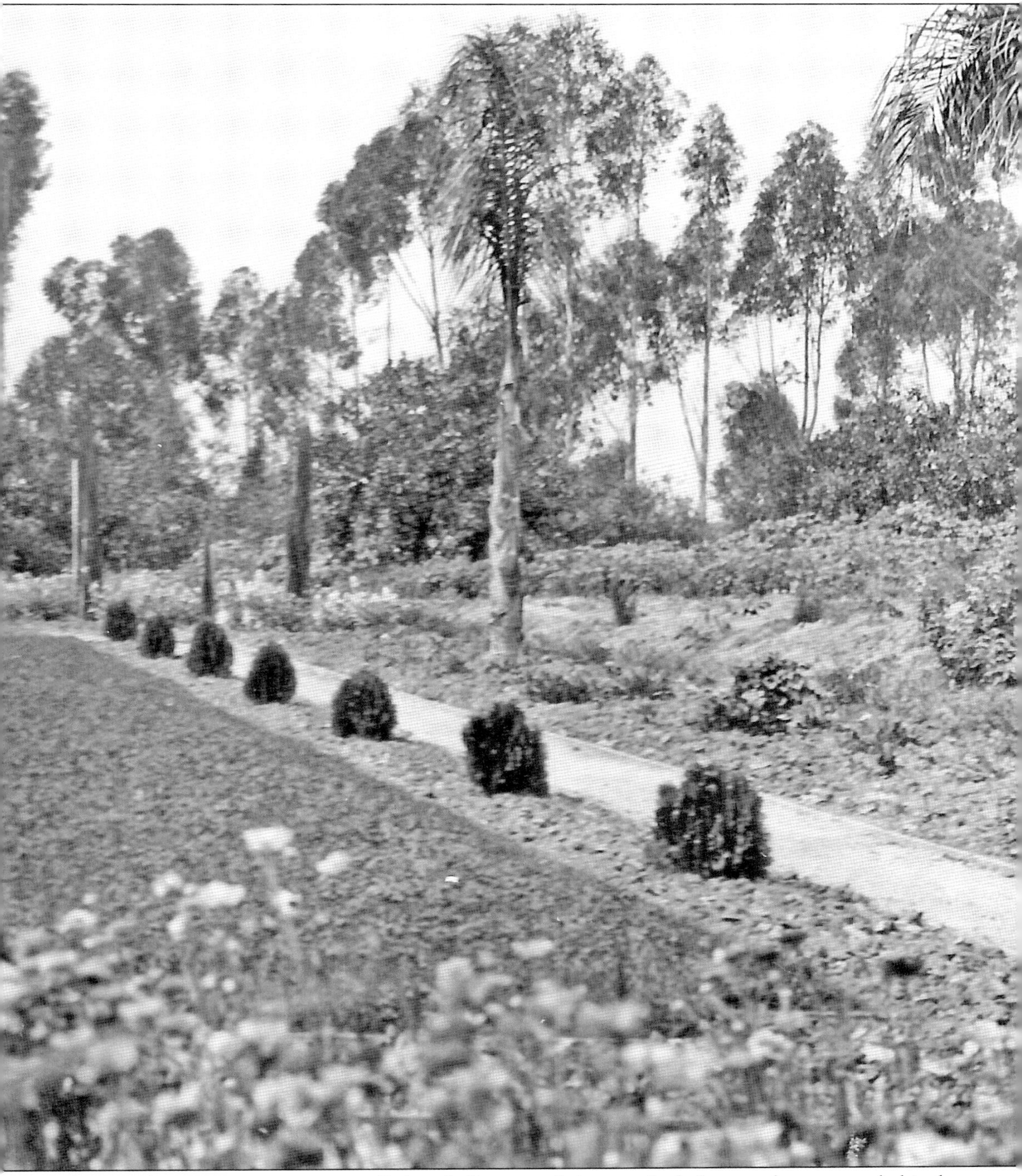

the foundation's catering partner, Colette's Catering. It is a magical place as the sun sets behind the palms. Flower sprays cover the new wrought iron gazebo, which is over the old goldfish pond. Brides and grooms exchange vows hoping to soak in a little of the aura that the Muckenthalers left after a generous life together and a marriage that lasted the rest of their lives. It is among the top three wedding spots in North Orange County. (Launer.)

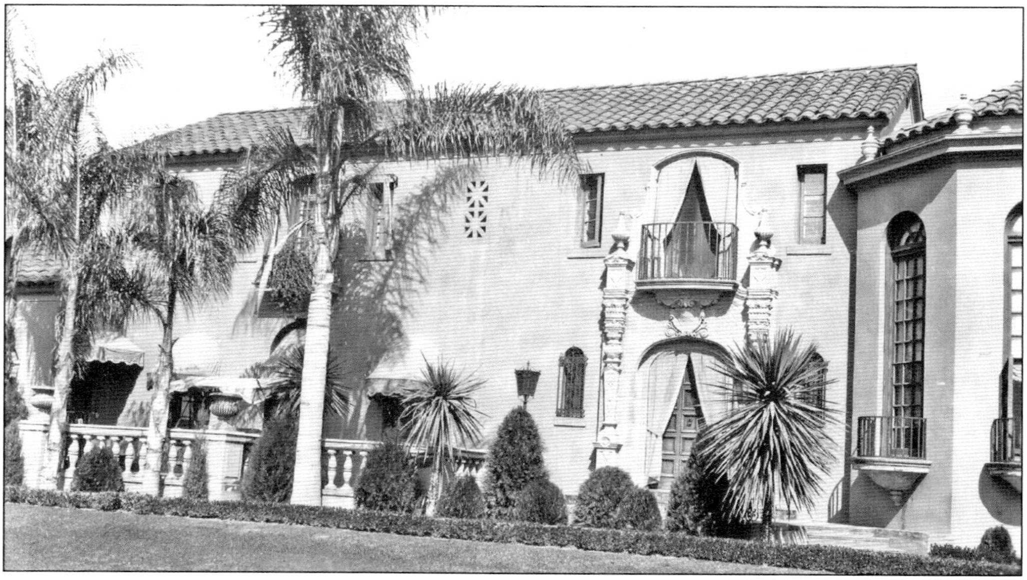

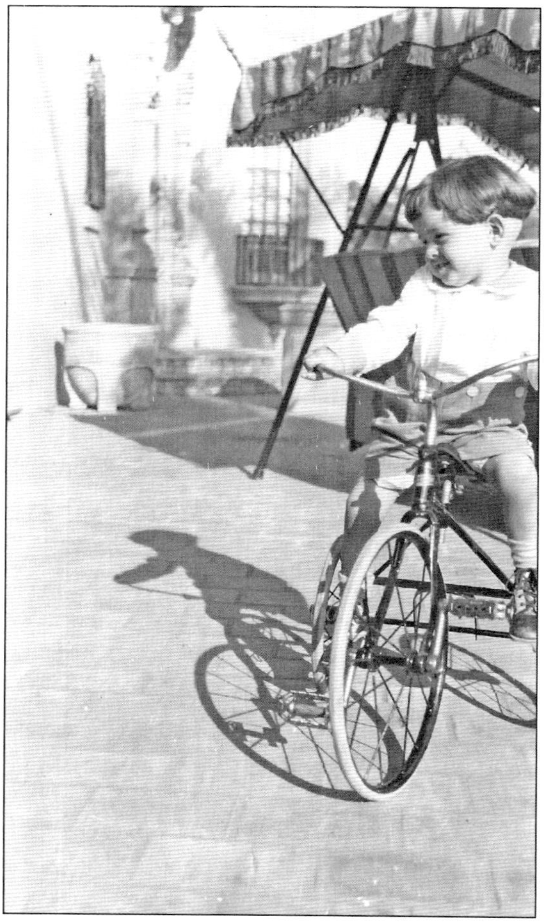

These heavy velvet curtains were hung on the outside of windows and doors as both a stylistic feature and a practical method of keeping the home cool during the hot summers of Fullerton before the advent of air-conditioning. During the winter, they retained the heat, keeping it from escaping through the drafty window areas. The curtains added to the Spanish style of the home. Granddaughter Peggy recalls that the curtains kept the bright California sun out of the room while she napped on a velvet love seat in the living room. At left, Harold rides his tricycle on the front porch next to the glider swing.

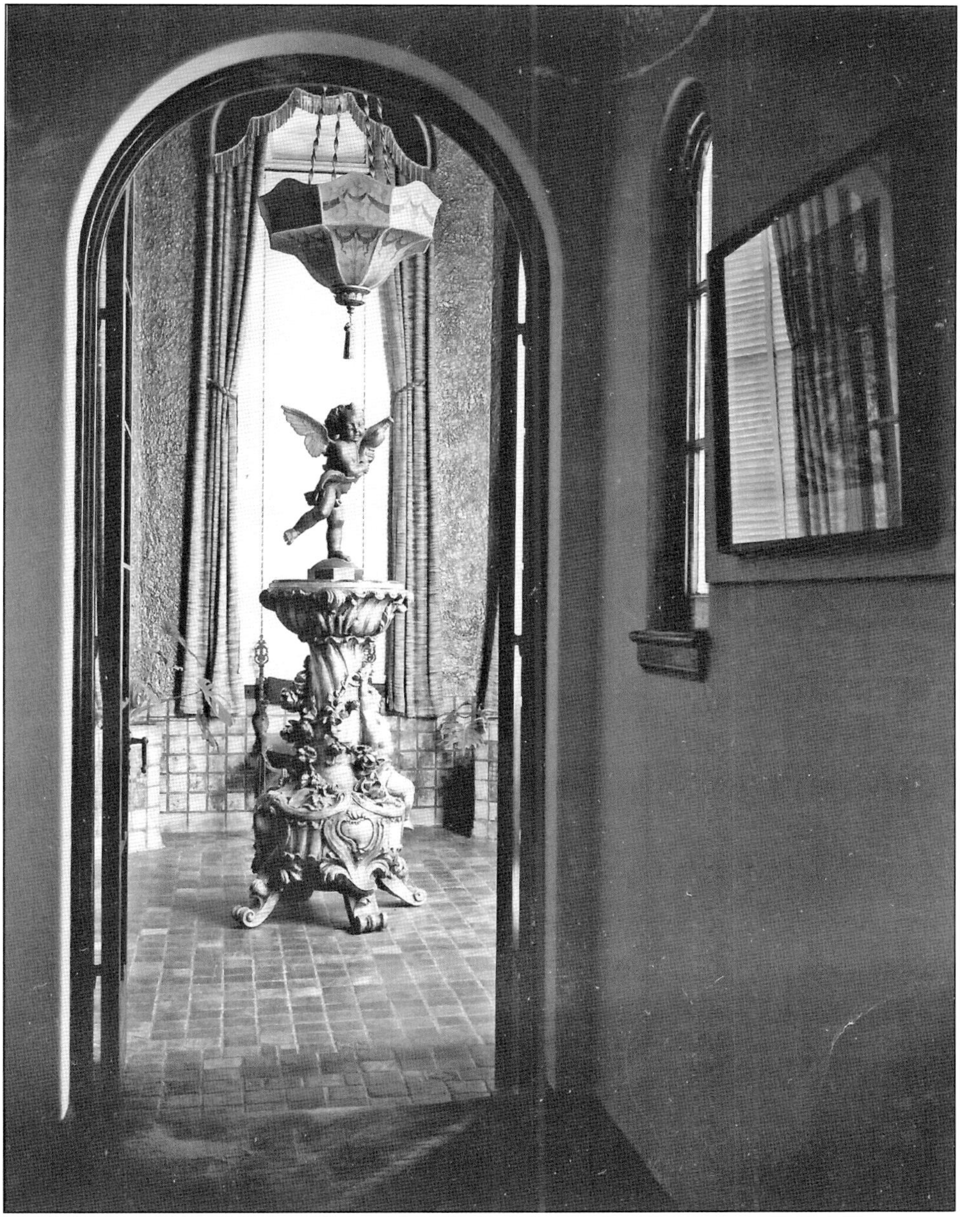

A classical cherub sculpture mounted on an elaborately hand-carved wooden pedestal was the centerpiece of the two-story solarium on the home's east side. Although it ultimately proved an unsuitable environment for many plants, the room was appreciated for its Batchelder tile floor, its planters, and its multipaned windows. The solarium was designed as a room from which to view the entire 80-acre ranch from the hill. Today, the solarium is used as the starting place for house tours, because the original ranch property is still visible for that vantage point. It is also used as a tearoom for guests of the gallery, and occasionally it is used as a bar area for weddings and corporate events. It has been used as a stage for site-specific dance and theater events. In 2011, the solarium doubled as Frankenstein's laboratory in a musical adaptation of Mary Shelley's *Frankenstein*. (Launer.)

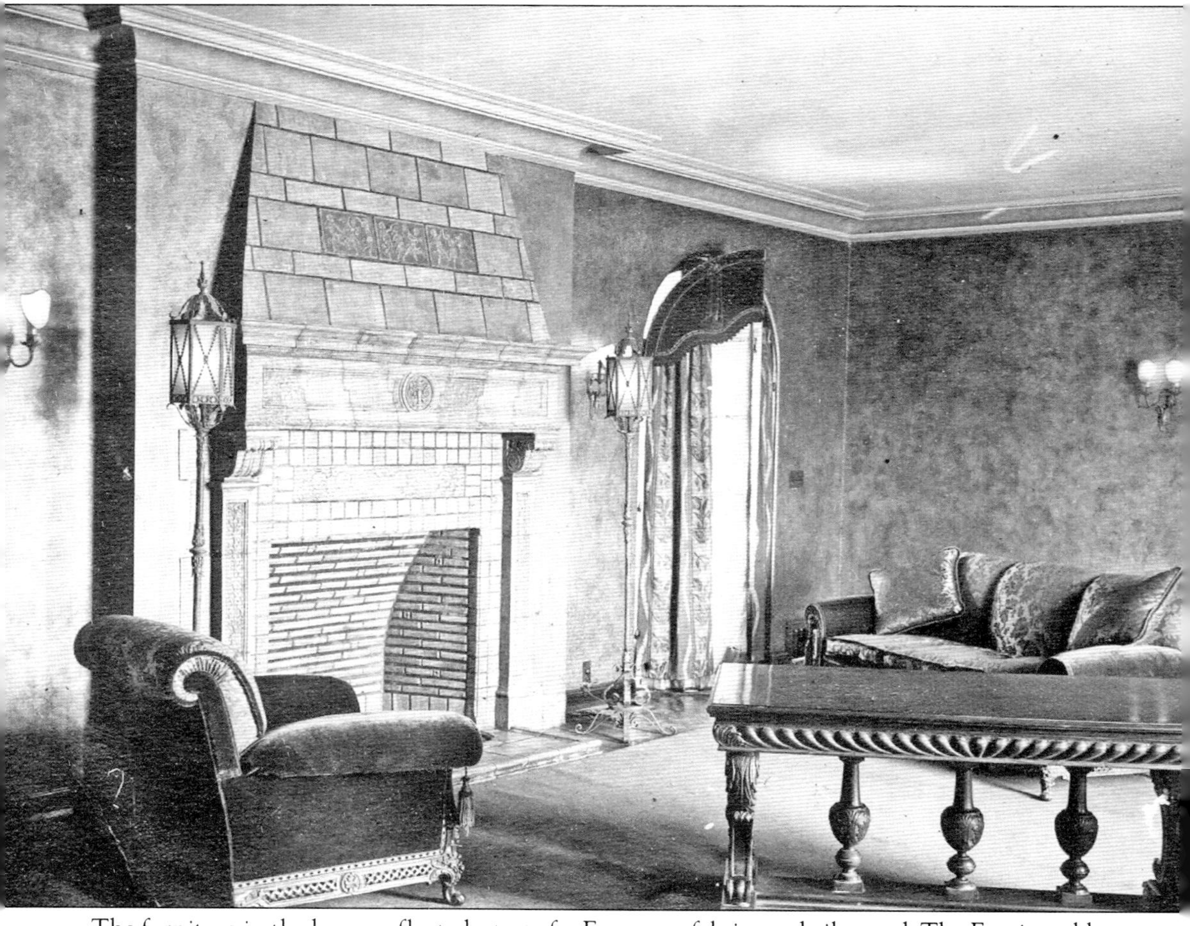

The furniture in the home reflected a taste for European fabrics and gilt wood. The Empire table, wrought iron lighting fixtures, and velvet upholstered couch perfectly suited the thick walls and deeply coved ceilings. Although many contemporaneous homes in the area featured Batchelder tile gas fireplaces, few could match the stunning floor-to-ceiling model that dominates the living room. This room was renovated in the 1980s and made an art gallery to showcase specialty art collections; the original Batchelder fireplace was maintained. The room is surrounded by arched French doors and windows, providing a beautiful frame of light and views (although many are covered now to showcase the art in the gallery). This beautiful carved and gold-gilded wood table serves at the Muckenthaler Center today as a desk for the executive director.

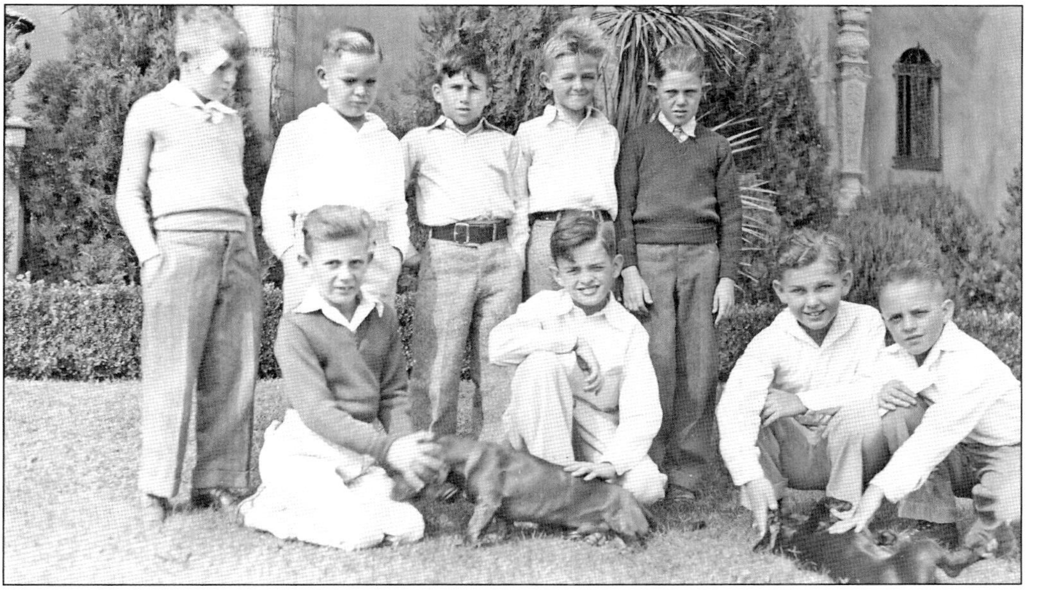

Above, Harold (first row, second from left) and his cousins are pictured in the front yard of the Muckenthaler estate. Below, Albert Muckenthaler, his sons Walter (center) and Martin, and their children relax on the front porch on the canopy-covered glider. Harold had 11 cousins in Anaheim. Today, many of the cousins—including Ron, Tom, and Norbert—attend the Muckenthaler festivities. They enter cars in the Motor Car Festival, attend gallery openings and concerts, and take cultural train tours. Norbert said that they hated coming to visit the Muckenthaler before because they had to be on their best behavior and dress to the nines. All they wanted to do was yell and scream and play. Judging from the pictures, they seemed to have found time to play as well.

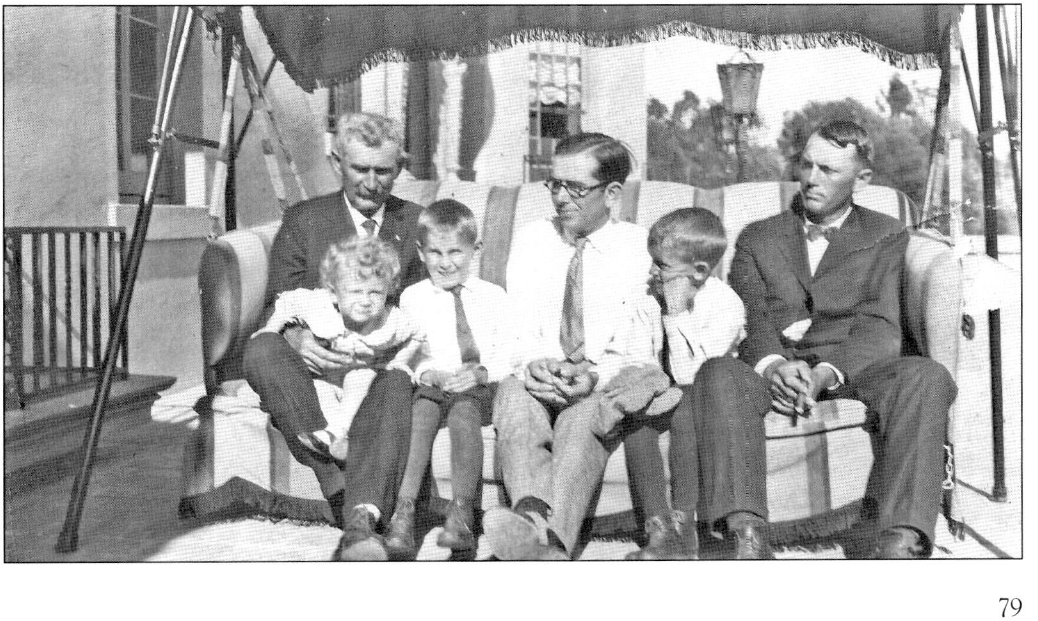

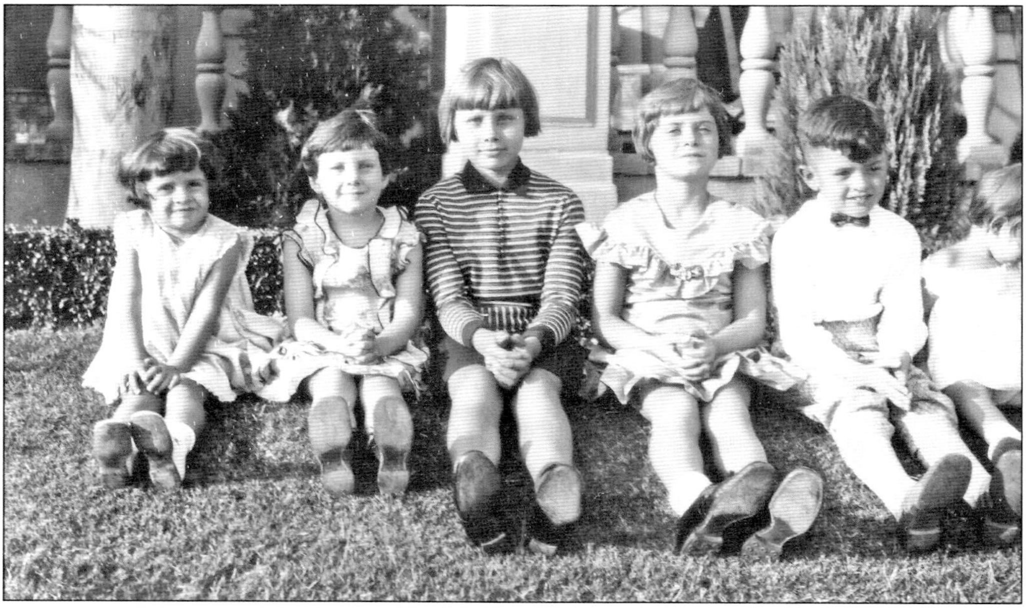

Not all of Martin's 11 children were boys. Harold had to pose with his girl cousins, too. Here, Harold and his cousins sit on the lawn in front of the cast concrete balustrade surrounding the front porch. Below, Augusta Muckenthaler (second from left) visits her son's home. Sitting on the front porch with her are, from left to right, daughters Vi and Gussie, daughter-in-law Adella, and daughter Abbie. There are many home movies that show the cousins and Harold playing at the Muckenthaler home. It was a kid's paradise, with a playground swing, exotic birds, and a pond to swim in. The men would meet in the garage to discuss cars and smoke cigars or go to the basement to play cards. The women would catch up while cooking. It was a great place for a family gathering.

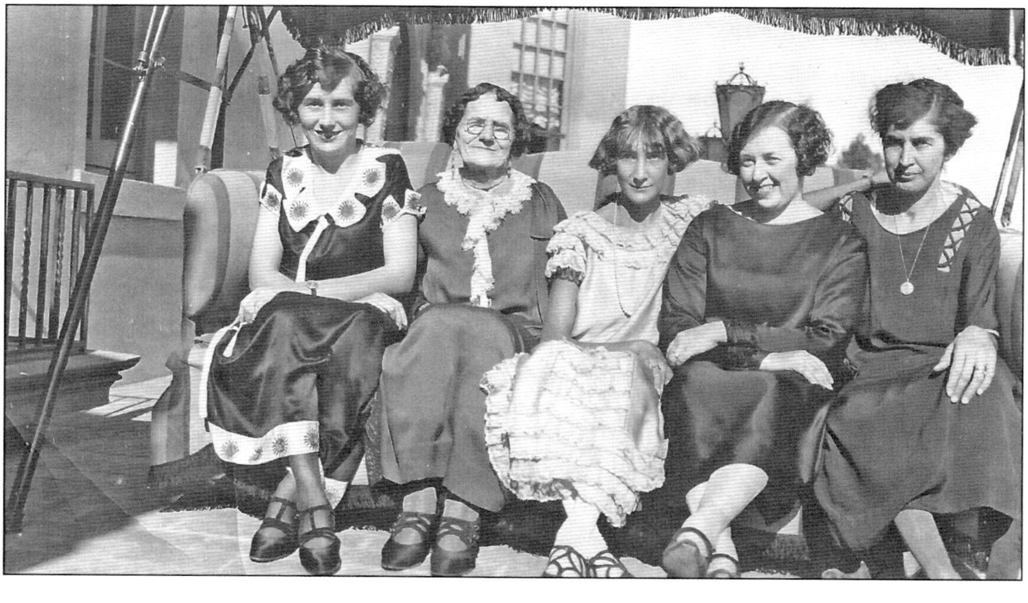

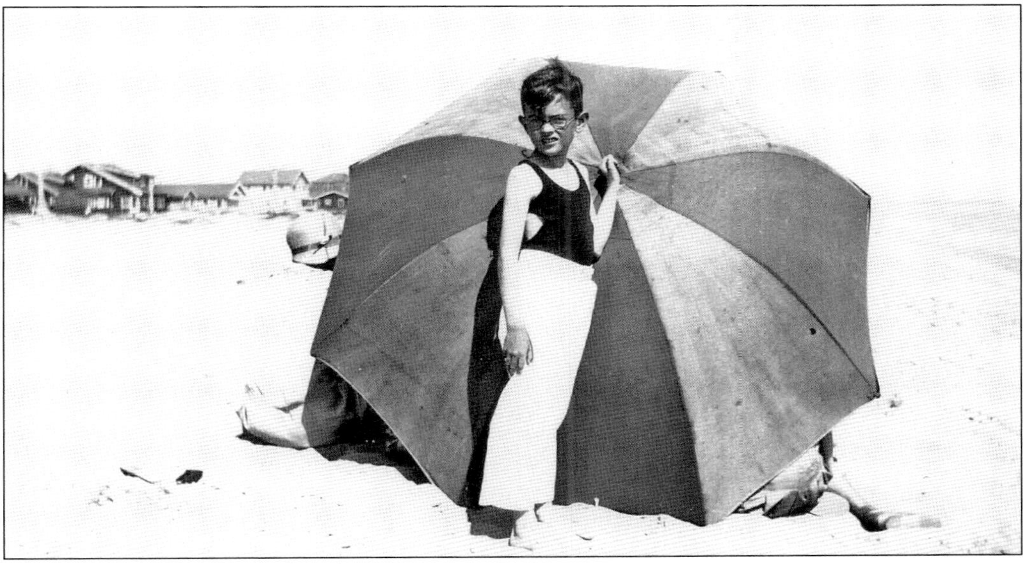

Harold enjoys a day at the beach, no doubt inheriting his father's love of the ocean (above). On Sundays, the family would often head for the shore to enjoy the sea air and play in the surf after attending church. At right, 11-year-old Harold holds one of his dogs on the front porch's cast concrete balustrade. The family loved dogs and had several over the years. It was a great life for both boy and dog, with 80 acres to run through and many more wilderness areas in the hills beyond the estate.

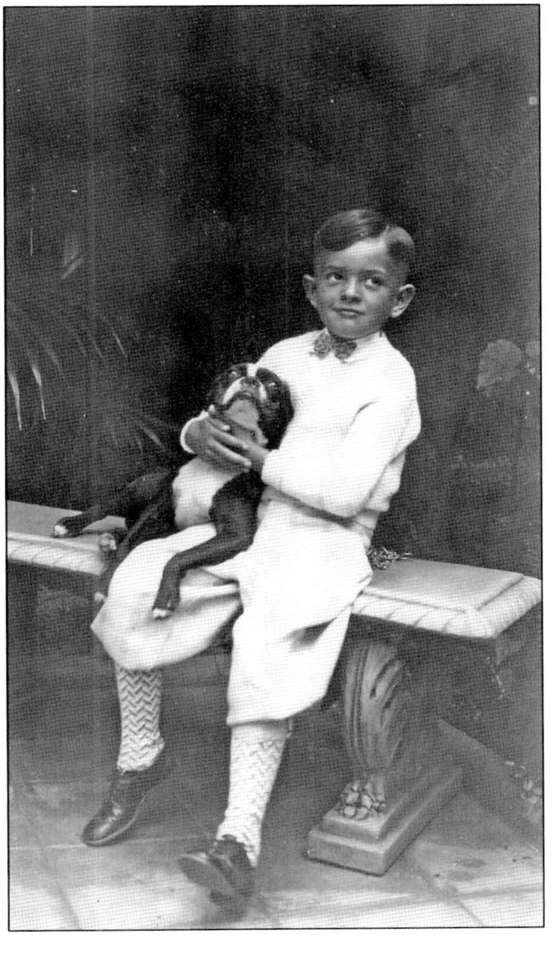

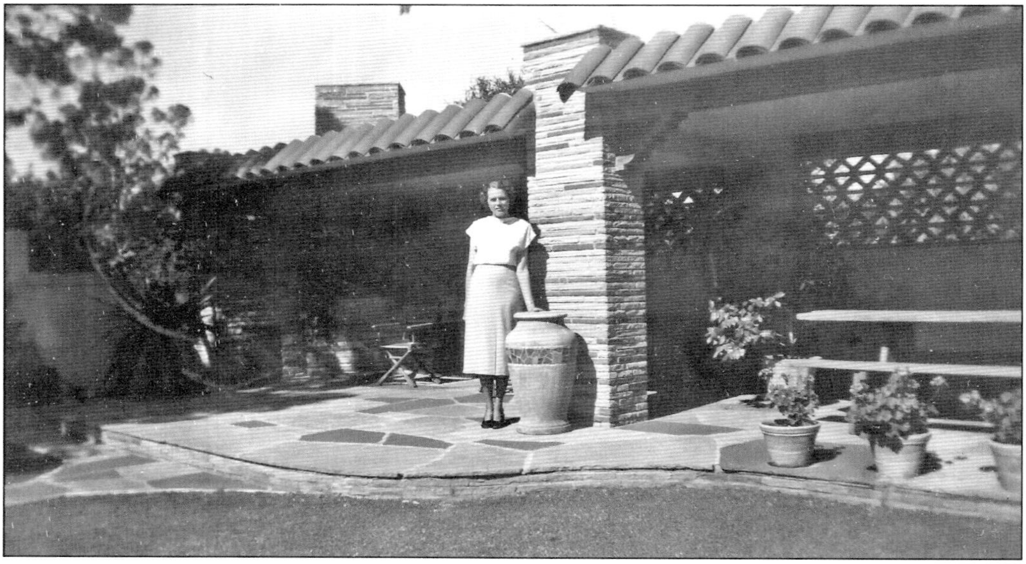

The flagstone barbecue is nestled in an open-air pavilion in the rear courtyard. Vista blocks provided airflow for a pleasant picnic area. Adella's sister Geraldine Chambers leans against one of the many large pots purchased by Walter for the gardens. Below, Walter and Adella are pictured with Geraldine Chambers on the back patio in 1951. This patio today is much as it was then, with part of it closed in for storage and the lawn cemented in. Now called the Center Circle Courtyard, it is home to poetry readings, concerts, and parties under string lights and a moonlit sky on warm summer nights. The tree pictured next to the barbecue has grown into a wonderful twisting marvel, a favored tree of many because of its elegant sculptural qualities.

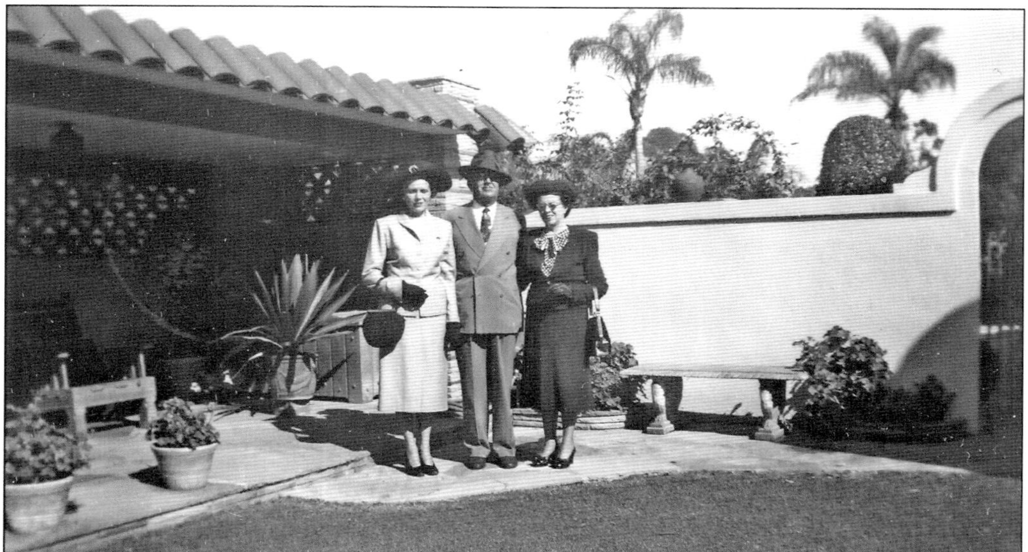

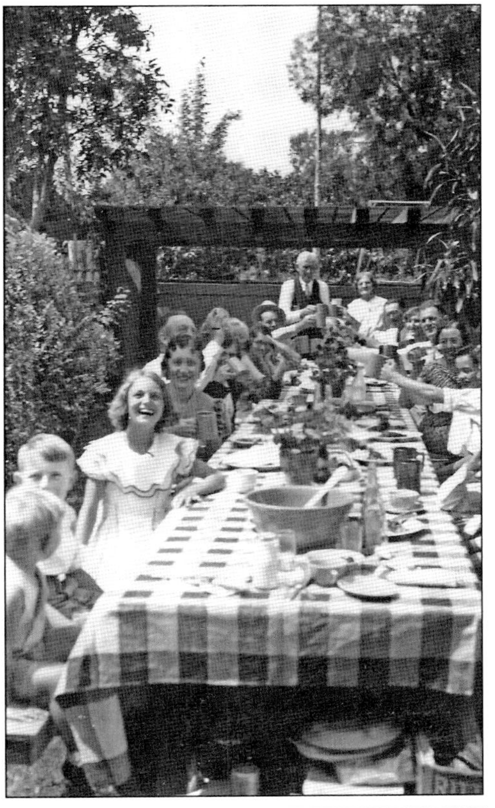

The other side of the barbecue area is a beautiful courtyard under a trellis. Just behind the kitchen, it was an easy place to serve outdoor meals and to hold parties. It was a frequent gathering space for entertaining. On this occasion, Albert Muckenthaler's many children and grandchildren celebrate his 72nd birthday in June 1934. Cousins often speak of regular dinners in the garden with the extended family. This tradition has led the cultural center to start a successful farm dinner series of fundraisers featuring local farm-raised food, wines, and guest chefs. The rear courtyard, with its original wooden trellises, provides partial shade for some of Walter's more exotic tropical plants. The gateway to the west led to the aviaries. The Italian Garden is just over the wall, where the once-tiny palms are showing impressive growth under the California sun.

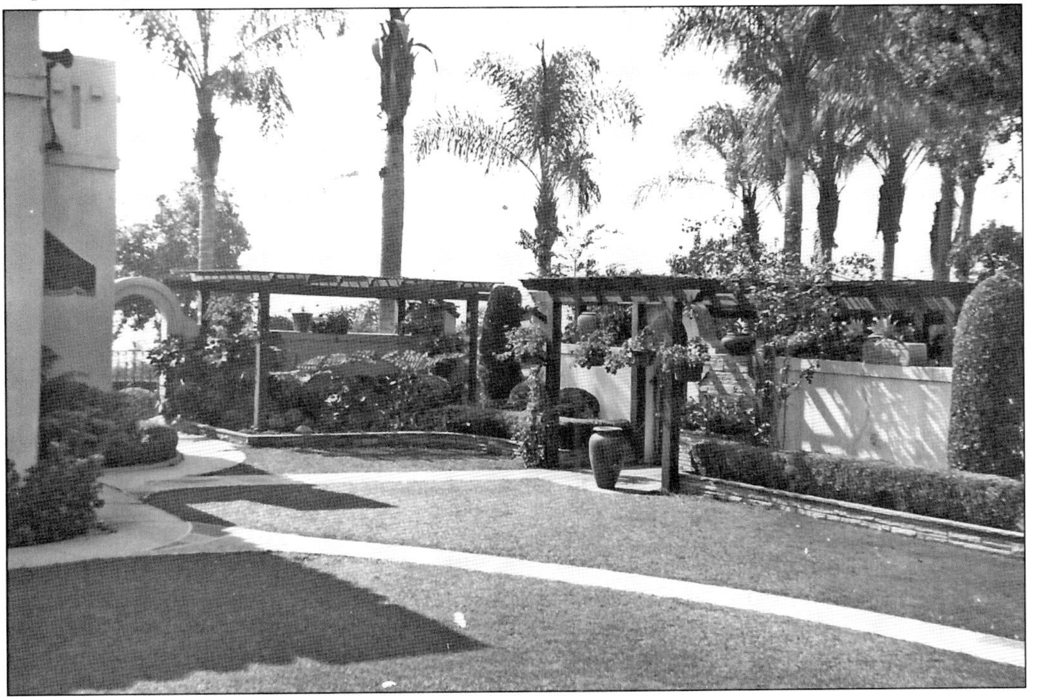

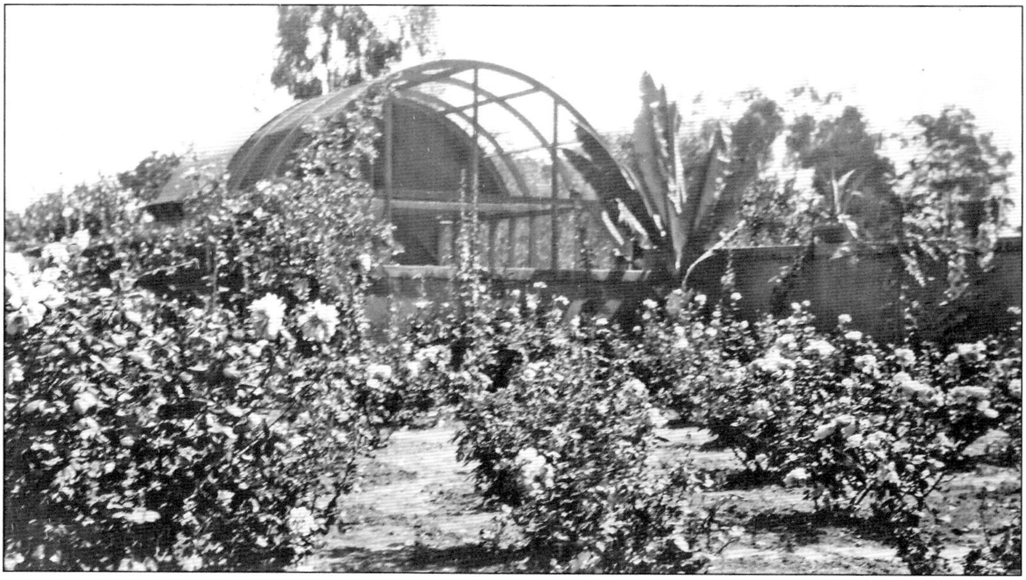

Just north of the house, Walter had a large aviary constructed. Guests were often surprised to see peacocks and other exotic birds wandering freely around the grounds. In front of the aviary is Walter's rose garden. The former site of the aviary and roses is now the Adella Lawn, used primarily for large wedding receptions, lawn sports, and games for children during outdoor festivals. Below, Albert and Augusta visit their son Walter's home along with Walter's brothers and sisters. From left to right are Martin, Augusta "Gussie," Albert, Augusta, Lawrence, Viola, and Walter. In the background is the aviary roof and gardens. (Above, Launer.)

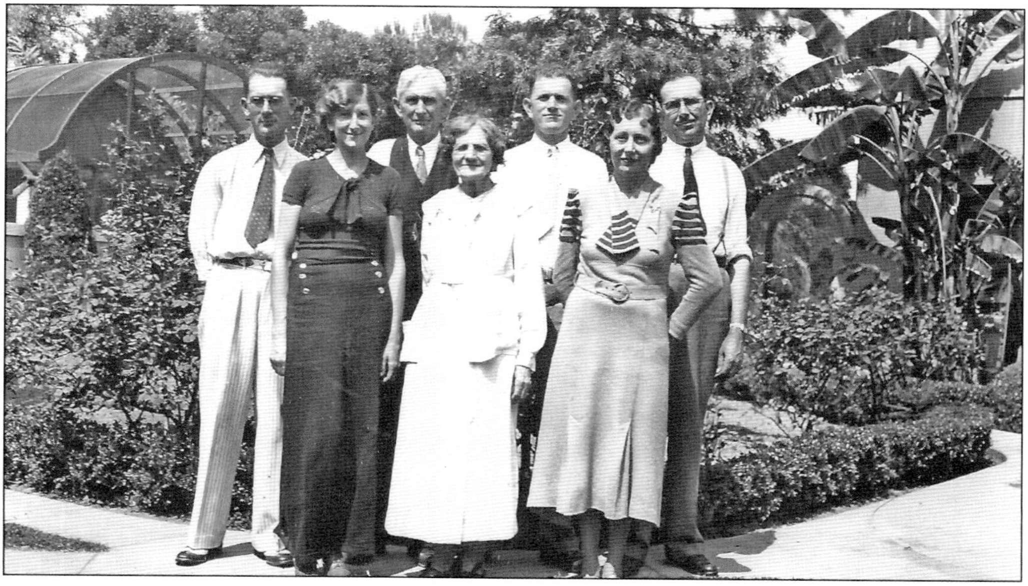

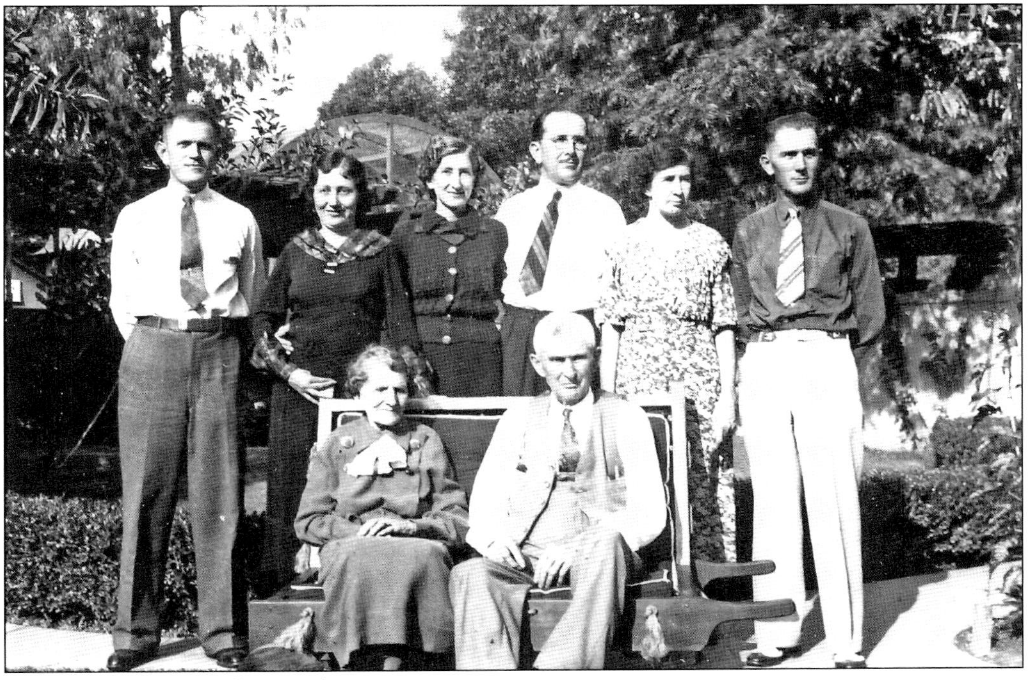

Pictured above are Albert and Augusta Muckenthaler (seated) with their children, from left to right, Lawrence, Viola, Augusta (Aussie), Walter, Abbie, and Martin. At right, Adella stands with the Kraemer women and Harold on the front lawn. The massive wooden door behind them was installed so skillfully that it opened and closed almost without effort. The south-facing main entrance was used by the family much less frequently than the west side door near the circular driveway. In all photographs, the family wears an amazing wardrobe of very fashionable clothes. All three of the family had their own walk-in closet and dressing area, a great luxury in houses of the time. The bedroom areas are now offices. The closets are so big that they are now used as offices for interns.

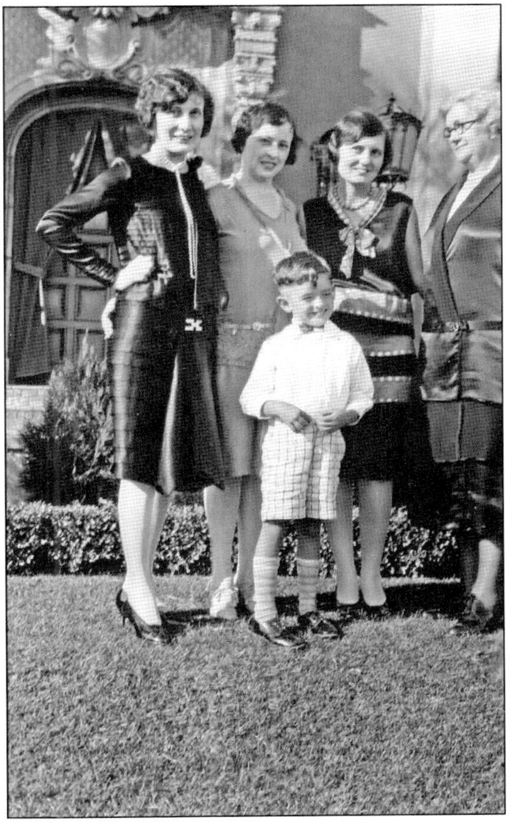

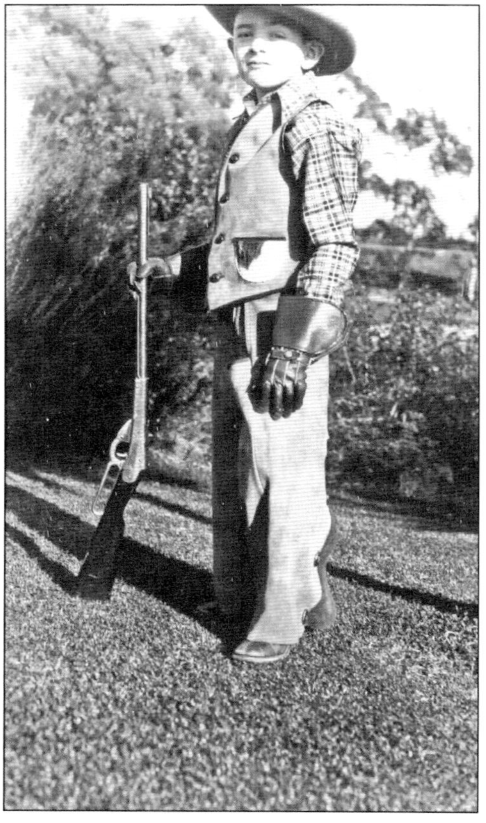

A young Harold dresses in cowboy attire as "a real man of the West." The undeveloped orchards and ranchlands of Fullerton doubled easily for the Wild West in his imagination during the 1920s. Most children of the era in United States grew up on Westerns and cowboy heroes like Tom Mix and Gary Cooper. But Harold actually lived the old West in his surroundings, just a few miles from where these films were shot. At a time when there was no television or video games, an only child had to be very imaginative to entertain himself. Harold honed an imagination that would serve him well his whole life.

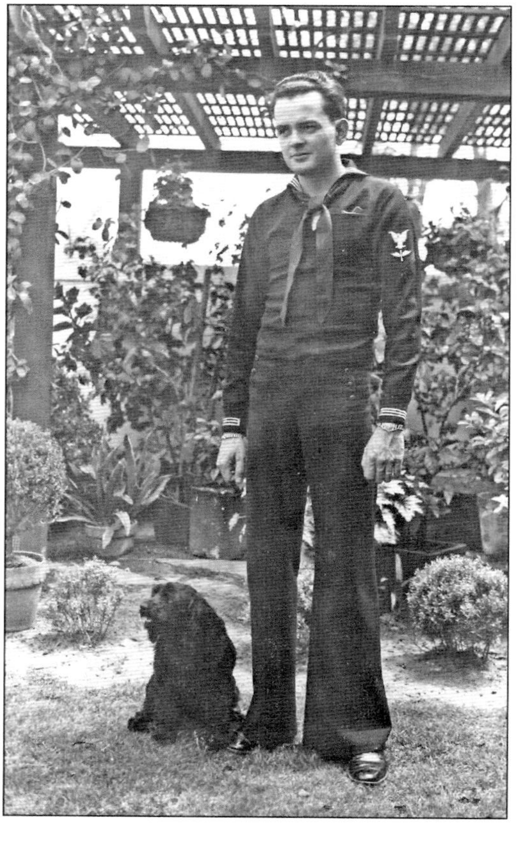

Harold shows off his World War II Navy uniform and one of his dogs on the rear patio while home on leave. His father Walter's naval service had been cut short by the discovery of a heart murmur. Walter was proud to see his only son enlist in the US Navy and serve his country in World War II.

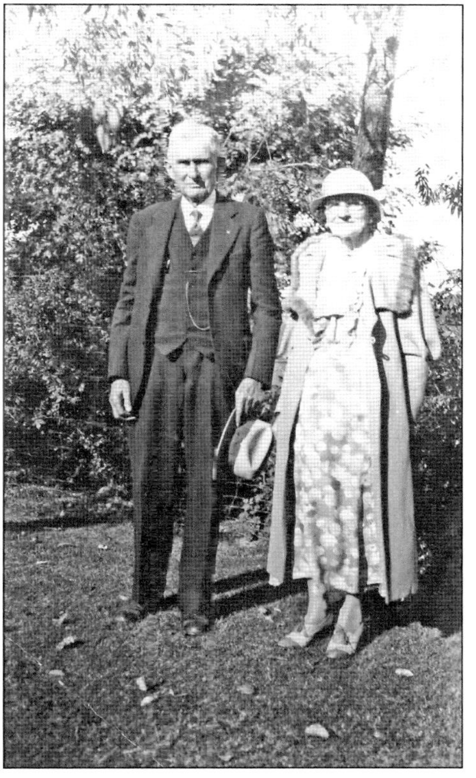

Albert and Augusta Muckenthaler are pictured here in their later years. They dared to sell most of what they owned in Kansas and move to Anaheim on the strength of their industriousness and vision for a better life in California. Decades later, they would visit the wondrous estate of their eldest son, Walter, who forged his own vision of the California dream atop a hill in Fullerton. Many of their grandchild and great-grandchildren visit the Muckenthaler Cultural Center and remain supporters of the cultural legacy their family so generously contributed.

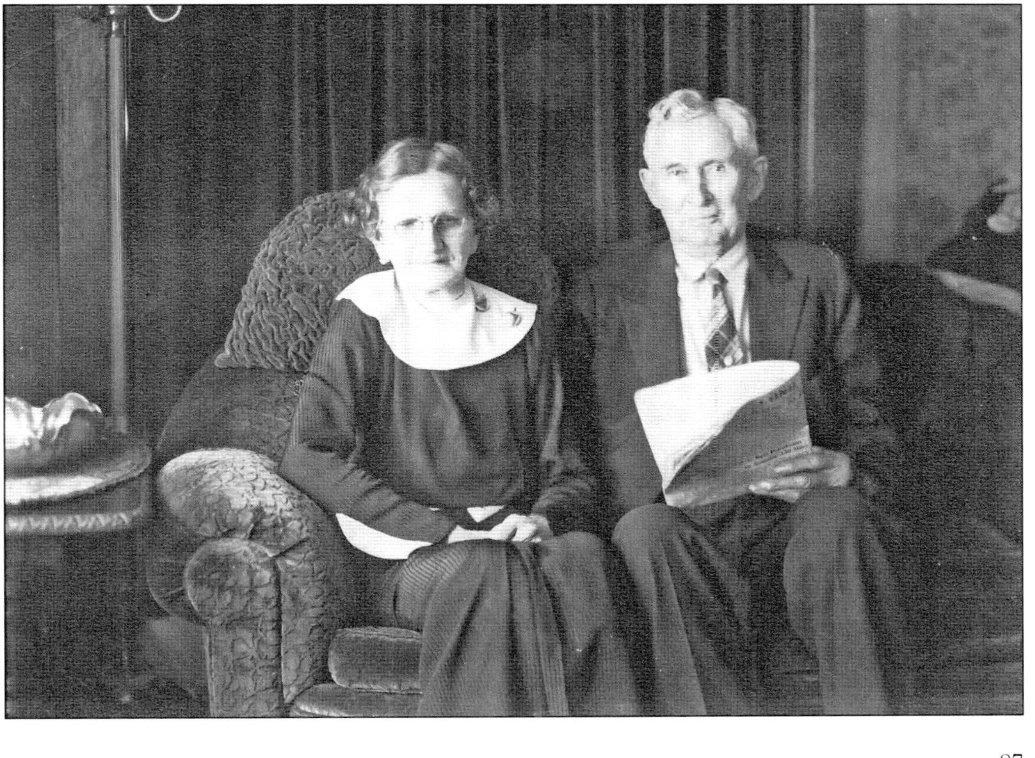

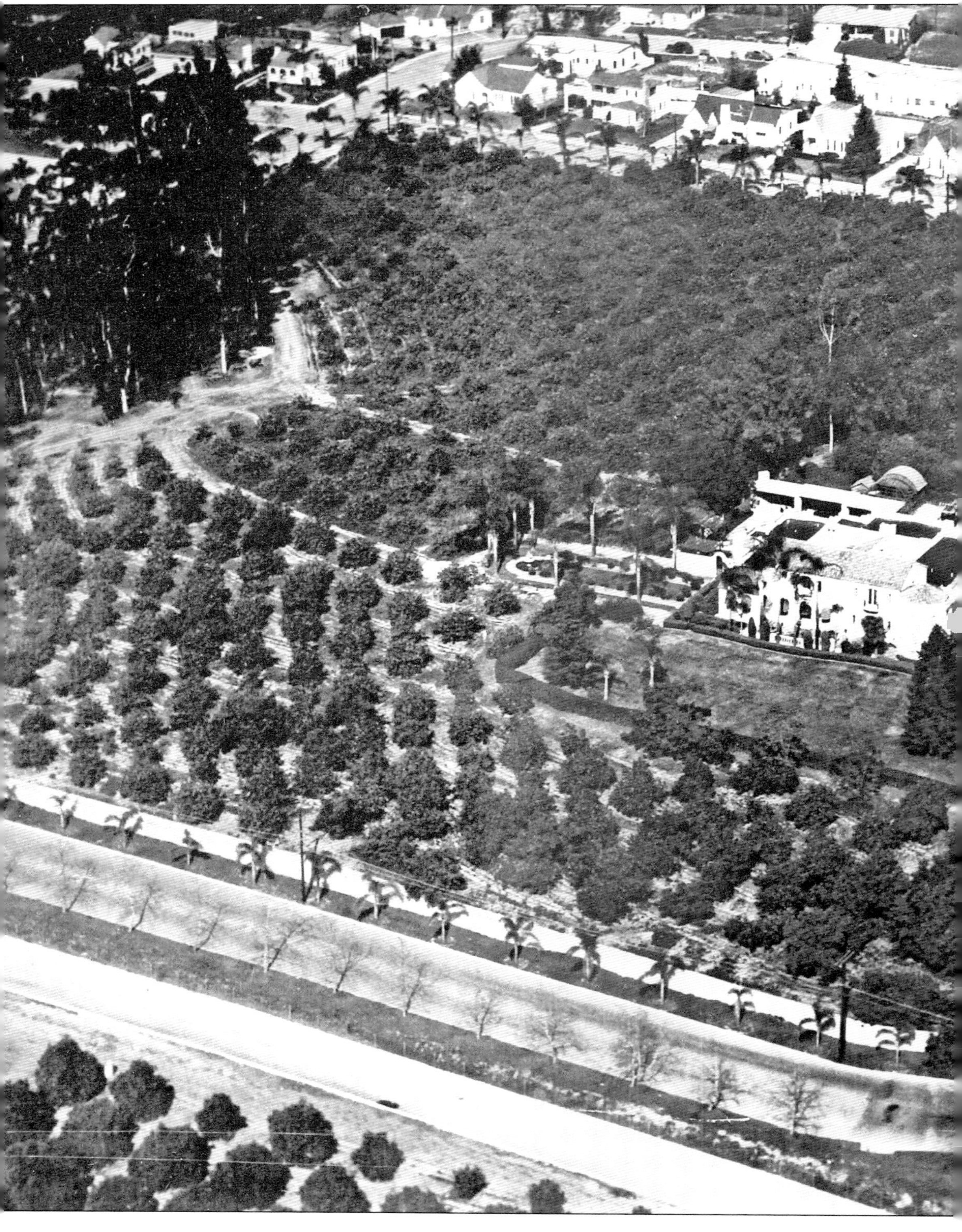

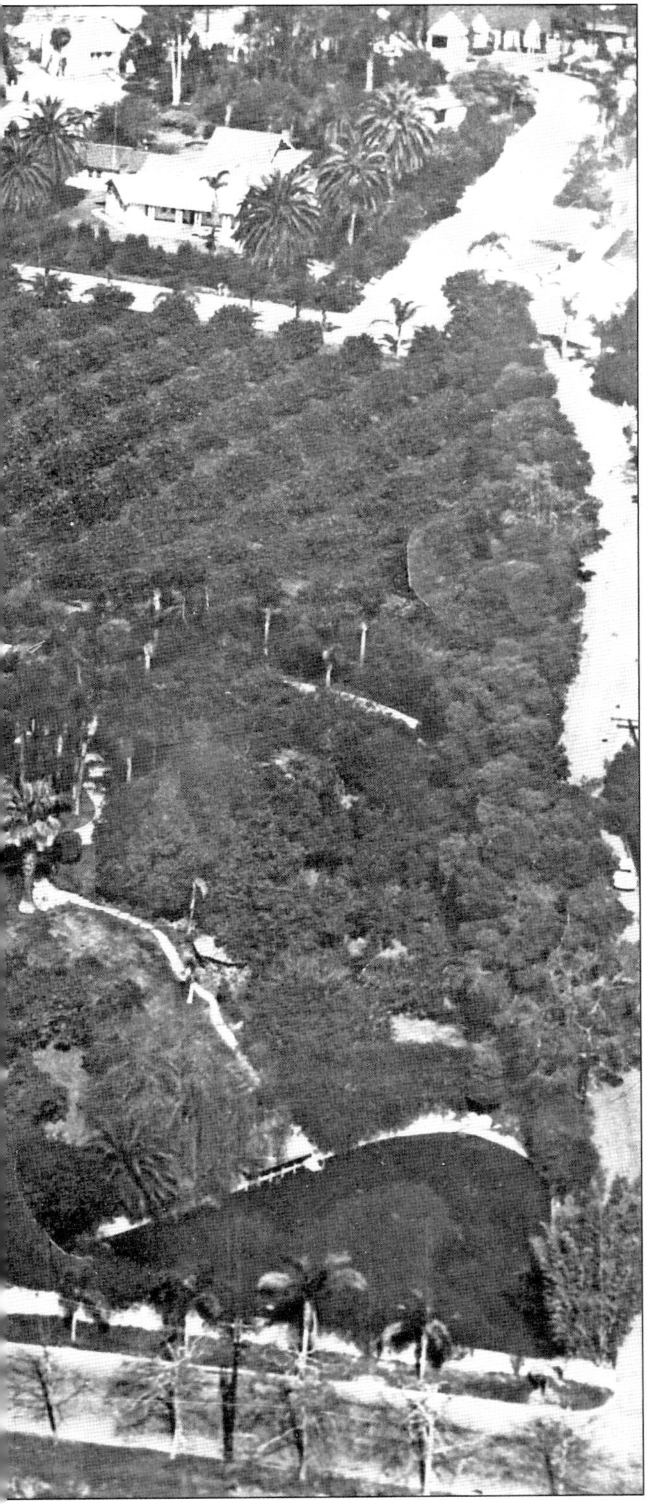

The 8.5-acre estate north of Malvern Avenue, seen from the air in 1931, includes a clear view of the stream leading to the reservoir in the southeast corner of the property. A small house located just to the northeast belonged to the manager of the orchards, some of which covered what is now a parking lot to the north and a sweeping lawn to the south. Just to the south were the 80 acres of orchards south of Malvern Avenue (not pictured), subsequently developed as a housing tract. The land pictured is still the Muckenthaler Center property line. The grove trees are gone and replaced by sweeping lawns for a community park, but the eucalyptus trees that border the property remain, echoing a time when the grove was here. (Launer.)

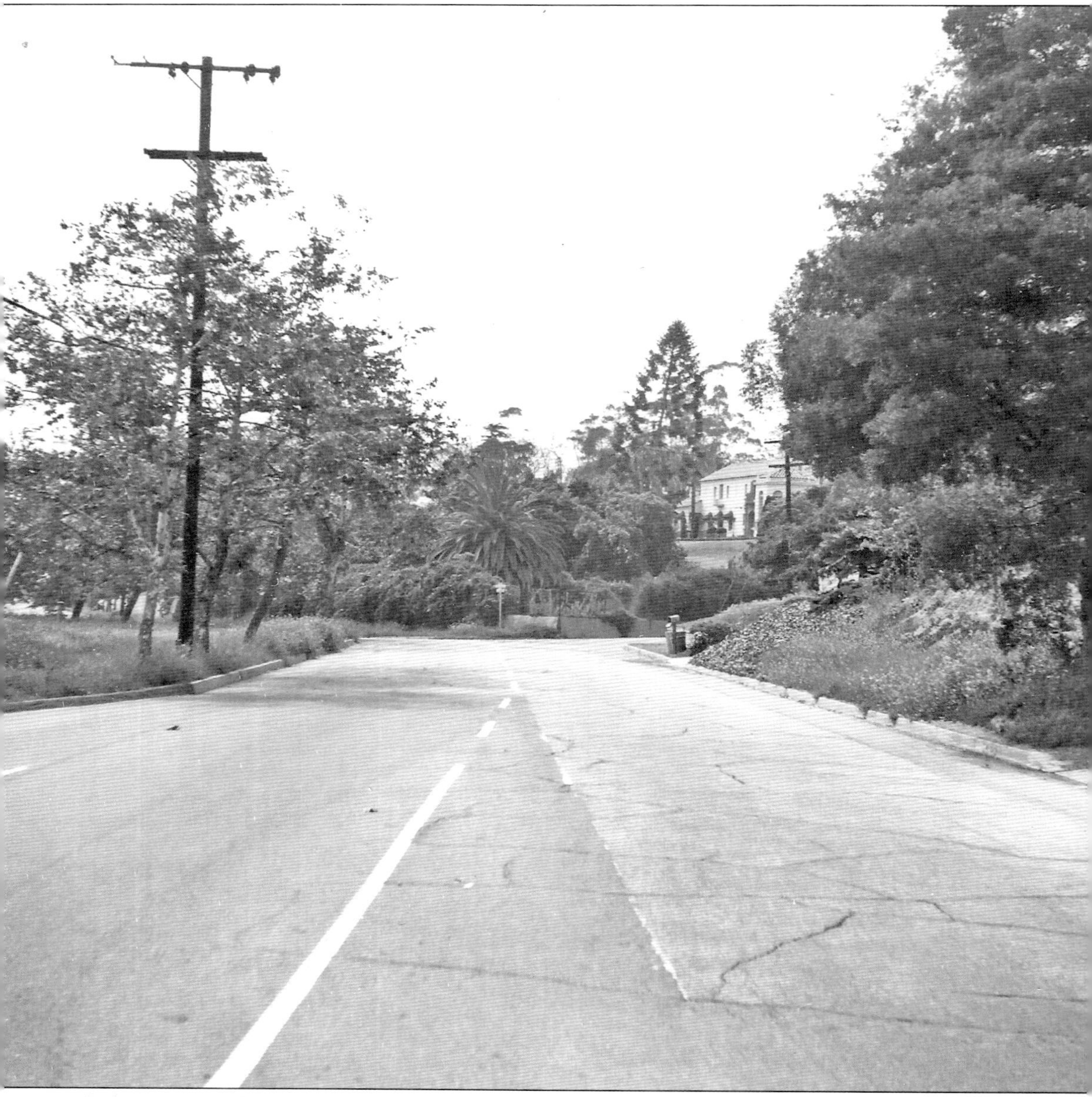

Before it was realigned to meet Chapman Avenue, Malvern Avenue led directly to the house from the northeast. Then a two-lane road, it was eventually widened to accommodate more automobile traffic as Fullerton grew. The neighborhood to the east and west of the ranch at the time contained other ranches. To the north was a small neighborhood of homes that housed many of the steady workers for the ranches. These homes are still along Rose Drive. Today, this section of Malvern Avenue is no longer a quiet, peaceful road; it is a busy thoroughfare bringing people to and from Buena Park and Amerige Heights to the west and into downtown Fullerton and California State University–Fullerton to the east. It also is a major connection to Interstate 5. (Launer.)

Five

Civic Life and Travel

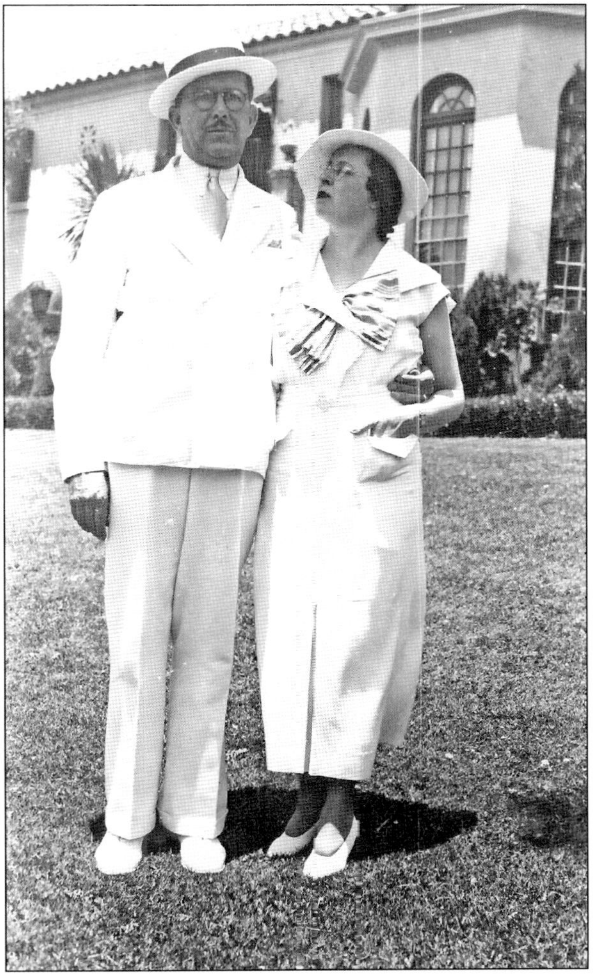

Walter and Adella posed for a portrait while dressed in tropical resort attire before embarking on a voyage to Hawaii. Walter purchased his suits from Stein & Strauss Company in Fullerton. Walter was a perfectionist and loved beautiful things, including clothes. He could work in the trenches, but when he dressed for occasions, he wanted do it right.

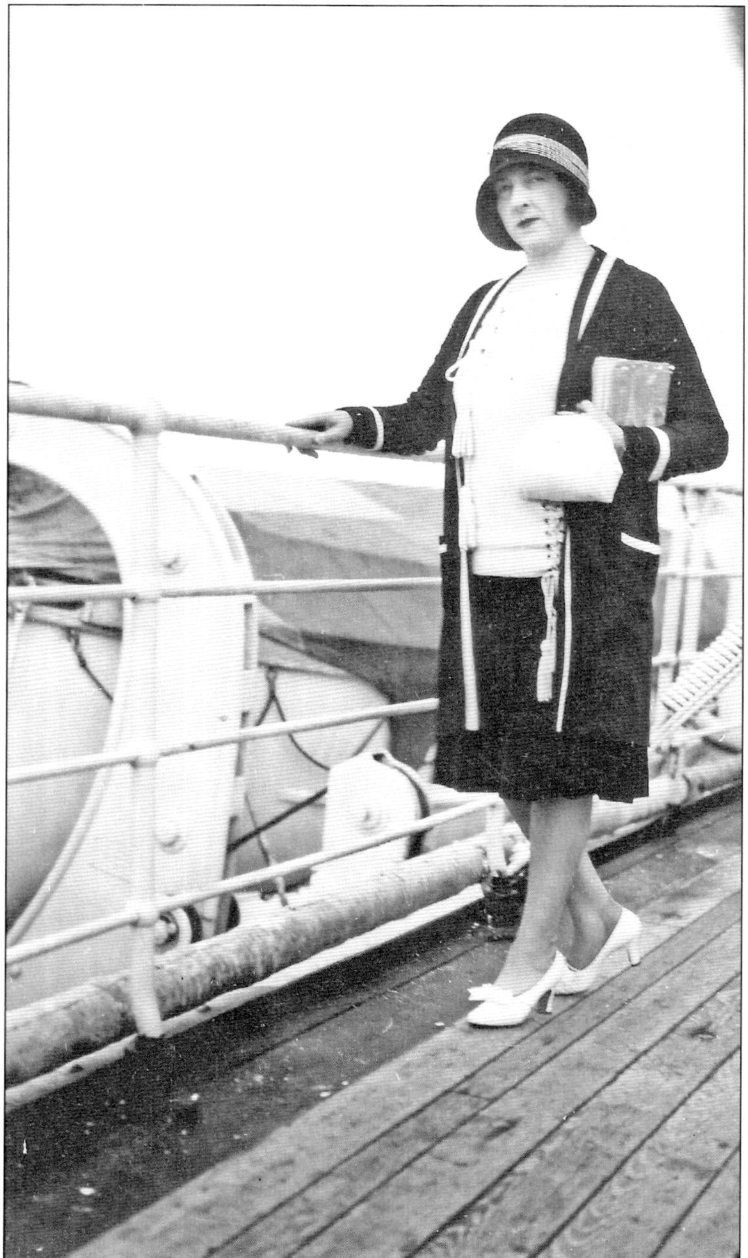

The Muckenthalers returned to the continental United States (Adella is pictured) by ship just three weeks before the stock market crash of 1929. Although their finances were certainly affected, they were better off than the many who lost everything in the worst economic depression of the 20th century. The oil and film industries helped California to fare better than many states. Citrus and other western agriculture escaped the catastrophic Dust Bowl that devastated the Midwest. People from Oklahoma and its neighboring states poured into California to look for work in the fields and orchards. The Muckenthalers weathered the Depression quite well and helped those in need.

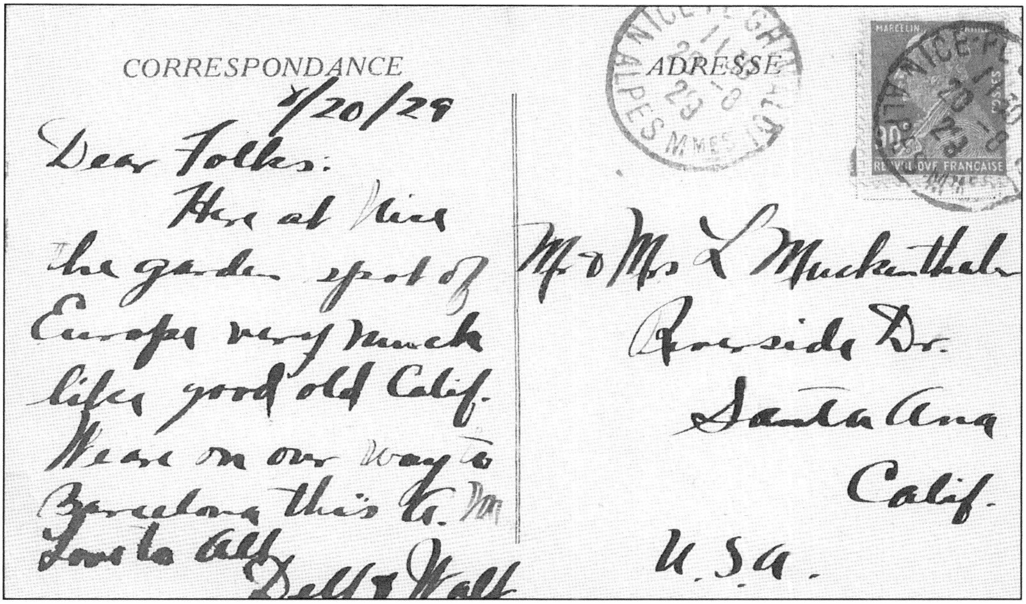

In 1929, the Muckenthalers toured Europe, visiting cities all over the continent. On their travels, they looked for fine furniture for their home. A postcard from Naples, sent in August 1929 to Walter's younger brother Lawrence and his wife, Nellie, in Santa Ana reads, "Dear Folks: Here at Nice, the garden spot of Europe very much like good old Calif. We are on our way to Barcelona this a.m. Love to all. Walt & Dell." In the second postcard, Walter writes to Lawrence and Nellie from Manhattan. "This is just a wonderful place," he wrote. "The Great White Way is a thrilling scene at mid-night. Tomorrow will go shopping."

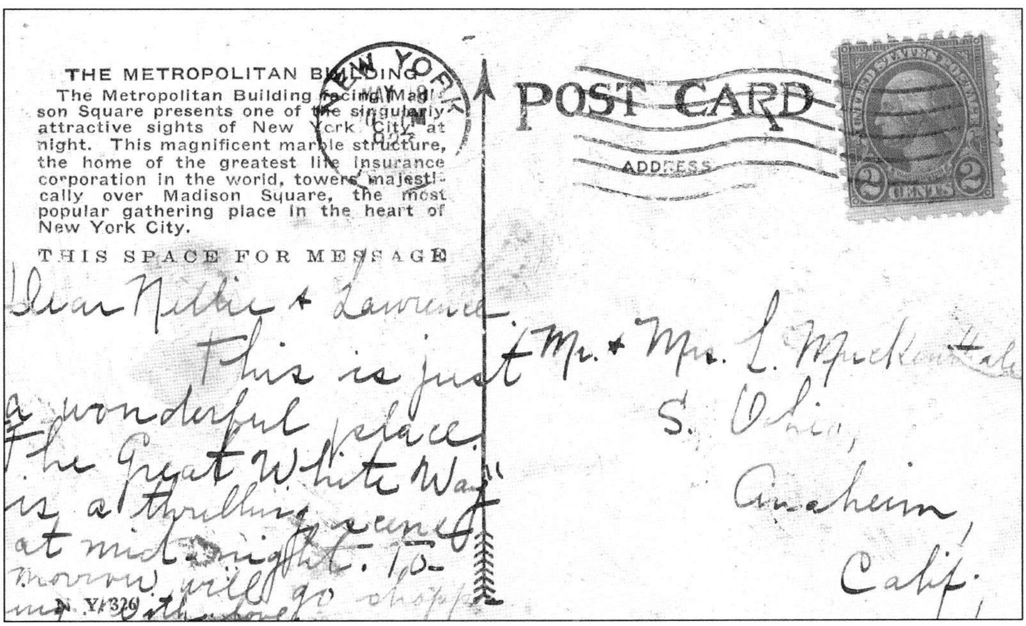

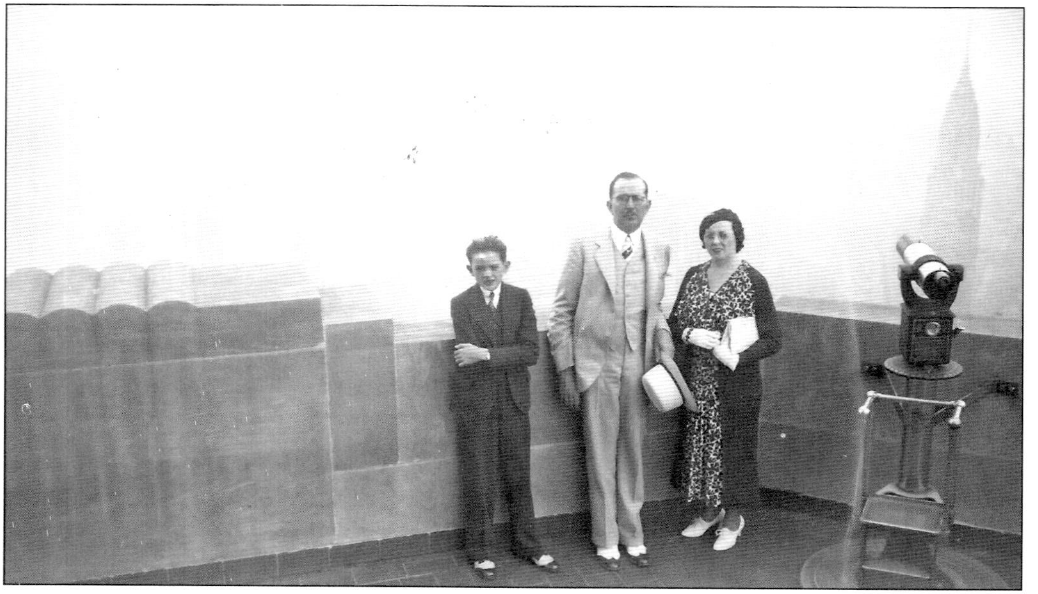

The family visited New York, New York, and stopped to take in the view from the observation deck on the 86th floor of the recently built Empire State Building (above). In 1936, the family sailed again for the Hawaiian Islands. A postcard showed their Honolulu hotel marked with an X. In the 1930s, there were only two hotels in Waikiki—the Royal Hawaiian and the Moana. The Muckenthalers stayed at the Moana, which is the oldest hotel in the area. The back of the postcard reads, "Hello Folks, Had a most wonderful trip over. Wasn't sick a day. Landing was most beautiful. It's a long story, so will tell you when we get back. I'm just thrilled about everything. Dell, Walt & Harold."

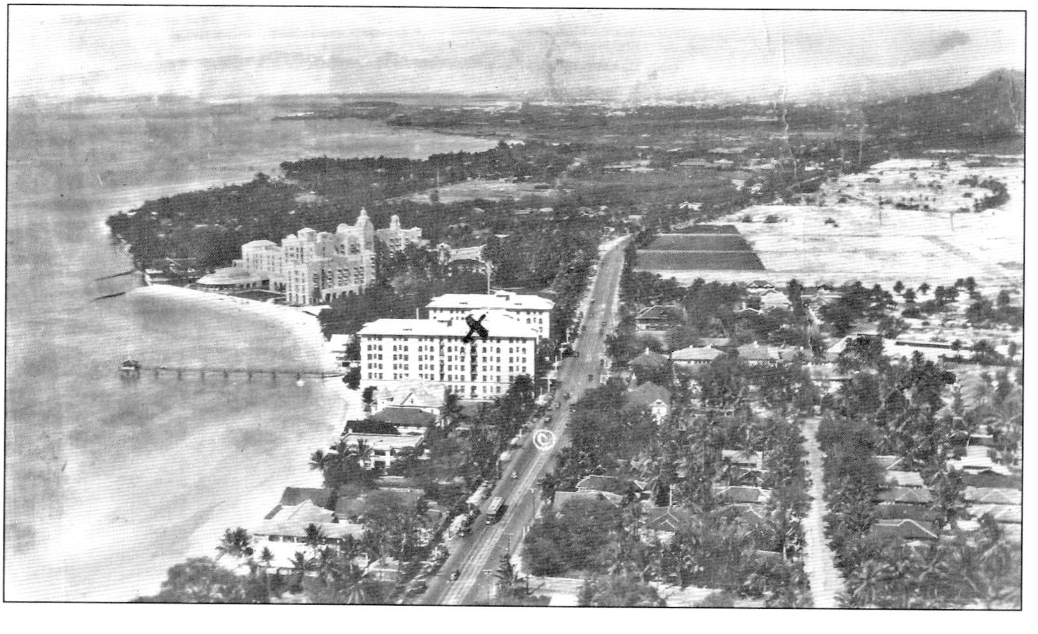

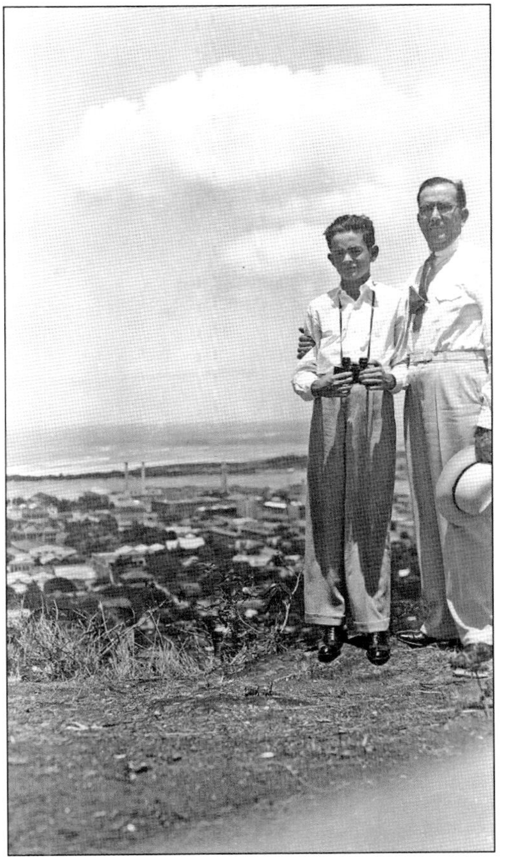

Harold and Walter enjoy the view of the ocean from the cliffs above Honolulu. The next time Harold would see Hawaii, it would be as a sailor coming into Pearl Harbor during World War II. He was happy to have a chance to see it first with his family during peacetime. They loved to spend time in the outdoors, taking full advantage of both the Sierra Nevada and more local getaways like Big Bear (bottom). They loved the beach, the mountains, and the desert. Walter was happiest when he was reveling in nature.

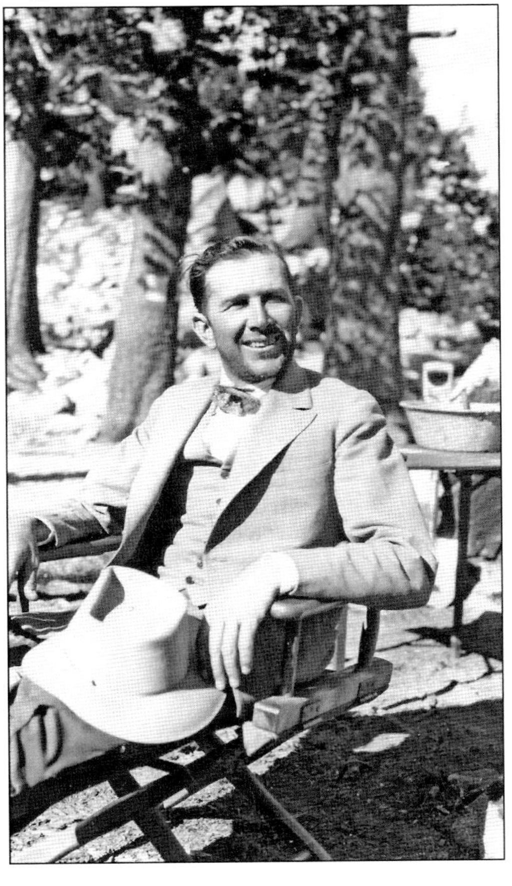

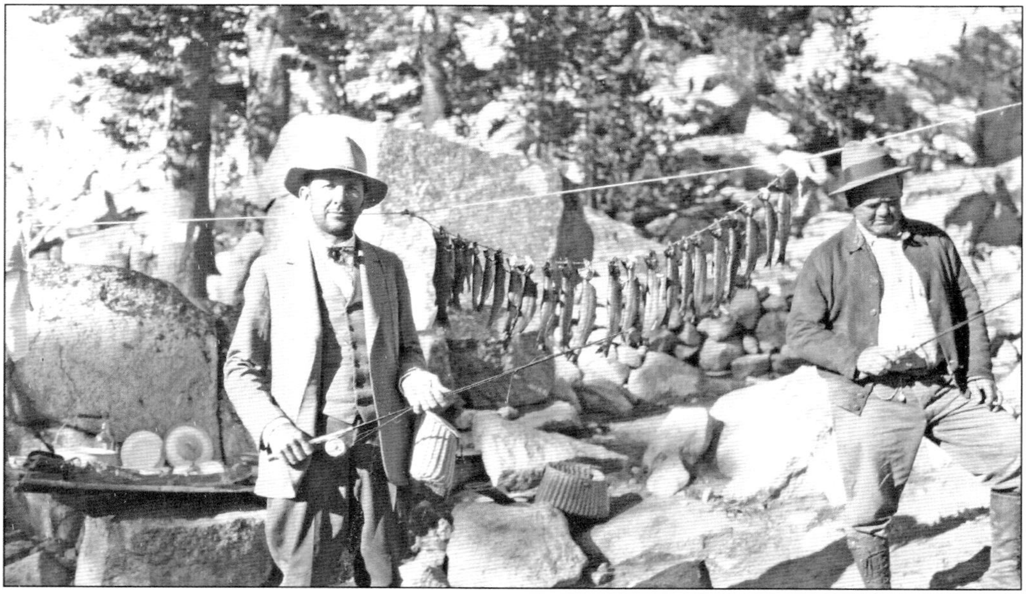

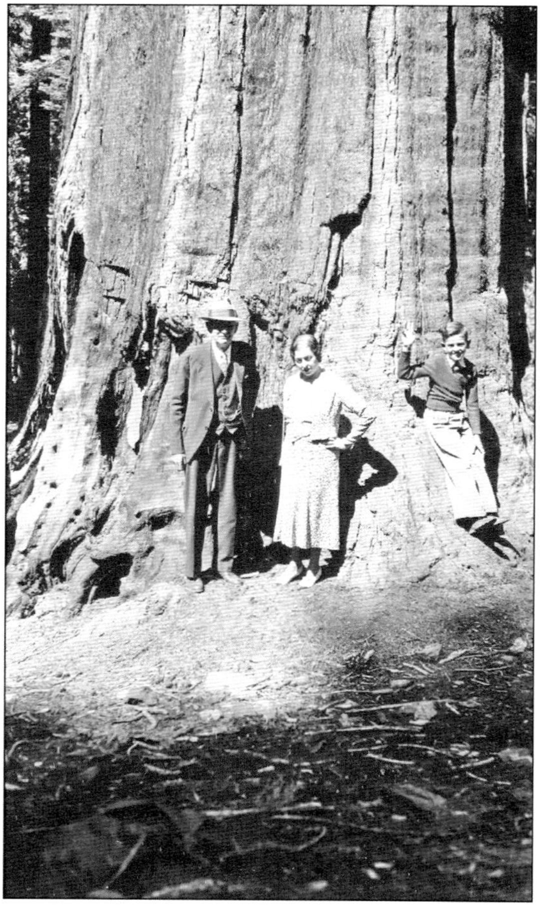

Walter enjoys a successful day of fishing, all the time wearing a three-piece suit and bow tie. He had a suit for everything, and this was his fishing suit. The family poses near a giant sequoia tree in the early 1930s at Sequoia National Park. Harold was more fortunate than most children of the time to be able to travel so extensively and see the world. It would help him later in life to have a worldview of things.

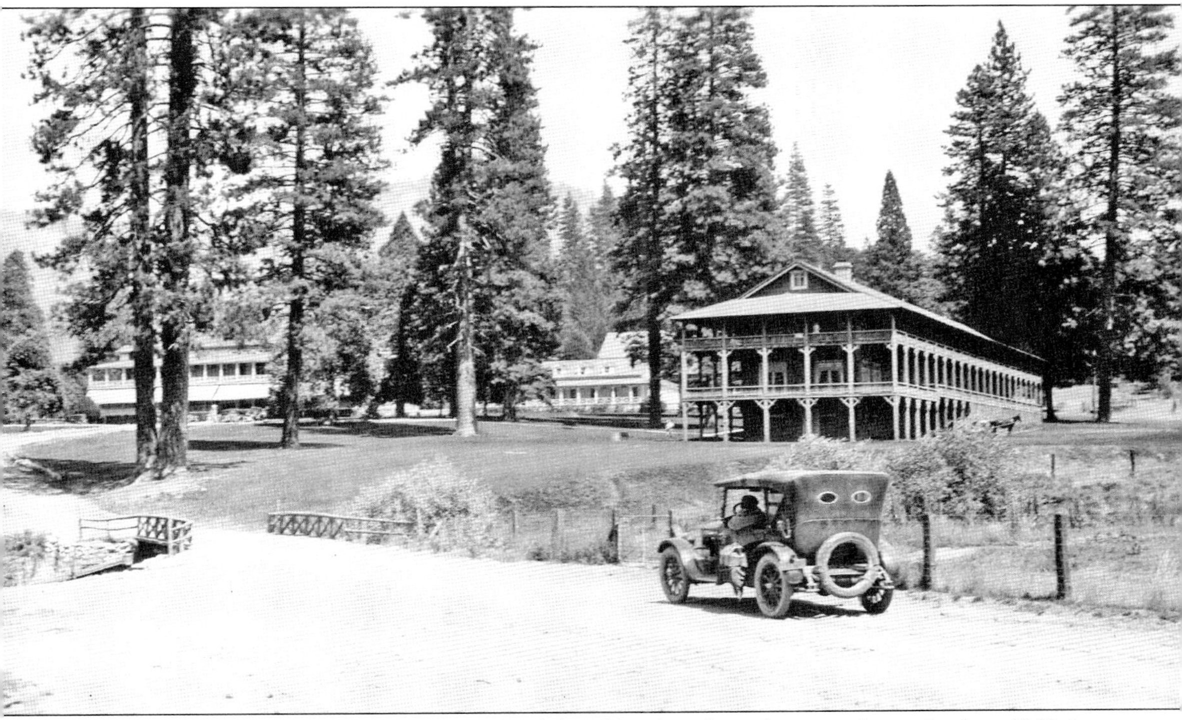

Wawona in Yosemite National Park is one of the oldest hotels in the area, dating back to 1860. In 1932, Wawona—which means "big tree" in the native language—was annexed to the national park. When the Muckenthalers visited, Wawona was run by the park service and Curry Company, which also ran Camp Curry with lower-end tents and rooms for rent. There were nightly performances and the famous Firefall, a summertime ritual (until 1968) in which embers were dropped a height of roughly 3,000 feet from the top of Glacier Point in Yosemite National Park down to the valley below, looking from a distance like a glowing water fall. Camp Curry also featured a dance pavilion, pool hall, soda fountain, nightly movies, swimming pool, gas station, service garage, and ice-skating rink.

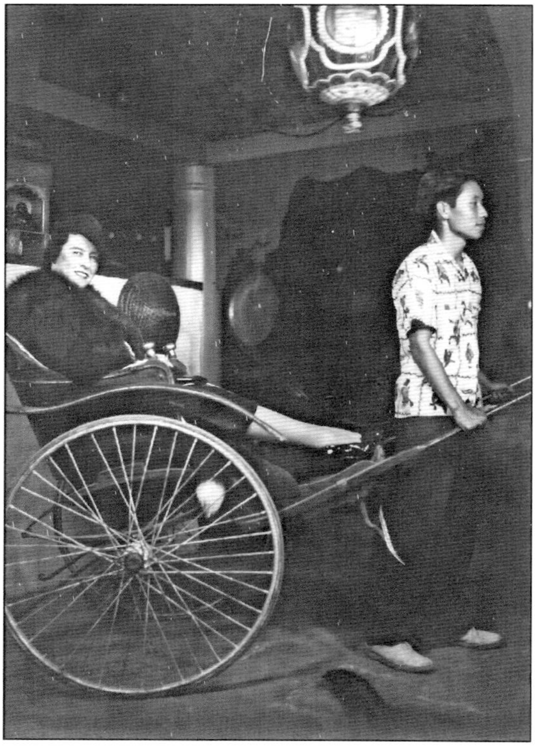

At left, Adella sits in a rickshaw. It's not clear whether this is from a trip Asia or in Los Angeles' Chinatown, which used rickshaws for tourists. A valuable purchase rides next to her. Walter may have loved the desert even more than he loved the beach (below). Family members recall that every time they went on short trips it was always to the desert, usually Palm Springs. The family says Walter liked to go to Palm Springs as often as he could and enjoyed hiking in the desert.

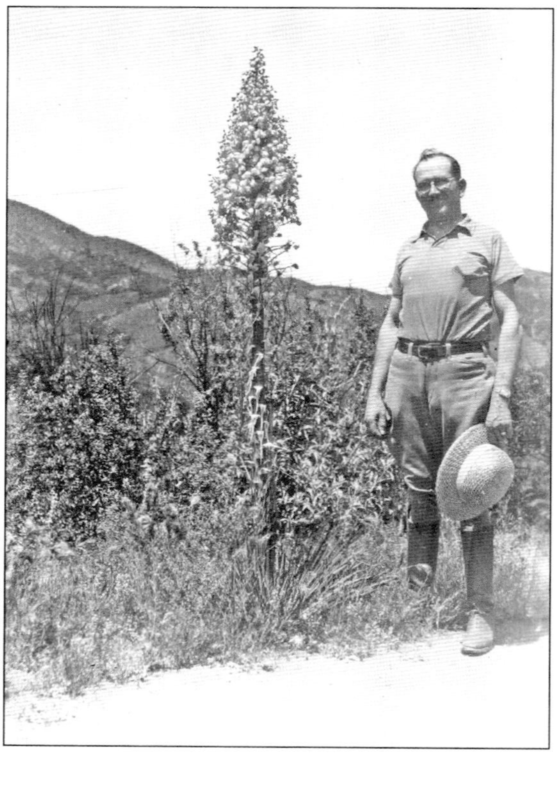

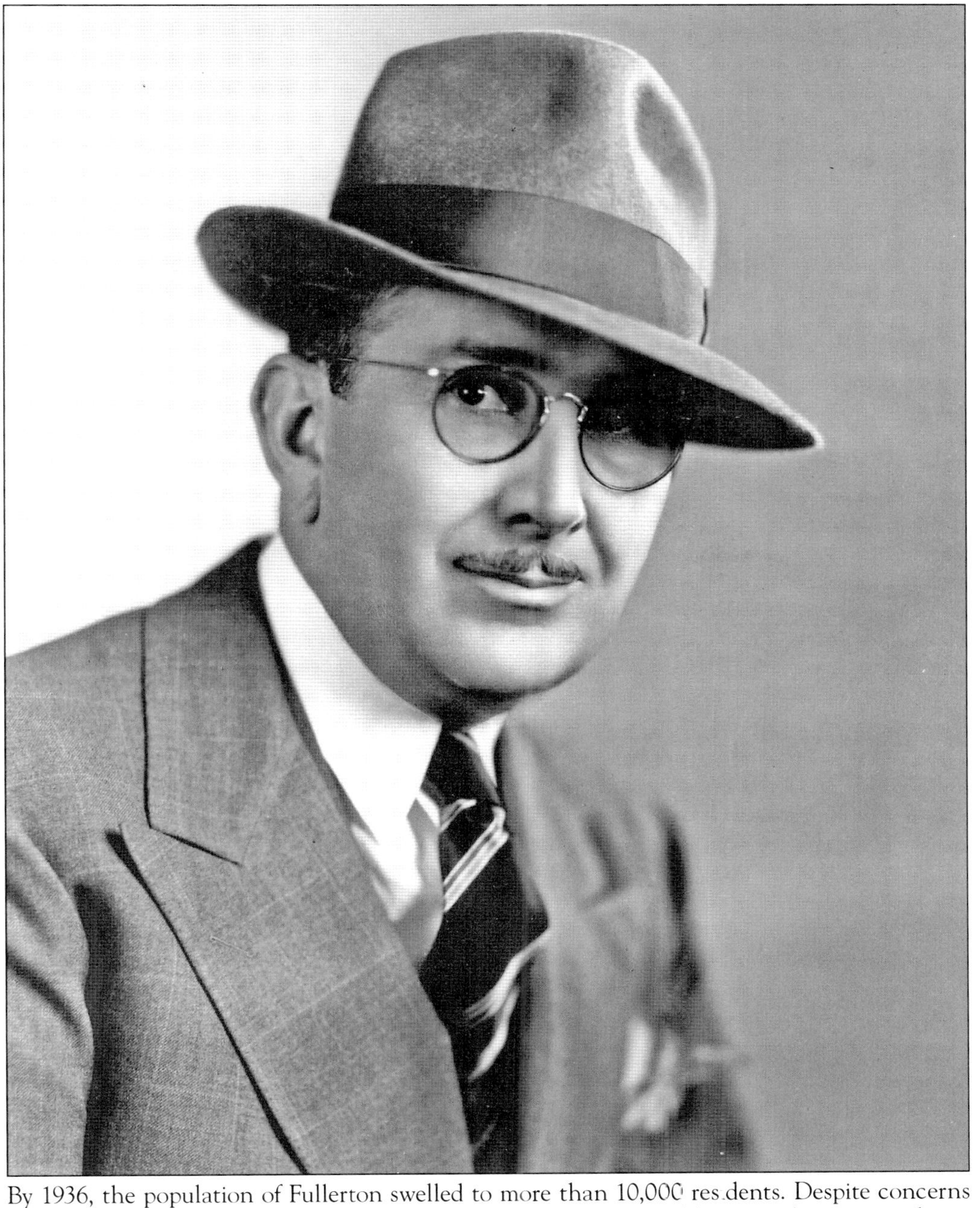

By 1936, the population of Fullerton swelled to more than 10,000 residents. Despite concerns by some community leaders that a Catholic would not be electable, incumbent councilman Tommy Gowen (who had a neighboring ranch and was a good friend to Walter) convinced Walter Muckenthaler to run for the city council. Both men were victorious in the campaign, with Walter actually garnering more votes than his friend. Gowen had known Walter for some time and was convinced that his friend's even temperament and solid principles would put him beyond the reach of special interests. Walter served on the council for eight years, starting in 1936. They accomplished amazing things during their time in office, including building much of the city's infrastructure.

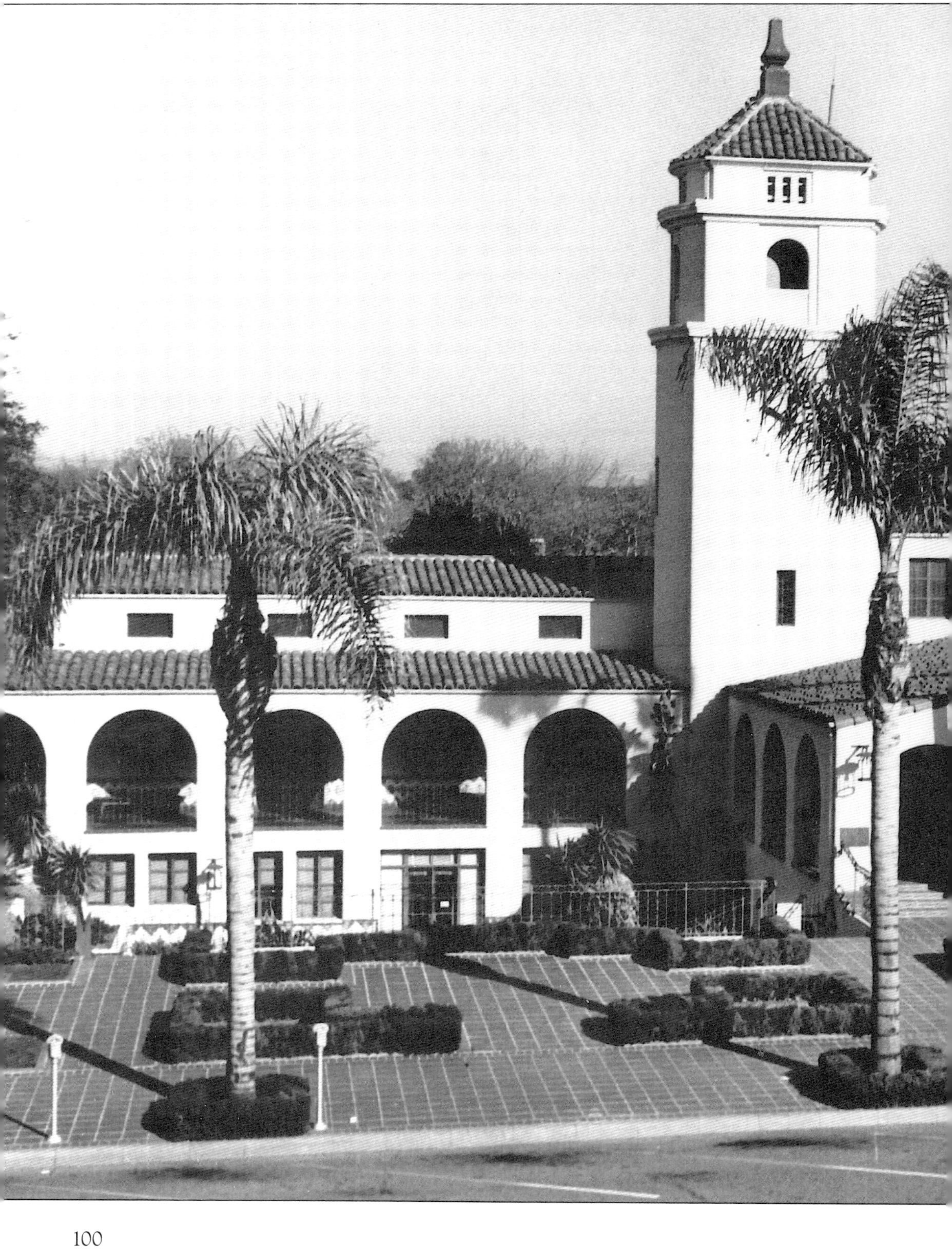

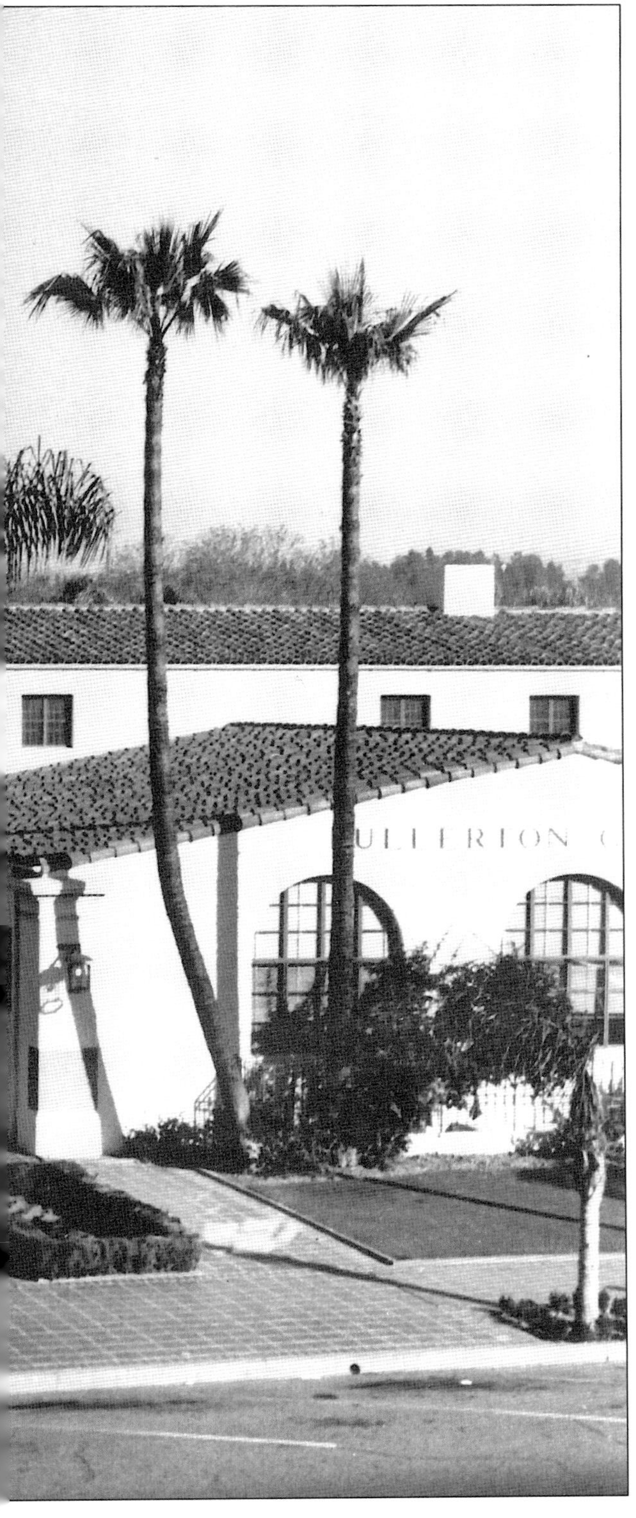

In the 1930s, most of Fullerton's civic offices were housed in a two-story building located behind the California Hotel on Wilshire Avenue and Spadra Road (now Harbor Boulevard). The city council met on the second floor in a large meeting space above the police station, city clerk's office, and fire department. A new space was needed for the council and larger offices for the city staff. In 1937, Pres. Franklin Roosevelt's New Deal spread federal funds to municipalities through the Works Progress Administration (WPA) for local improvement projects. Once funding was secured, the city moved ahead quickly with the new city hall. Ground was broken on the site in September 1939, with the mayor and members of the city council in attendance. A site on the corner of Malden and West Commonwealth Avenues was eventually chosen by the council because more automobile parking would be available there. (Launer.)

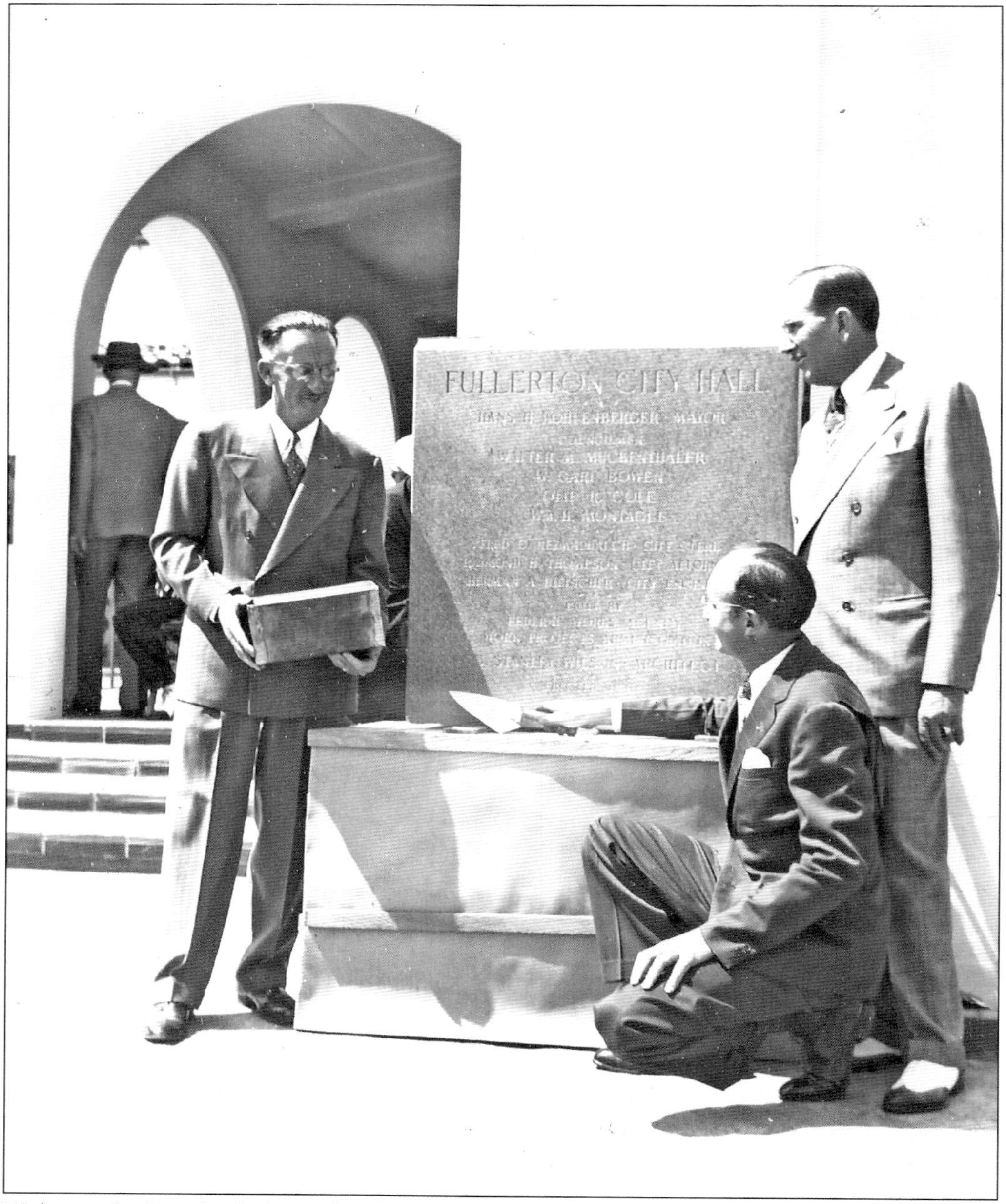

Walter and others (including other council members) formed the Forward Fullerton Committee to advocate passage of a special election ballot measure to approve construction of a new city hall to house the city offices and council chambers. The planning and execution of the building, accomplished with WPA money, would include WPA murals by Helen Lundeberg that can be seen today in the old council chambers, now known as the Mural Room. Again Walter's love for art was evident in the new building. Laying the cornerstone are, from left to right, Mayor Hans Kohlenberger, Councilman W. Carl Bowen, and Councilman Walter Muckenthaler. (Launer.)

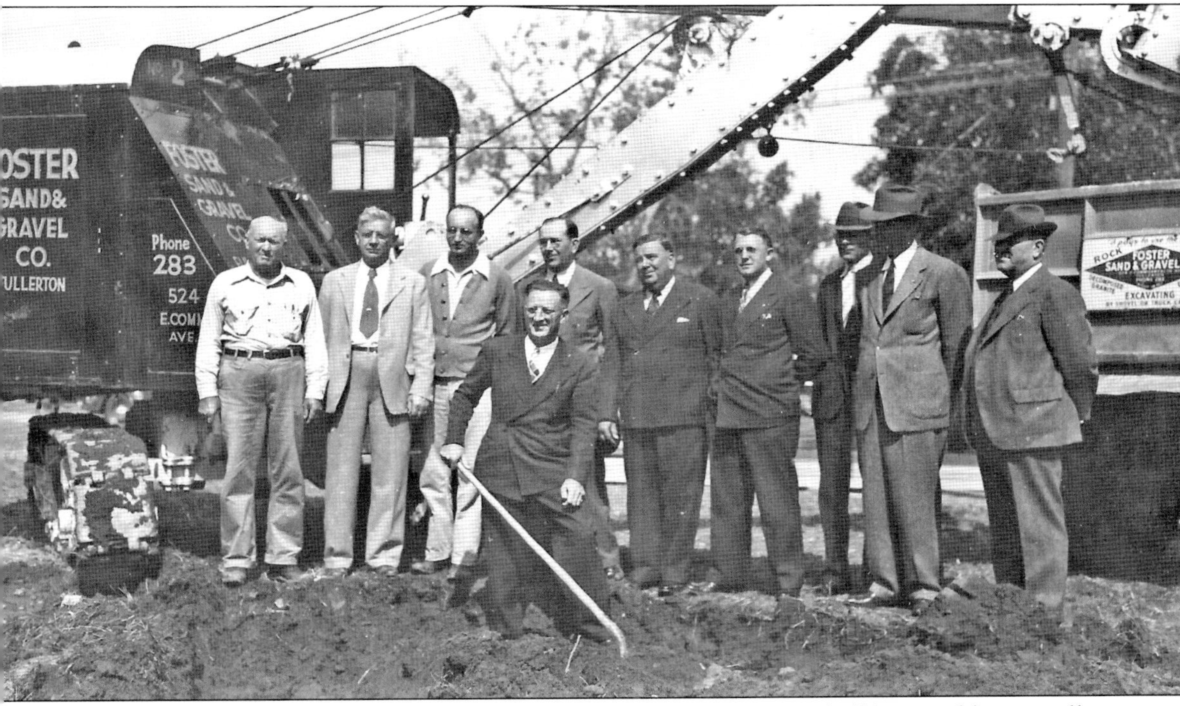

Walter influenced the design of the building that became the new city hall but would eventually house Fullerton's police department. The white stucco walls and red tile roof recall features of Walter's own elegant home, right down to the tiled patios and wrought iron details. Its soaring clock tower beckoned residents of the city to spacious outdoor courts and welcoming archways. The opening of the building was celebrated in June 1940. Walter M. Muckenthaler's name can still be seen on the bronze plaque placed there that day. Mayor Hans Kohlenberger holds a shovel full of dirt at the ground-breaking ceremony in September 1939. Councilman Walter Muckenthaler stands directly behind him surrounded by other unidentified city officials. (Launer.)

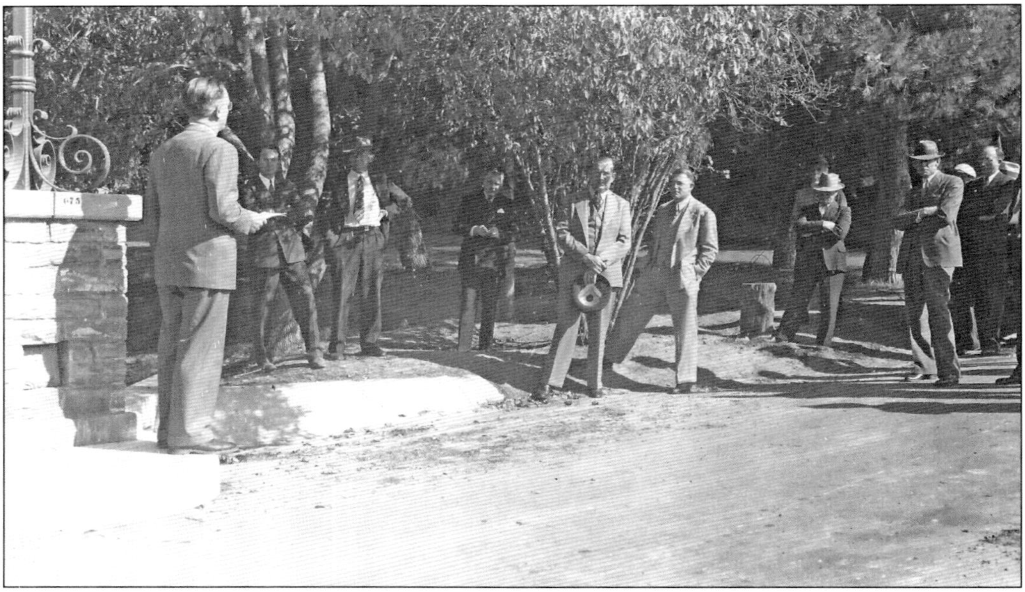

In 1938, five days of continuous rain swelled the Santa Ana River, causing it to overflow its banks. Many people died as torrents of water lifted houses off their foundations and swept them away. Dams in Santa Ana Canyon burst, sending water into the natural flood plain of Orange County. In Fullerton, Spadra Road became a veritable waterway. Up on its hill, the Muckenthaler estate escaped the floodwaters, but the orchards below did not. The earthen sides of the barranca on Malvern Avenue partially collapsed, inundating property to the south. Using WPA funds, the city council approved lining Fullerton's waterways with cement to protect the town in another flood. Most importantly, a new dam was approved above Spadra Road. The Brea Dam was dedicated in November 1940. Walter Muckenthaler, second from left, and other unidentified city officials toured the new flood-control channels in a flatbed truck (below). (Both, Launer.)

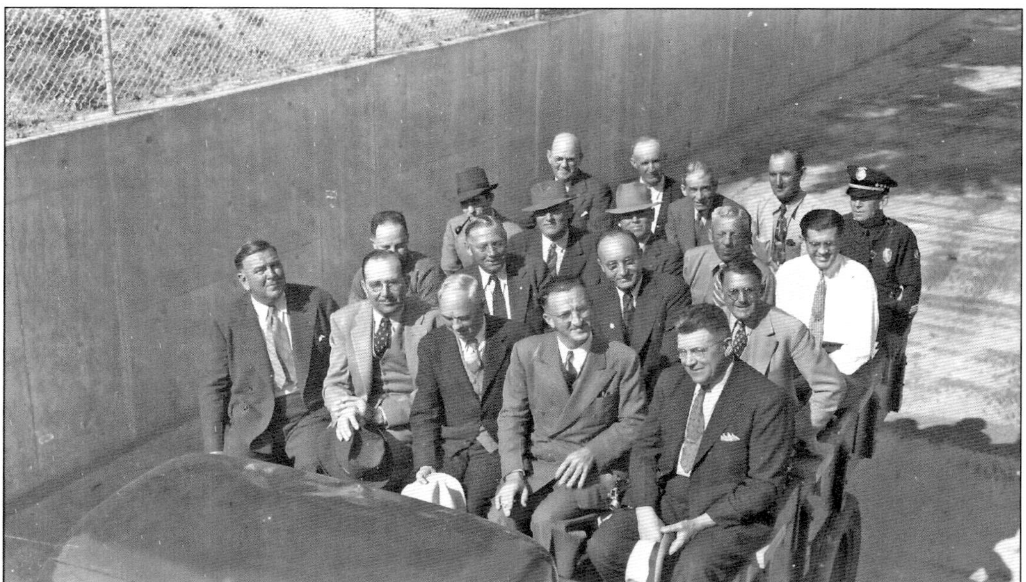

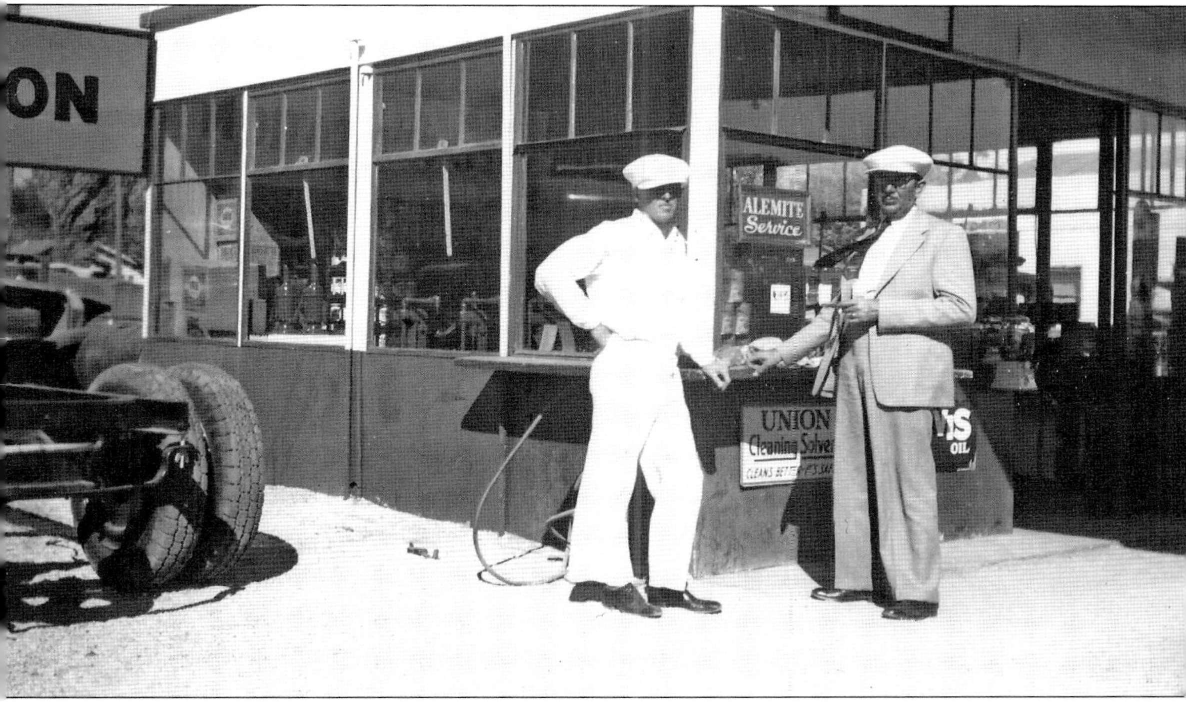

Declining to run for another term on the Fullerton City Council after eight years of service, Walter accepted an appointment in 1944 to the town's planning commission, where his love of architecture and his civil engineering background would be put to good use. His term as a commissioner helped influence Fullerton's retention of some of its agricultural heritage while it transitioned to light industry. Walter's years of public service were boom years for Fullerton. He had a hand in much of the development of the town.

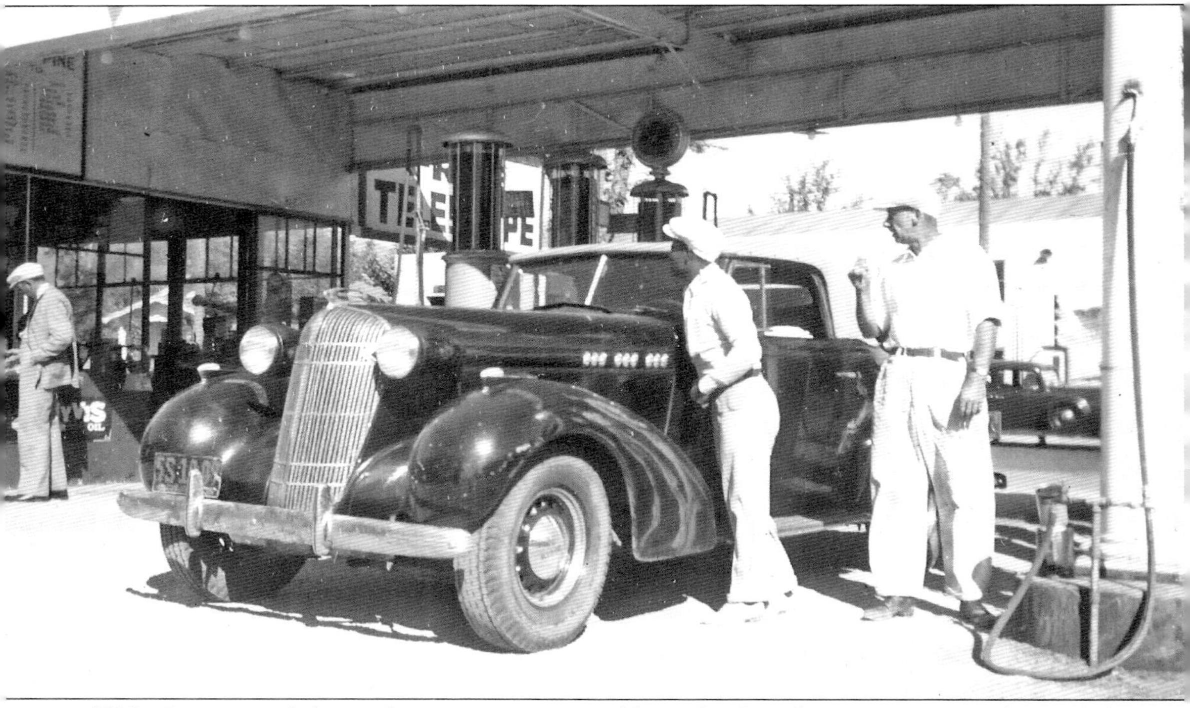

Walter's many and diverse business interests tied him closely to his community and provided increased financial security for his family in years to come. Walter owned a gas station, among other business interests. As he and Adella aged, they inherited parts of their parents' Kraemer and Muckenthaler estates and became very busy managing all their business interests for their heir, Harold. Harold gained his father's sense of civic duty and also his business sense. It was a combination of the two that led him and his mother to gift the estate to the city as a cultural center years later.

Six

Harold and Shirley

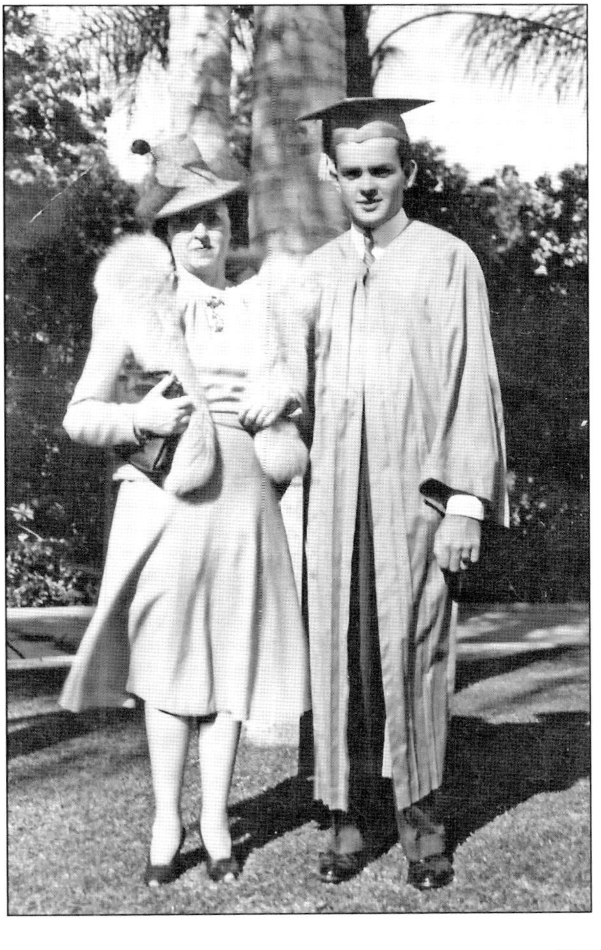

A proud Adella Muckenthaler poses in the circular driveway with her son, Harold, on the day of his graduation from Fullerton Union High School in 1941. He graduated just in time to be the first class of men signing up for the war effort. In June 1941, the world was full of promise for high school graduates, but by December, they would be defending their country in World War II.

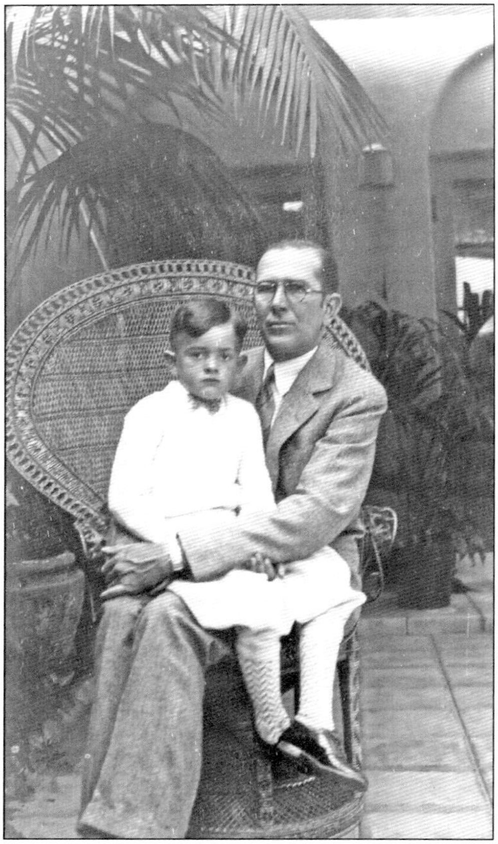

At left, a young Harold sits on his father's lap in the atrium of the villa around 1932. Shirley Zoeter's family had come from Colorado to Fullerton when she was a child. She and Harold Muckenthaler met at Wilshire Junior High School in Fullerton. Walter was a friend of Shirley's brother. Harold and Shirley were childhood sweethearts through high school. Harold enlisted in the Navy in 1942, just two months after the United States joined World War II. He was assigned to North Island Station, the same naval training facility his father had been sent to more than 20 years earlier. Below, Harold plays with his dog in the rear courtyard of the villa while visiting home on leave. Unlike his father, Harold had no physical problems to keep him from active duty.

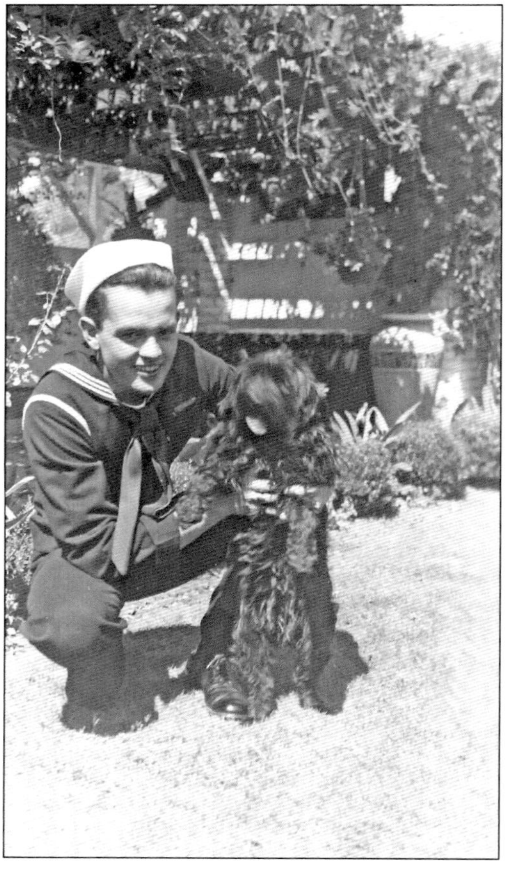

Mrs. E. M. Zoeter

requests the honour of your presence

at the marriage of her daughter

Shirley Irene

to

Mr. Harold Walter Muckenthaler

United States Naval Reserve

on Sunday afternoon, the fourteenth of February

Nineteen hundred and forty-three

at half after three o'clock

St. Mary's Church

Fullerton, California

Shirley Irene Zoeter and Harold Walter Muckenthaler were married on Valentine's Day, 1943. Their wedding invitation is pictured. The ceremony was held at St. Mary's Church in Fullerton, where the Muckenthalers were parishioners. St. Mary's Church was founded in 1912. Maria O. Bastanchury donated the land and the altar. In 1923, St. Mary's moved the church building (picked it up and wheeled it) to its present site across the street. In 1968, a disastrous fire completely destroyed St. Mary's Church. The current church was built in 1970.

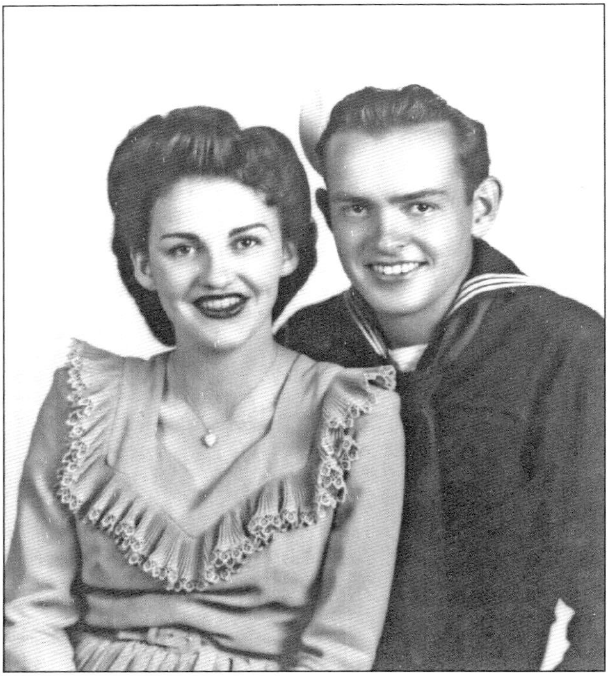

Harold obtained leave to marry his fiancée on Valentine's Day, 1943. Shirley was radiant in her wedding gown; Harold wore his Navy uniform (left). Following the wedding, the couple traveled back to Los Alamitos, California, where Harold was stationed. Harold spent the war years in a naval uniform. He is flanked by his mother, Adella, and new wife, Shirley (below). Harold was fortunate to spend most of the war stateside in California, with occasional trips to ports in Hawaii and Alaska. He had much more opportunity to see his new wife than most servicemen did at that time. Harold and Shirley were married for 67 years, until Shirley's passing on January 3, 2010, at their home.

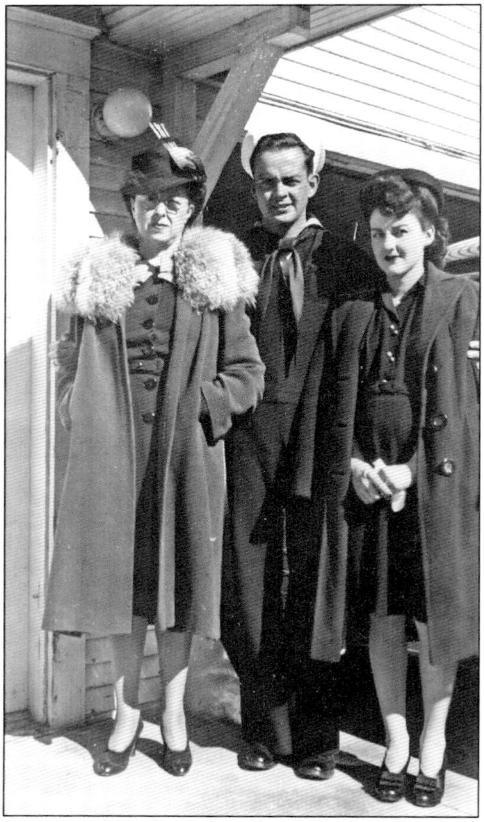

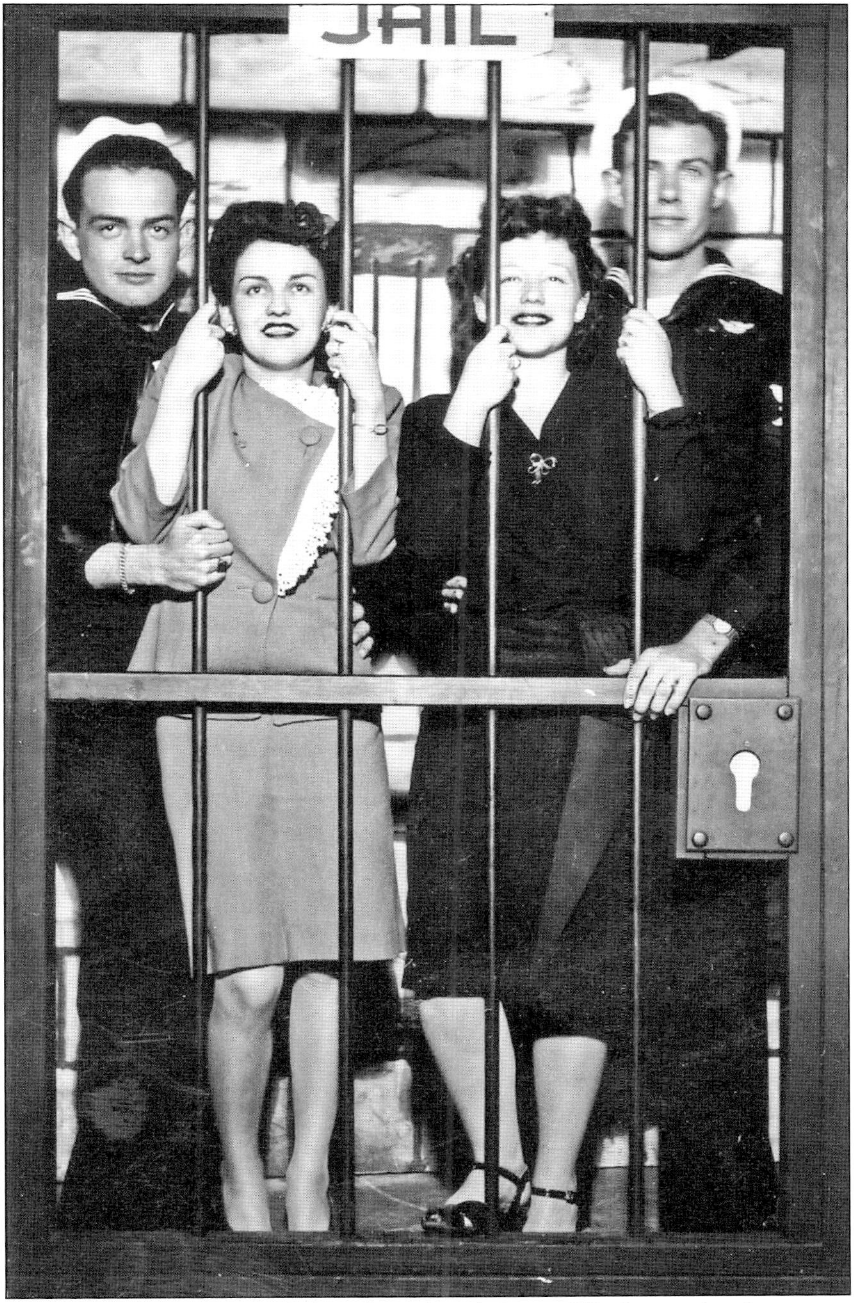

Harold and Shirley are pictured with friends Dick and Harriet Wrigley at a local tourist attraction at the Long Beach Pike during the war years. Harold and Dick remain good friends to this day. The Pike was a favorite destination for Southern Californians and tourists. It was a large amusement park—likened to New York City's Coney Island—and had a unique swimming facility called the Plunge, which brought saltwater in from the ocean. Thousands vacationed there during summers. Long Beach was also a Navy port. The Pike was a favorite spot for sailors and their girls during the war years but eventually closed down in 1979 after falling into disrepair.

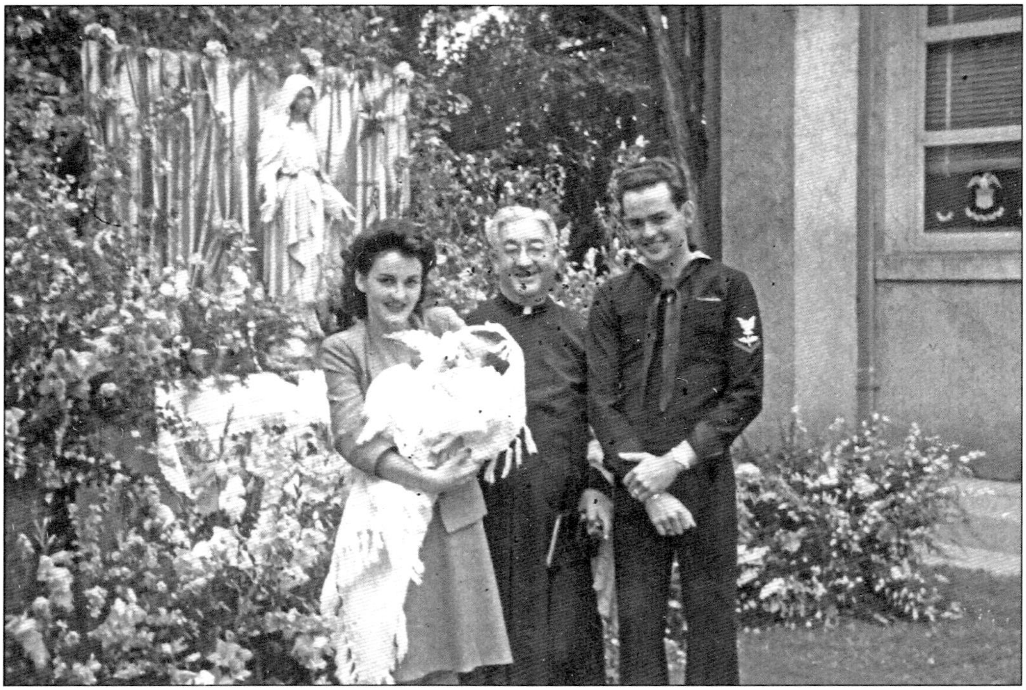

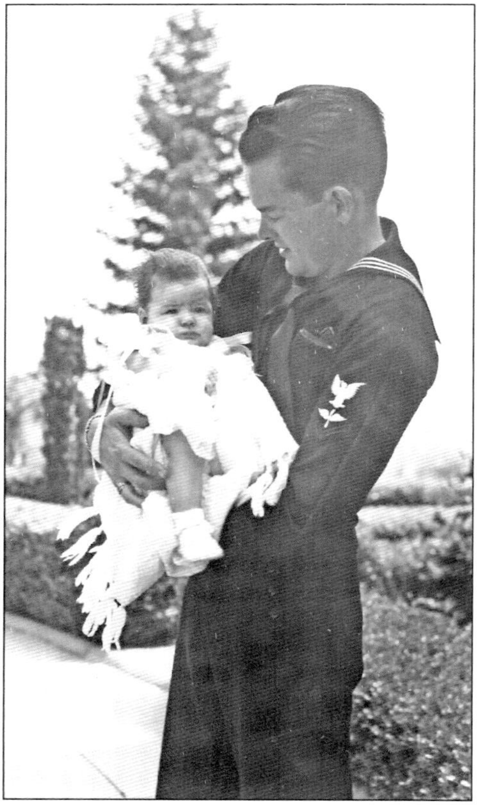

By spring 1944, Harold and Shirley had started a family of their own. Their first child, Peggy, was baptized at St. Mary's Church in Anaheim by Father Lehain. Peggy is held by her mother above and her father below. Shirley later had two other daughters, Sherryl and Kathleen. Following his discharge from the Navy, Harold started a gas station business with a friend from the service. As Walter's health declined, Harold would also take over the family ranch. Like many orchards in Orange County, the Muckenthalers' land was eventually developed for housing and commercial centers. The Stater Brothers commercial center on Euclid Avenue is still owned by the family.

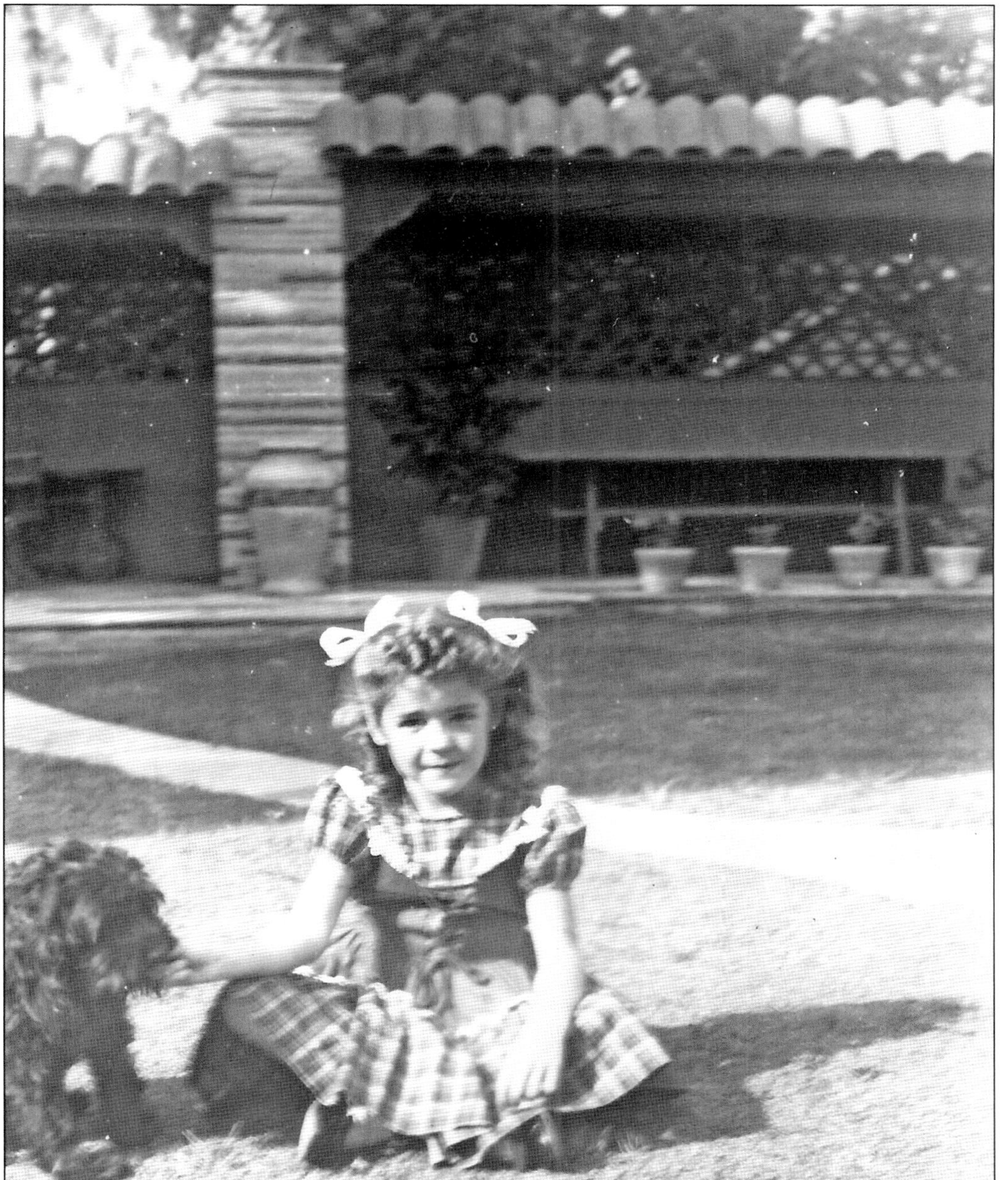

Peggy loved visiting her grandparents on the hill, where she played in the gardens. She plays with her father's dog Pudgy in the villa's rear courtyard in this photograph from 1949. Harold, Shirley, and their family lived just one mile away on West Amerige Avenue in a lovely Spanish-style home that still stands. They later donated their home on West Amerige Avenue to the Fullerton Interfaith Emergency Services (FIES), where it now serves as housing for families in need. Peggy is very active at the Muckenthaler Cultural Center as a board member, historian, docent, and president of the Center Circle guild that her mother cofounded. She has devoted her life to the center. Her husband, Don Albert, is a top volunteer, fixing things around the center. He also donated and installed the security system.

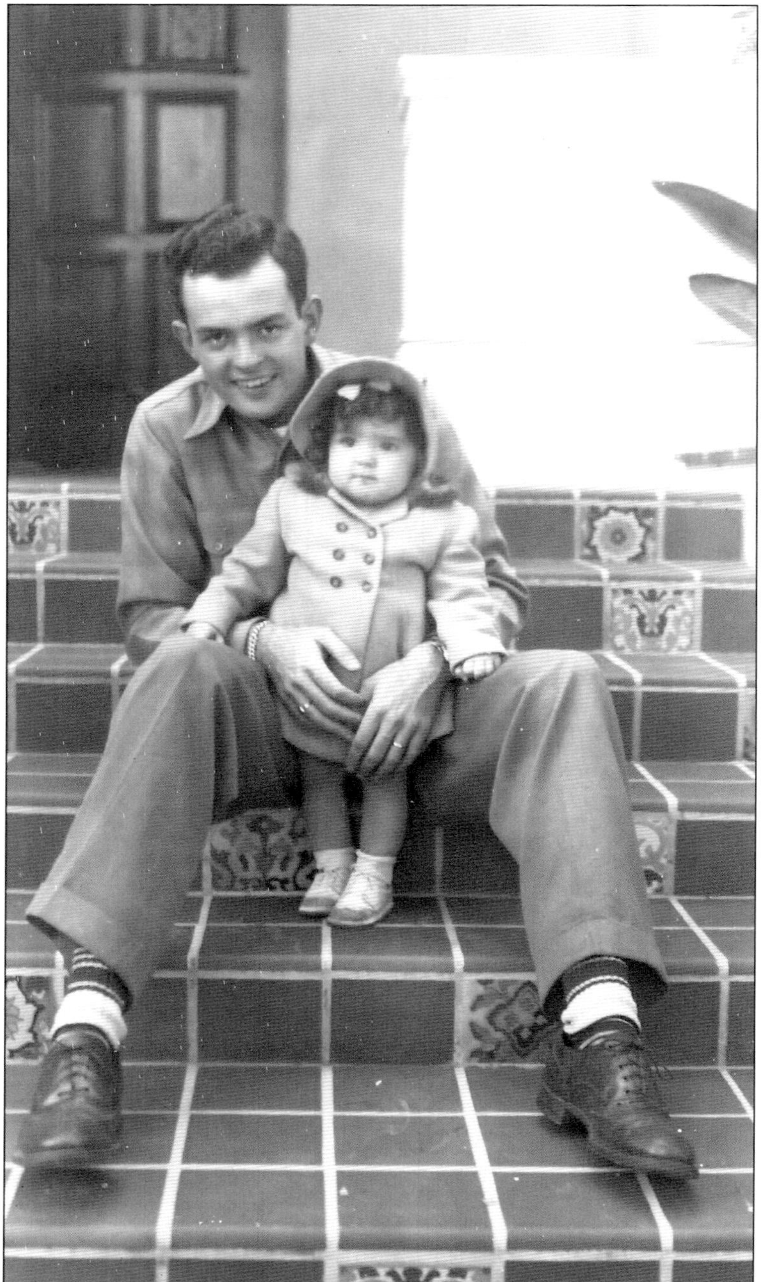

Back in civilian clothes, Harold visits his boyhood home with his new family. As he grew into his adult life, Harold began to assume some of his father's business responsibilities. Like his father, Harold enjoyed photography. He captured many moments of Fullerton's history in brilliant Ektachrome slides. After Walter's death, Harold and his mother looked at many options for the estate. They considered gifting it to the church for a school, but the church wanted to tear down the house. Harold did not want to see his home demolished, so it was gifted to the city as a cultural center.

Seven

THE LATER YEARS

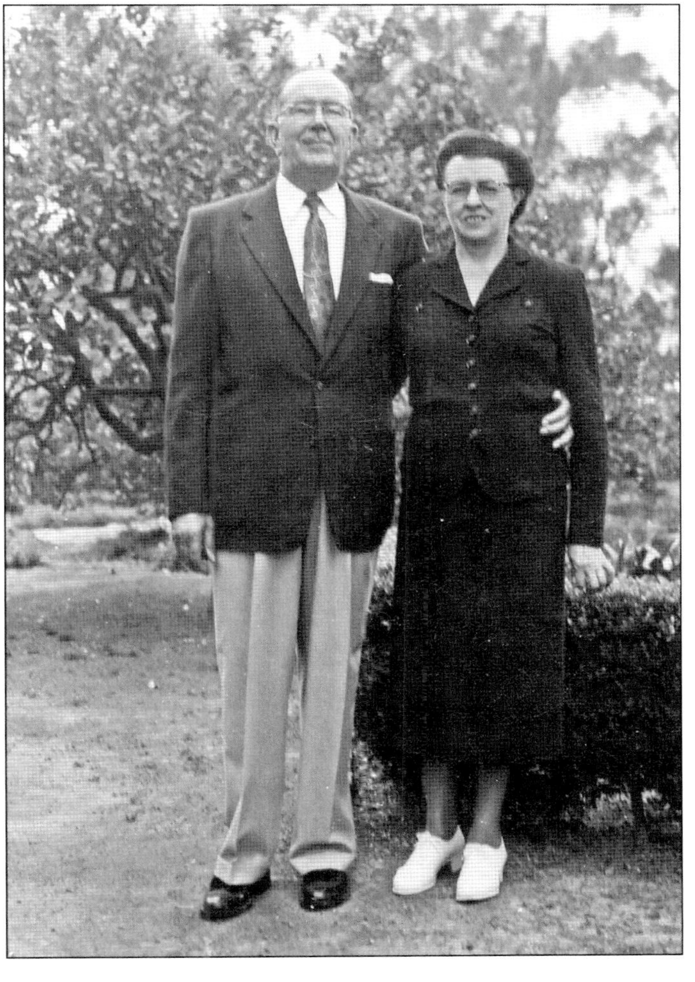

Through inheritance and his own astute dealings, Walter's business ventures began to grow beyond Fullerton, including real estate, commercial development, residential development, and more citrus orchards located as far away as Corona, inland, and Ventura, north of Los Angeles. He even purchased a building on the corner of Fourth Street and Broadway in Santa Ana.

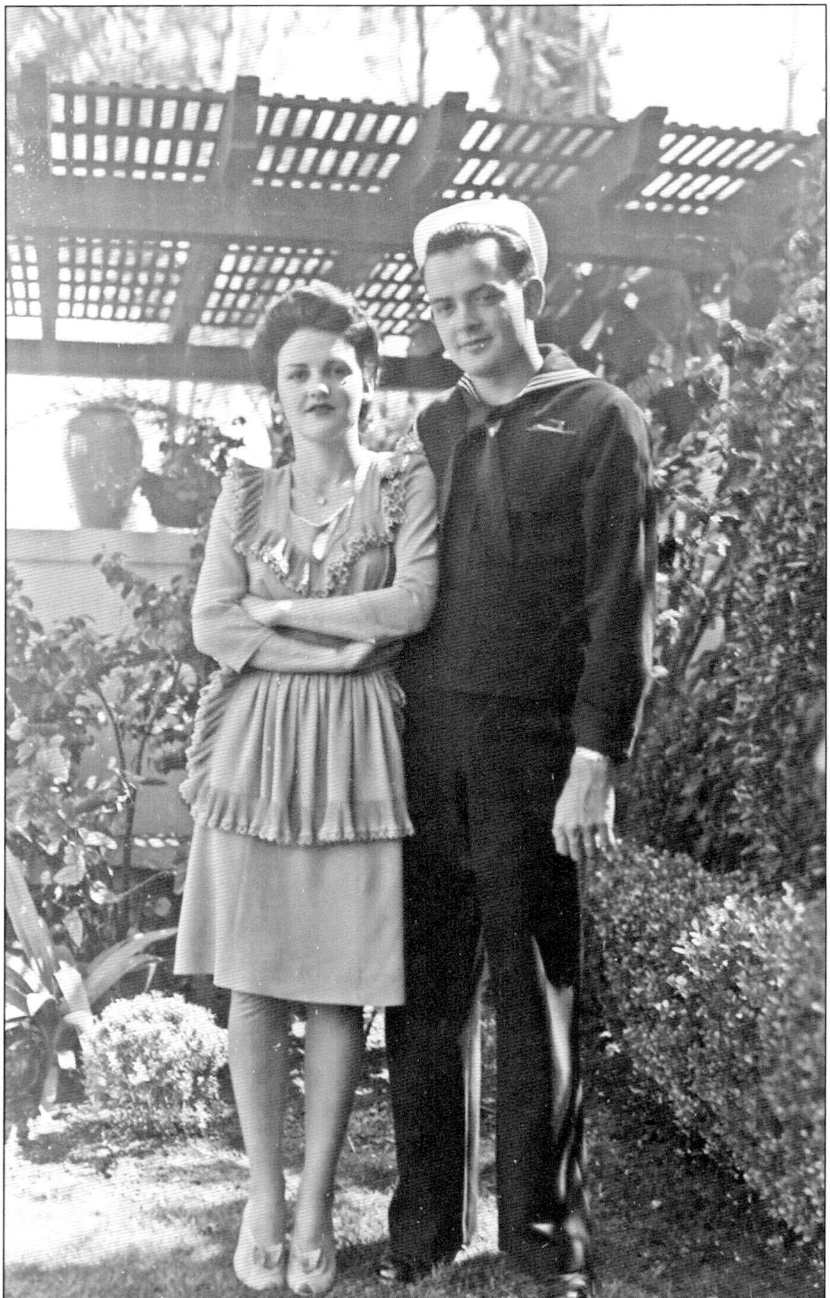

Harold and Shirley pose for a photograph before Harold heads off to war. While his son was serving in the Navy, Walter became a deputy marshal for civil defense in Fullerton. His work as both a past city council member and planning commissioner gave him the valuable experience and the respect of his community during a time of great national struggle and sacrifice. Although qualified for a higher priority gas-rationing card, he chose the same A sticker assigned to most other motorists and sometimes even used Harold's bicycle to attend meetings downtown.

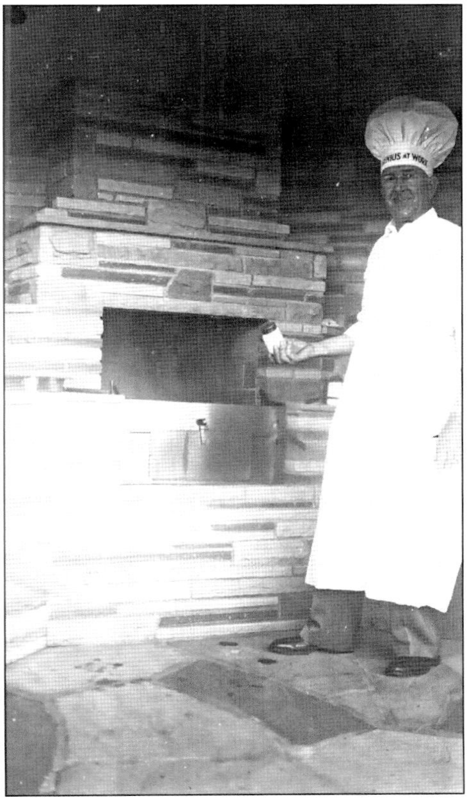

Walter wears a chef's hat as he cooks at the barbecue built into the back patio (right). The flagstone construction mirrored the large fireplace installed in the atrium when it was enclosed in the early 1950s. The barbecue is now used as a small stage area for outdoor events in the courtyard. Occasionally, when the center has farm dinner fundraisers, it is used for its original purpose. The estate evolved with the family's lifestyle, incorporating more modern features without compromising its original vision as a Mediterranean-style villa. Harold and Adella pose with Shirley in the newly enclosed atrium, in front of the mural that covers the former back porch (below). Walter had commissioned the mural two decades earlier through the WPA.

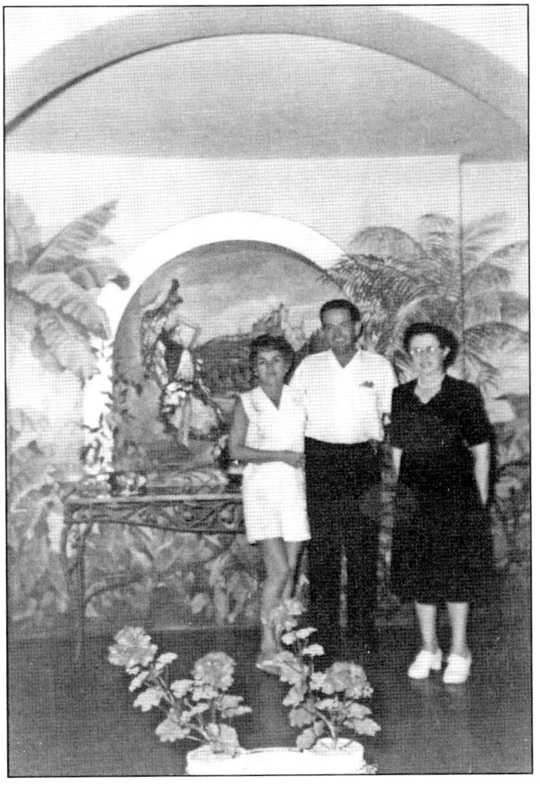

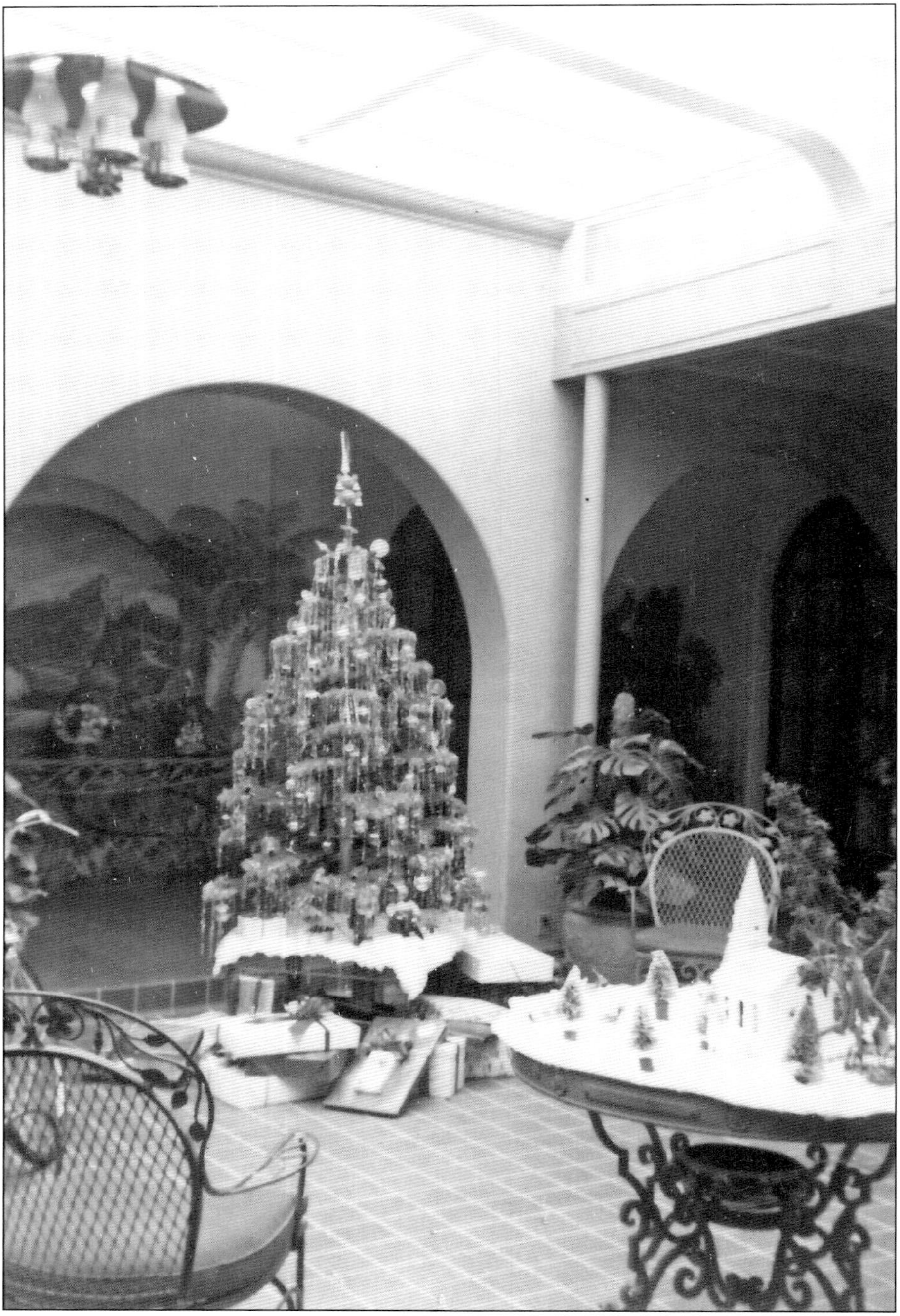

In 1951, a skylight was built to enclose the atrium as an indoor patio, providing more space for Christmas and other family gatherings. A new sunroof spanned the ceiling, filling the space with brilliant sunlight during the day. Sturdy but elegant wrought iron furnishings allowed the family to relax, surrounded by the glass panel doors leading to the other rooms in the house. This room is now the main gallery and is also used for meetings, performances (with excellent acoustics), cocktail parties, and small weddings and functions in winter.

Adella holds her first grandchild, Peggy, on the steps of the side porch. By this time, the original Craftsman tiles had been replaced with highly polished red tiles interspersed with Catalina designs. As a special treat, Peggy or her sisters, Kathy and Sherry, would be invited to spend the weekend at the villa.

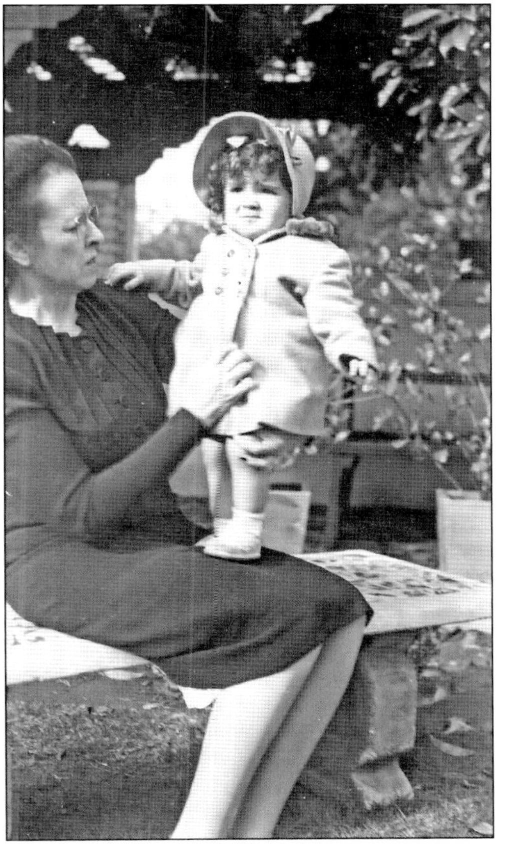

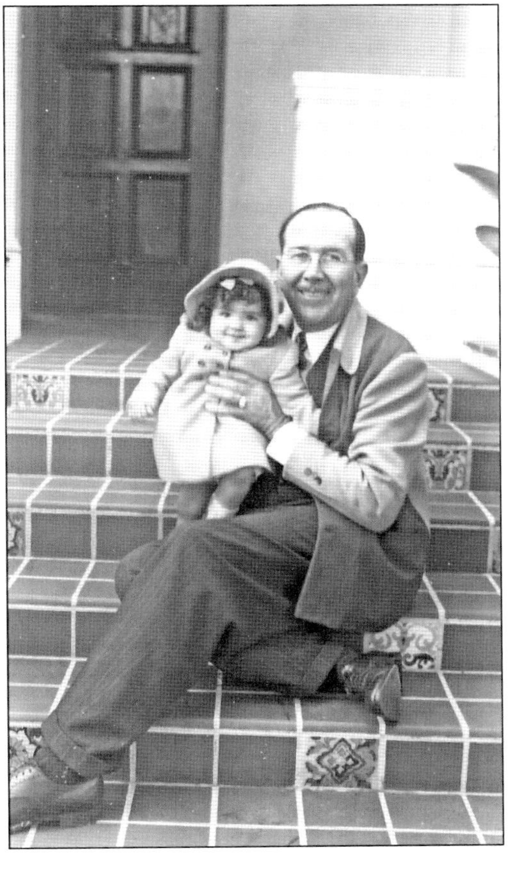

Walter holds Peggy on the steps of the front porch. Walter's youth on a Kansas farm made him an early riser throughout his life. He would stroll through his gardens in the dawning light, inspecting the plants and feeding his exotic birds. Returning to the house, he would squeeze fresh orange juice for Adella and take it to her upstairs before returning to the kitchen to prepare breakfast.

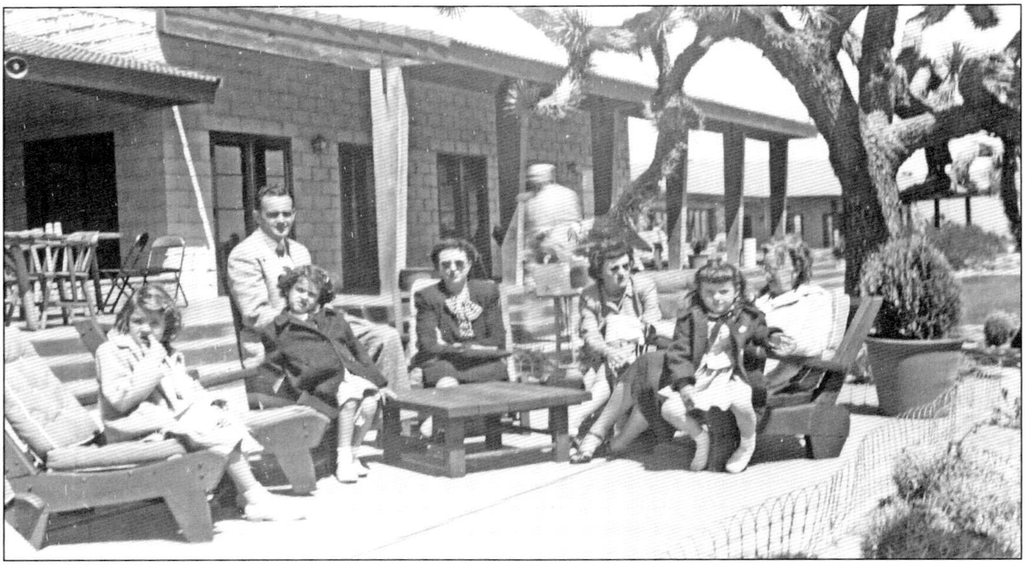

The family often visited Apple Valley or Palm Springs at Easter. Above, they are pictured relaxing on the patio of the Apple Valley Inn some time during the 1950s. Closer to home, Walter and Adella enjoyed mass at a variety of churches throughout the county. Below, the family poses in front of a church. Walter studied the architecture of each structure, comparing them from week to week with other chapels.

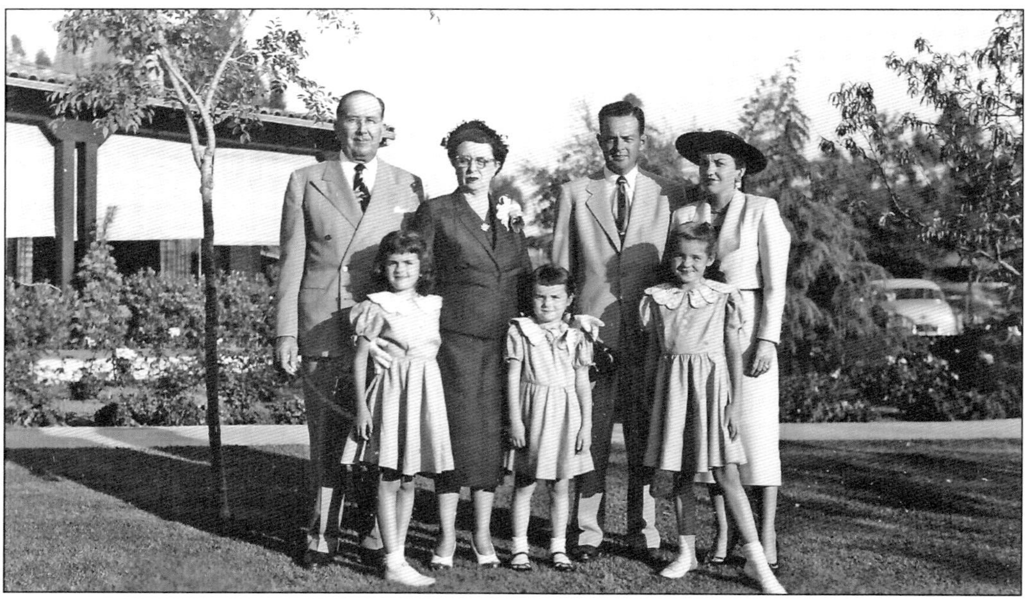

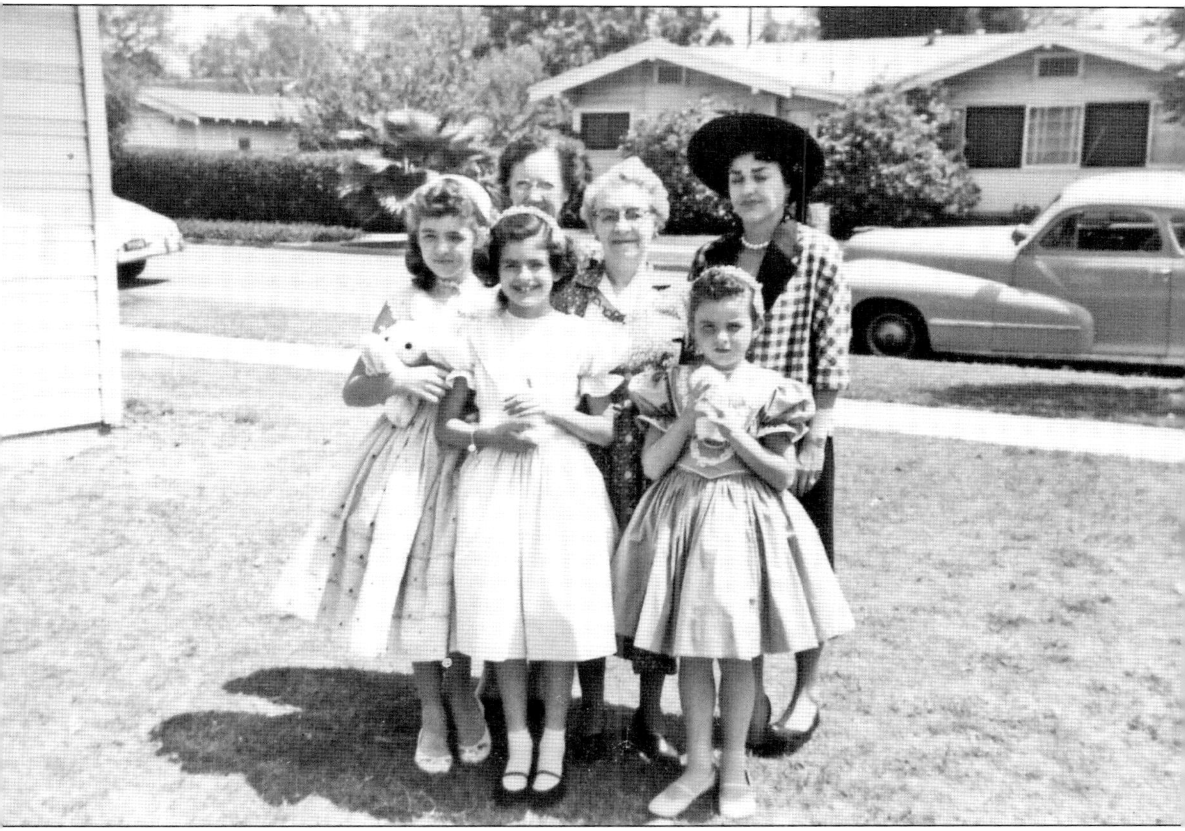

Shirley, her mother, her great aunt, and her daughters pose for a photograph on Jacaranda Street in 1951. Harold and Shirley's three daughters were the apples of their eyes. Sherryl passed away from cancer in 2009, just prior to her mother's passing one year later. The Muckenthaler family has provided funds to the cultural center to dedicate programs and endowment money for programs in perpetuity to both women in their names. The women are greatly missed.

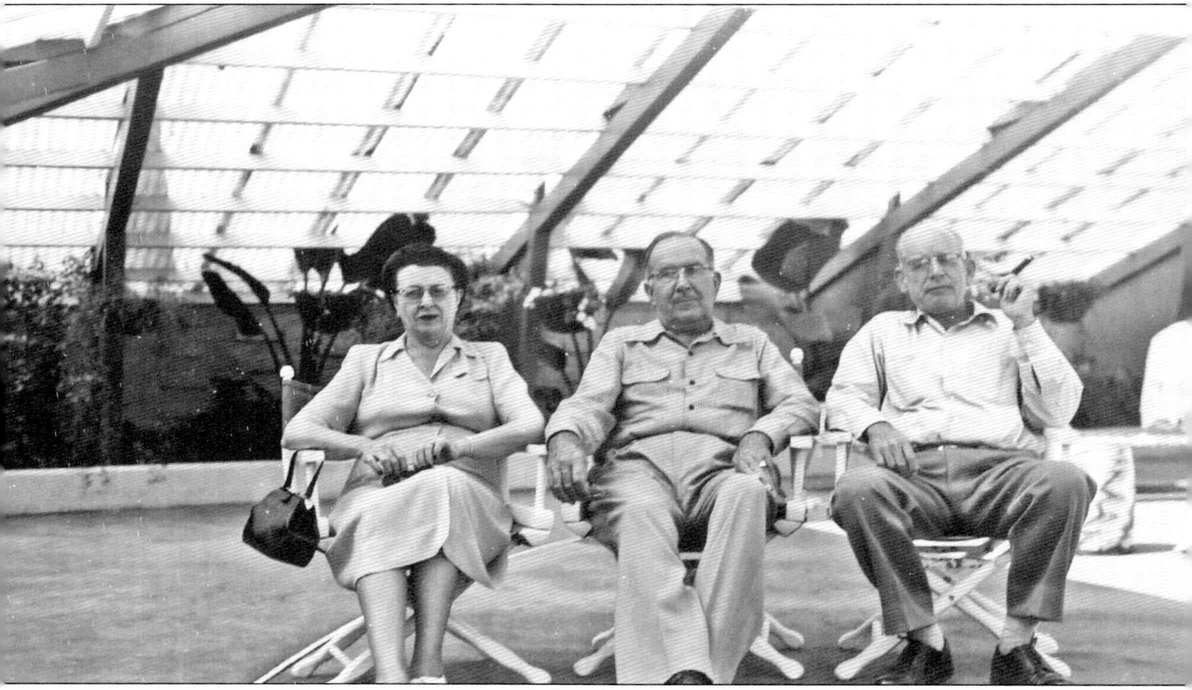

In 1953, the normally vigorous Walter began to feel increasingly fatigued. He consulted G. Wendell Olson, the family's doctor. Tests sent to Los Angeles showed that Walter was suffering from leukemia. He struggled with his condition, which was complicated by hepatitis contracted through a blood transfusion. Unable to negotiate the grand staircase to his bedroom, Walter moved into the guest room near his downstairs office. He died one month after his 64th birthday, on April 20, 1958. The Muckenthaler Cultural Center, now a city park and National Historic Registry building, will remain a testament to him for generations to come.

Eight

The Muckenthaler Cultural Center

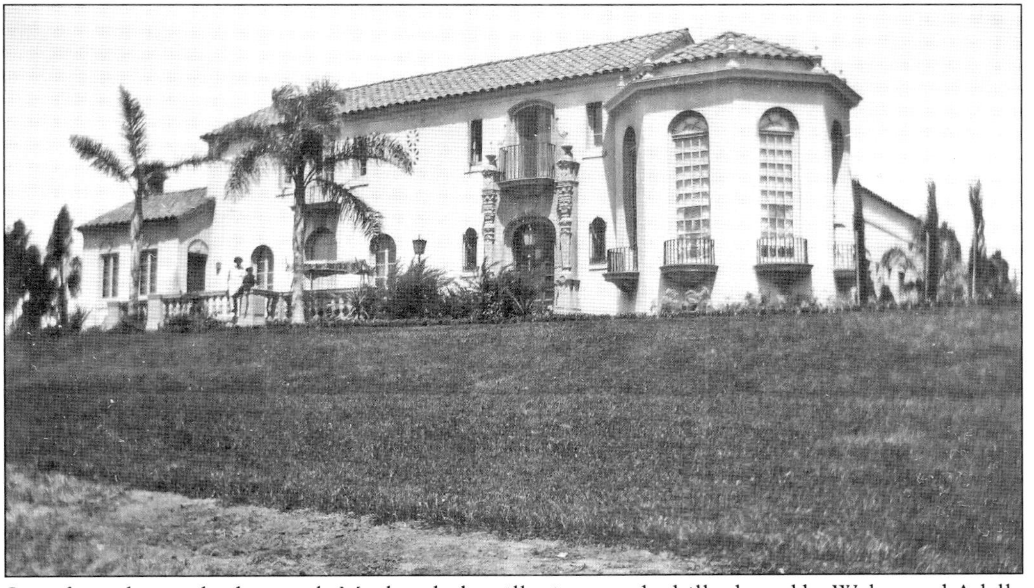

Seen from the south, the stately Muckenthaler villa sits atop the hill selected by Walter and Adella as the site of their dream home. Although some changes have been made to the surrounding grounds and structures, the home still looks much as it did when the family lived in it. Older Fullerton residents (who recall a time when they played on the front lawn or swam in the reservoir) and new generations now visit and enjoy more than 60 annual art exhibitions and performances and the center's popular Motor Car Festival, held every May.

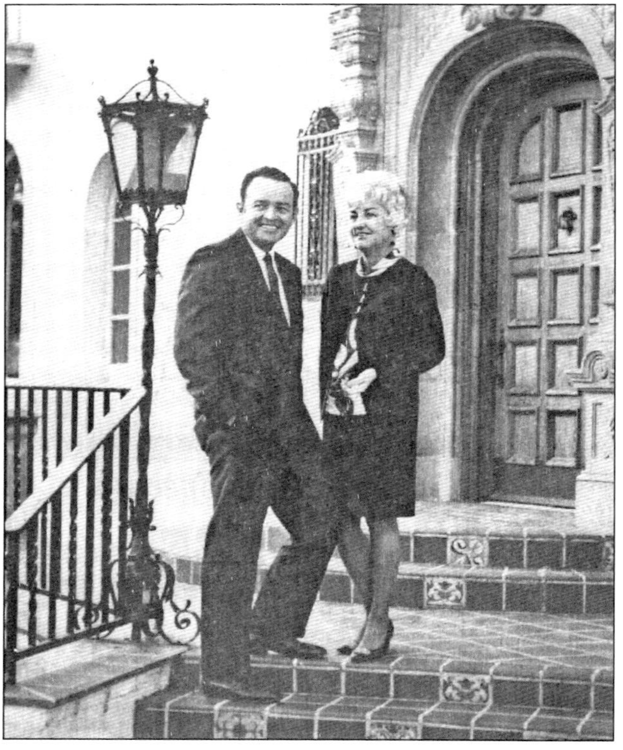

Harold and Shirley Muckenthaler actively supported the center's transformation into a cultural center. Shirley Muckenthaler stayed active in the Fullerton community by participating in the Assistance League of Fullerton, PTA groups, Girl Scouts, and the Muckenthaler Center Circle, which she helped found. She was a frequent and beloved visitor up to the time of her passing in 2010.

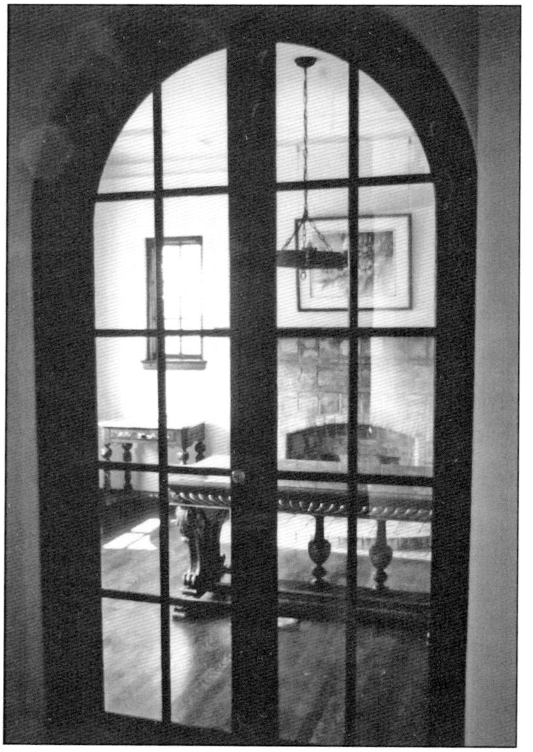

The library, with the smaller of the home's two Batchelder fireplaces, is seen through glass-paned, oak-stained doors. Paintings are often hung above the pictorial fireplace for exhibitions. Visitors can peak through the west windows to see a 246-seat outdoor amphitheater, often filled with patrons enjoying dance, drama, music, and other performances and festivals. (Launer.)

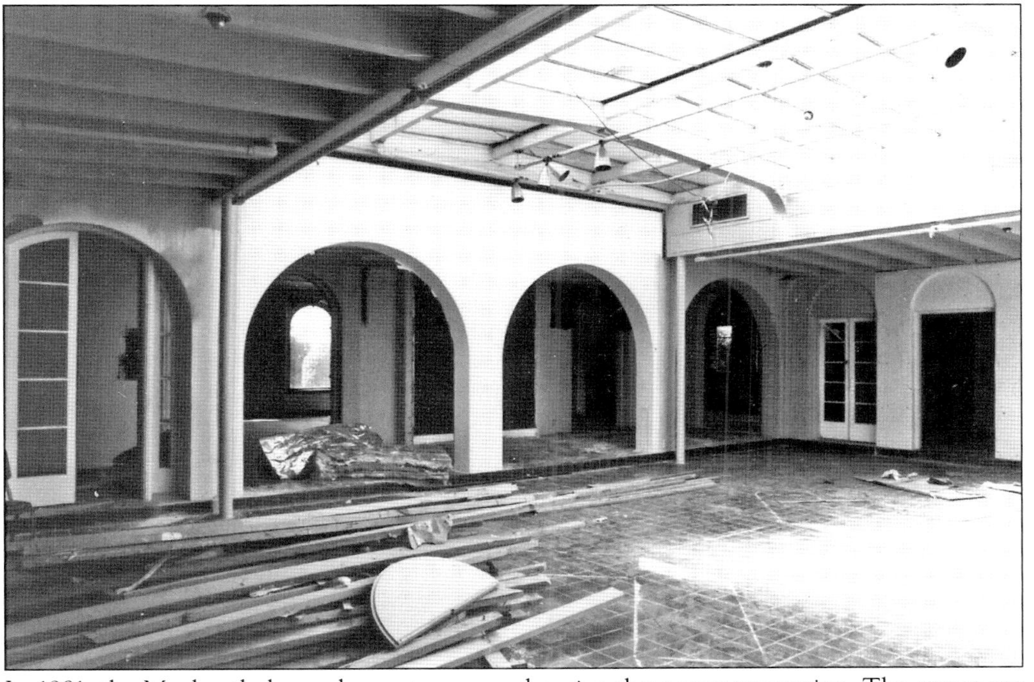

In 1981, the Muckenthaler underwent a comprehensive three-year renovation. The spaces are now designed to exhibit paintings, photographs, and other two-dimensional work. The tile patio often serves as a stage for indoor performances, as well. Although the Muckenthaler estate was turned over to the city in October 1965, it took three years before the center foundation was incorporated to help raise funds; the Center Circle was also created in 1968 as a women's auxiliary for the same purpose. City renovations made by 1970 would make it accessible as a cultural center. In 1989, a new master plan brought the addition of a grand entrance and a new theater space, which was completed in 1995. In that year, the Muckenthaler Cultural Center Foundation was formed by contract with the City of Fullerton to manage the facility. Plans have begun for more renovations to be completed by 2015 to celebrate the Muckenthaler Cultural Center's 50th anniversary. (Both, Launer.)

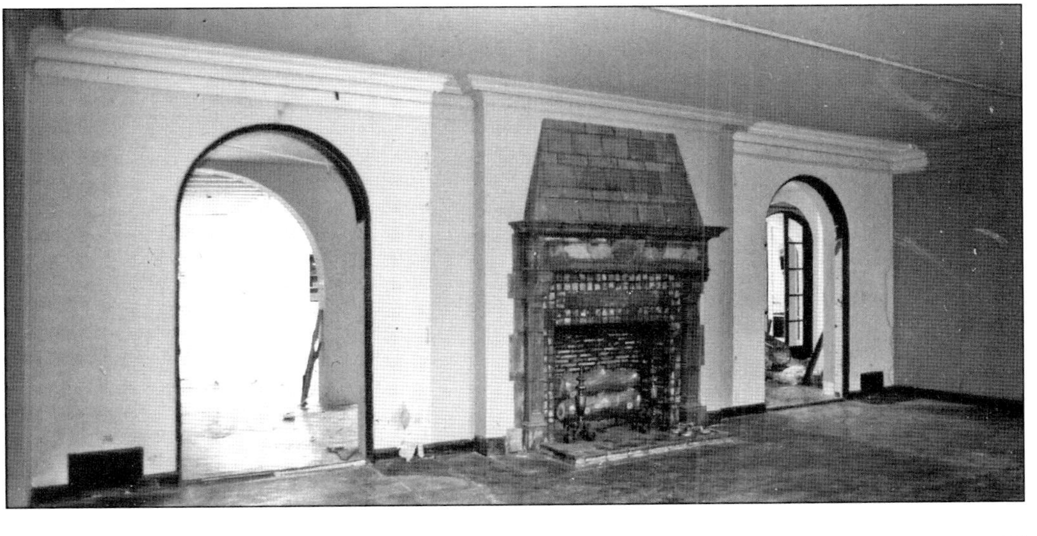

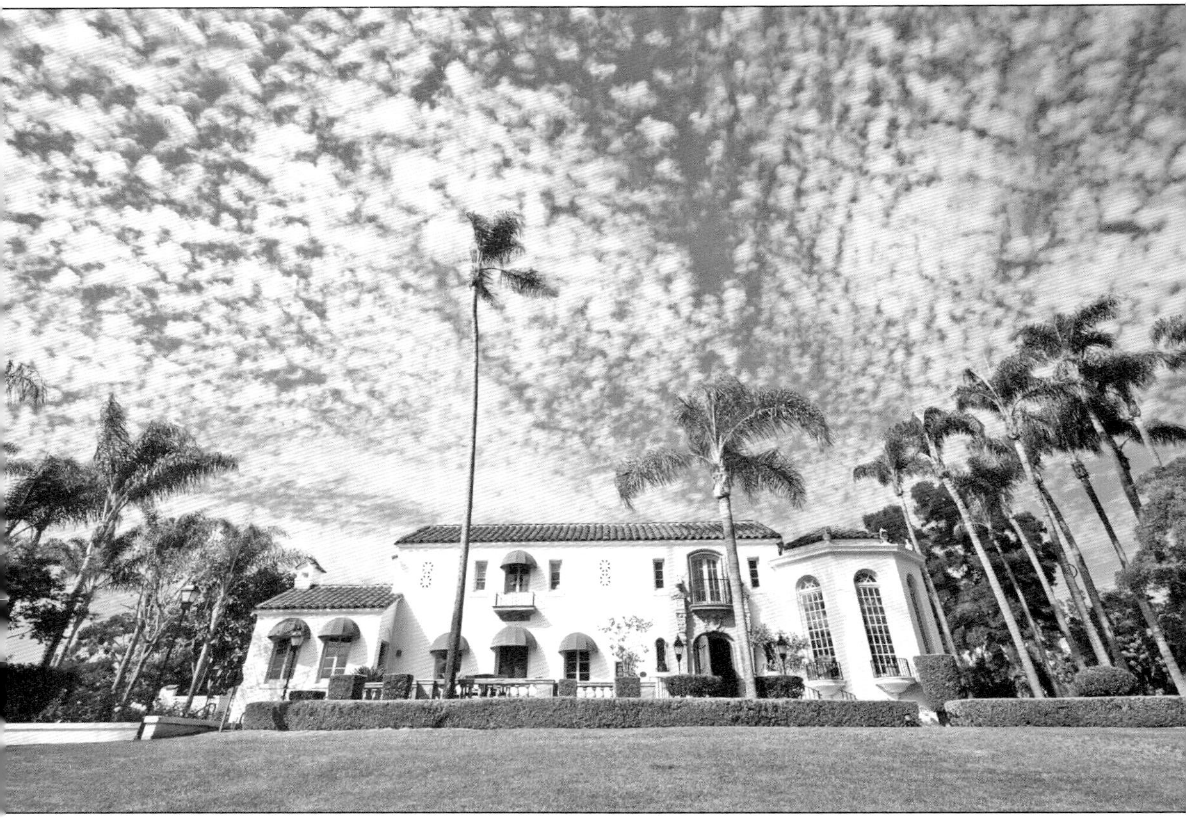

In this 2010 photograph taken during a wedding on the property, the beauty of Walter and Adella Muckenthaler's dream endures under blue skies in Fullerton, California. Today, third-graders come and learn about the Muckenthaler, Kraemer, and Yorba families and their contributions to the county; youth and adults create and view art; and newlyweds kiss in the shadow of this homestead of arts, culture, love, and history in the heart of North Orange County. (Courtesy of Zach Hodges.)

About the Organization

Now in its 46th year, the Muck, as staff and patrons affectionately refer to it, produces more than 100 performances, gallery exhibits, and classes each year, serving more than 25,000 people annually. The center also hosts more than 75 weddings and corporate events, welcoming over a 100,000 attendees each year, to help fund these cultural activities. Recent years have seen many awards and recognitions, including the 2008 Best Historic Site and Best Cultural Center awards from OC *Parenting* magazine, the 2009 Fullerton Chamber of Commerce's Quality of Life award for best nonprofit organization in the city, and the 2010 award for Best Arts Organization of the Year from Arts Orange County.

The Muckenthaler Gallery is open Wednesday through Sunday from 12 p.m. to 4 p.m. On Thursday evenings from February through October, the Muck hosts performances, festivals, and gallery openings with extended gallery hours. Over 25 hours a week of classes are taught at the center. Arts education programs include free seniors' classes, school tours for third-graders, outreach programs, and after-school programs. The Muck provides arts education programs to local foster care families, hospitals, Boys and Girls Clubs, and tutoring groups. Visit our website at www.themuck.org or call 866-411-1212.